FORMAL METHODS
OF PROGRAM VERIFICATION
AND SPECIFICATION

FORMAL METHODS
OF PROGRAM VERIFICATION
AND SPECIFICATION

H. K. BERG
Honeywell Corporate Computer Sciences Center, Bloomington, MN

W. E. BOEBERT
Honeywell Systems & Research Center, Minneapolis, MN

W. R. FRANTA
Department of Computer Science, University of Minnesota

T. G. MOHER
Department of Information Engineering, University of Illinois at Chicago Circle

PRENTICE-HALL, INC., Englewood Cliffs, New Jersey 07632

Library of Congress Cataloging in Publication Data
Main entry under title:
Formal methods of program verification and speci-
  fication.
  Includes bibliographical references and index.
  1. Computer programs—Verification. 2. Computer
programs—Specifications. I. Berg, Helmut K.
QA76.6.F658   001.64′25   81-22719
ISBN 0-13-328807-2   AACR2

Editorial/production supervision by Linda Mihatov Paskiet
Cover design by Edsal Enterprises
Manufacturing buyer: Gordon Osbourne

Prentice-Hall Software Series
Brian W. Kernighan, advisor

QA
76.6
.F658
1982

Printed in the United States of America

10 9 8 7 6 5 4 3 2 1

ISBN 0-13-328807-2

PRENTICE-HALL INTERNATIONAL, INC., London
PRENTICE-HALL OF AUSTRALIA PTY. LIMITED, Sydney
PRENTICE-HALL OF CANADA, LTD., Toronto
PRENTICE-HALL OF INDIA PRIVATE LIMITED, New Delhi
PRENTICE-HALL OF JAPAN, INC., Tokyo
PRENTICE-HALL OF SOUTHEAST ASIA PTE. LTD., Singapore
WHITEHALL BOOKS LIMITED, Wellington, New Zealand

8110748

7.1.85 AC

CONTENTS

5

APPROACHES TO PROOFS OF TOTAL CORRECTNESS   56

6

CORRECTNESS OF PARALLEL PROGRAMS   86

7

APPLICATIONS OF THE VERIFICATION APPROACHES   118

8

APPROACHES TO SPECIFICATION   128

9

STATE OF THE ART AND SUMMARY   179

LIST OF SYMBOLS

Certain mathematical symbols used throughout this text are:

	Symbol	Sample Usage	Meaning
1.	$:$	$A: B$	The expression or statement given by B is assigned the name A.
2.	$\in$	$a \in A$	Element a is contained in (is a member of) the collection (set) of elements denoted by A.
3.	Z^+	$i \in Z^+$	Z^+ denotes the set of positive integers. The usage implies i is a member of the set.
4.	$\vdash$	$\vdash S$	It is true that the statement S is valid.
5.	$\longrightarrow$	$A \longrightarrow B$	A implies B.
6.	( )( )	$(\forall i)(A(i) \longrightarrow B(i))$	For the quantified variable contained in the leftmost parentheses, the statement in the right set of parentheses is valid.
7.	$\forall$	$(\forall a \in A)(S)$	Universal quantifier. The usage reads: "For all elements a contained in the set A the statement S is valid."
8.	$\exists$	$(\exists a \in A)(S)$	Existential quantifier. The usage reads: "There exists an element a contained in the set A such that statement S is valid."
9.	$i..j$	$k \in i..j$	Definition of an integer interval containing the integers from i through j, $i \leq j$. In the usage, k denotes any of the integers in $i..j$.
10.	$\vert\ \ \vert$	$\vert i..j \vert$	The cardinality defines the number of elements in a set or the length of a sequence, $\vert i..j \vert = j - i + 1$.

PREFACE

The developmet of software systems in the recent past has been plagued with difficulty and outright failure to such an extent that the phrase "software crisis" has become a cliché. Software practitioners have taken action in both applied and theoretical areas to meet the crisis. In the applied area, they have begun to replace the craft of programming with software engineering. In the theoretical area, they have investigated the role that formal mathematical reasoning might play in the development of software.

The principal application of formal methods lies in the area of verification, where mathematical techniques are used to argue that a given program is correct. Such an argument requires a rigorous definition of correctness; this definition is given by a formal specification. This book is an introduction to the fundamental techniques in both specification and verification.

Such an introduction is naturally selective in the techniques it covers and must sacrifice rigor for clarity in its presentations. We apologize in advance to those workers in the field whose efforts have been overlooked and to those whose efforts have been included without treatment of the finer points. The reader who wishes to investigate any of these techniques further will find additional material listed in the references.

We wish also to note that this volume has been prepared in a spirit of explanation and not advocacy. We recognize that formal methods have their limitations, that their effective use requires extensive machine support, and that the techniques as presently developed have difficulty with programs that are as large and complex as those typically encountered in practice. On the other hand, we believe that the principles underlying formal specification and verification provide excellent guidance for the development of correct and maintainable programs. Thus, while we do not argue that every program should be formally specified and verified, we do argue that every programmer that aspires to professionalism should be at least casually acquainted with these techniques and their mathematical foundations.

The book can be read at two distinct levels. At the first level the reader can glean the ideas without attention to the details of our example proofs. At the second level, with proofs, the material becomes more meaningful, more complete. We hope the reader will profit at one or both of these levels.

The authors gratefully acknowledge the help given by Elaine Frankowski and Connie Galt in the preparation of this manuscript.

H. K. Berg
W. E. Boebert
W. R. Franta
T. G. Moher

FORMAL METHODS
OF PROGRAM VERIFICATION
AND SPECIFICATION

1

INTRODUCTION

1.1 FORMAL METHODS

The formal methods that we will describe seek to do for programming what mathematics has done for engineering: provide symbolic methods whereby the attributes of an artifact can be described and predicted. The artifacts in which we are interested are computer programs, which are themselves strings of symbols; it should be possible to define transformations upon strings of symbols that constitute a program, the result of which will enable us to predict how a given computer would behave when under the control of that program. If this prediction is independent of specific values of the input data of the program, then it becomes a general statement about that program. If the general statement is formed so that it provides an argument that the program achieves its purpose, then it becomes the desired replacement for exhaustive testing and we call it a *proof of correctness*. If we are to employ this approach, the notion of program purpose must be made rigorous. This formalization becomes the *program specification*, which serves to state precisely the requirements and objectives the program is to satisfy.

1.2 THE VERIFICATION PROBLEM

From the earliest days of their craft, programmers have faced the task of showing that their programs achieve some intended purpose; this task has come to be known as *program verification*. The early computers were devoted to mathematical computation, and their programs could be verified by a simple process of manually duplicating the computation for some subset of the data. As computer applications expanded, the task of verifying programs became more difficult. This resulted in the development of an elaborate technology based on testing [1]—that is, on the idea that a computer program is an artifact whose detailed attributes must be discovered by a process of experimentation.

Testing strategies are inherently limited, because the number of test cases required to completely exercise even a small program is prohibitively large. As a consequence only a subset of the cases can be tried, and successful completion of a subset is a necessary but not sufficient condition for proving that the program is correct. Despite these limits, programmers have almost exclusively used testing as a verification method. There has, however, been considerable research into more rigorous methods of program verification [2]. This research has been motivated both by the movement of computers into application areas (such as the processing of highly sensitive information) where no affordable level of testing is adequate and by the powerful intellectual challenge raised by the problem of placing a mathematical foundation under the craft of programming.

1.3 THE SPECIFICATION PROBLEM

A specification is the embodiment of the requirements a system is to satisfy—a precise, formal statement that expresses desired behavior in a manner intelligible to an implementor. The set of specified behavioral attributes can also be viewed as a description of the system, much as a blueprint is a description of a mechanical object such as a machine part. Formal specifications share certain attributes with other forms of description: they are more abstract than the object being described, and they often show artifacts that derive from the descriptive notation being used but are not part of the object being described. Thus a blueprint may contain lines (such as section or dimension lines) that give information about the object but that do not directly represent aspects of the object the way a line describing an edge does. Also, conventional notation may be used; for example, blueprints represent the complex helical shape of a machine screw, not in detail, but as a set of dashed lines.

The problem of separating artifacts of the descriptive method from essential aspects of the described object is complicated in the case of formal specifications of programs, because the object being specified is itself an abstraction. The reader of a blueprint immediately recognizes that he is dealing with a description (paper, lines) rather than an object (solid material). A formal specification of a piece of software, however, is a symbol string that is not obviously different from a program and may use notational devices (for example, if ... then ... else) that are misleadingly familiar to a programmer. The distinction between the described object and its description is further blurred by the existence of informal specification techniques (such as "design languages") that are themselves programming languages.

The formal specification techniques discussed later in this book maintain a semantic distinction between description, which we refer to here as the specification, and the described program, which we refer to here as the implementation. Loosely speaking, a *specification* describes behavior in terms of results, whereas an *implementation* defines behavior in terms of procedure. This distinction gives rise to the informal notion of describing "what" (specification) as opposed to "how" (implementation), and hence to the notion that specification languages are "nonprocedural" in nature. The point can be further illustrated by an example. Consider a single element of behavior: setting the elements of an array to zero. An implementation might take the form

$$i := 0;$$
$$\underline{\text{do while}}\ i \leq 100$$
$$A[i] := 0;$$
$$i := i + 1;$$
$$\underline{\text{endo}}$$

while a specification would describe the result

$$(\forall a_i \in A)(a_i = 0).$$

Note that the implementation contains two elements of information missing ("abstracted out") from the specification: the size of the array and the order in which the elements are to be set to zero. The decisions necessary to develop this information constitute the craft of programming.

For purposes of discussion we will define three users of a specification, each distinct from the author of the specification: the validator, the implementor, and the verifier. The *validator* is the person who acts as the representative of the sponsor of the system. His or her concern is that the specification is complete, consistent, and relevant—in short, that it properly embodies the requirements. The *implementor* is concerned with producing a procedural and ultimately executable definition of the behavior described in the specification. The *verifier* is concerned with the correctness of the implementation, *where correctness is defined with respect to the specification*. The verifier's task is, therefore, to show the consistency between two representations of the same behavior, one substantially more detailed than the other.

In general, the validator seeks a specification language (technique) that enables arguments to be made about the properties of the described implementation, such that it will be secure or fault-tolerant or will exhibit other behavior consistent with the sponsor's goals. The implementor seeks a specification language that describes desired behavior in the least constraining way, so that the implementor has maximum freedom in producing that behavior from a program that must fit the constraints of a real computer. The verifier seeks a specification language that describes behavior in a manner easily mapped into one of the techniques used for formal verification. Not surprisingly, these three uses occasionally conflict, and no consensus on the desirable features of a specification language has yet emerged.

1.4 PROGRAM CONSTRUCTION AND PROGRAM VERIFICATION

Earlier we broached the subject of program verification—the business of showing that a computer program achieves its intended purpose. There is naturally a complementary task, which begins with a program specification and results in a program; we call this task *program construction*.

We can, in fact, decompose the programming task into several steps, each of which is defined by the information it requires as input and produces as output. This decomposition is shown in Figure 1.1.

The programming task begins with some idea of the purpose the program (or program system) is to achieve. The idea of the purpose is used to guide a step we call requirements engineering. *Requirements engineering* identifies the major functions and constraints of the program to be constructed. The resulting requirements definition provides two classes of information about the proposed program. (1) The *functional requirements* informally describe the required behavior of the program. (2) The *attributes* (such as security, reliability, robustness, and viability) define the features the program must possess for all possible executions. In particular, security requirements have been defined [3] that are independent of any set of functional requirements; they simply state that a given program, irrespective of what it sets out to achieve, must not cause any information to be transferred in violation of a set of codified relationships between information sensitivity and user trustworthiness.

The functional requirements, or required behavior of the program, and the attributes that are independent of a particular execution behavior become the basis for a step we call nonprocedural design. *Nonprocedural design* formalizes the functional requirements and attributes given by the requirements definition. The result of nonprocedural design is a *program specification*. The program specification differs from a program in that it states "what" the program is to achieve, rather than "how" it is to achieve it. It consists of two parts, which are both stated with the same formal machinery. The first part, *specification of properties*, is the formal statement of attributes. The second part, the *functional specification*, is a formal statement of the functional requirements.

The program specification serves to drive a step we call procedural design. *Procedural design* converts the program specification into algorithms that state "how" the "what" is to be implemented. As these algorithms do not yet constitute the concrete programs of an implementation, we call the result of pro-

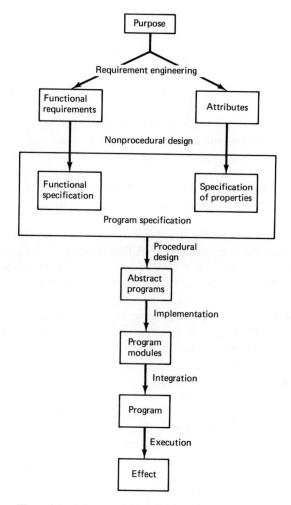

Figure 1.1 Decomposition of the programming task

cedural design *abstract programs*. That is, procedural design produces blueprints for the program modules to be implemented. The nonprocedural and procedural design steps may be repeated in order to refine the blueprints for program implementation to a degree that lends itself to the formulation of program modules in a programming language.

Implementation generates executable program modules that embody the blueprints provided by the procedural design. *Integration* coordinates and couples the program modules so that the assemblage results in an entire concrete *program* (or program system). This program written in some programming language can then be submitted to a computer system and by a step we call *execution* achieve an *effect*. The effect is achieved as the result of a sequence of algorithmic steps performed by the computer system to calculate a result, to perform an administrative task, or to control an industrial process.

Although the decomposition shown in Figure 1.1 may at first appear arbitrary, we believe that these steps and their results can be identified for any purposeful programming project. A single programmer working on a single program may have only an informal mental picture of the program's purpose, may only sketch the functional requirements, may accept any set of constraints that a given computer will impose on program execution, and may design while he or she programs. Large programming projects, on the other hand, involving a programming team, may require elaborate documentation of functional requirements, attributes, program specifications, and abstract programs, and implementation and integration will proceed only after extensive design review [4, 5].

As we mentioned before, the informal methods of program verification are largely based on a process of executing a program, observing its effect, and then comparing that effect with functional specifications and properties. The formal methods we discuss in this book replace this process of informal verification for certain of the steps in the programming task; the formal methods provide "backward mappings" that serve as proofs that these steps were conducted correctly with respect to information provided as inputs to these steps. The verification methods for the programming task that are pertinent to this treatise are identified in Figure 1.2 as additions to the steps of the programming task shown in Figure 1.1.

The most basic of the formal methods, and those that were developed first, are concerned with proof of correctness of existing programs. A somewhat later development is concerned with the interleaving of program construction and proof of correctness. Both approaches to proof of correctness use the functional specification as the embodiment of the program's purpose. Very little exists in terms of formal methods to devise notations for functional requirements and attributes or to demonstrate, other than by inspection, that they conform to the statement of purpose. As a consequence, inspection remains the only tool for confirming correspondence between functional requirements and functional specification. Some work has been done, however, in formally proving properties of functional specifications such as nonfunctional attributes (for example, security), and we discuss this work in Chapter 8.

1.5 ORGANIZATION OF THIS WORK

This book is organized in the following way. We begin with a short discussion of fundamentals, including the application of the mathematical technique of abstraction to the problem of developing a rigorous model of the consequences of running a program on a machine. We then present the various aspects of

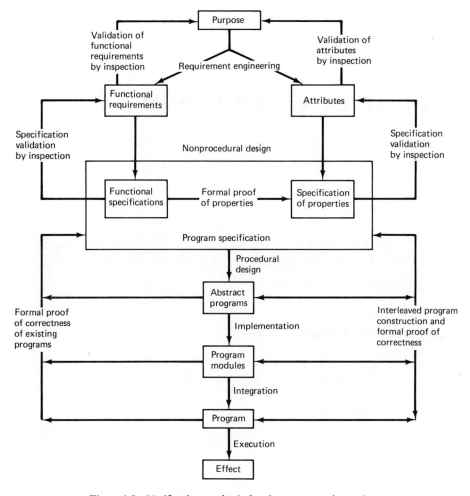

Figure 1.2   Verification methods for the programming task

formal verification. This subject is presented before that of specification because it provides the motivation for specification efforts and because the verification of simple examples can be presented without advanced specification techniques. In addition, an understanding of the verification problem is needed for a full appreciation of the specification problem.

Next we present the various aspects of formal specification, including the major approaches to specification languages, the problem of reasoning about specifications, and the way each specification approach is used in program verification.

We conclude with a summary of the state of the art at the time of this manuscript's preparation, including the progress that has been made in applying formal methods to practical problems.

2

MODELS OF COMPUTATION

2.1 NATURE OF A FORMAL MODEL

In order to reason about any subject we require a representation of its various elements. If the reasoning is to be carried out with mathematical rigor, the representation must be a formal model of the subject. Such a model must satisfy three requirements:

1. It must be complete. It must represent all the essential aspects of the subject being modeled.
2. It must be predictive. Conclusions drawn from the model must correspond to the results obtained by observing the subject itself.
3. It must be well formed. The model should not permit fallacious or ill-formed reasoning.

In this chapter we discuss the problem of producing a formal model of computation. We begin with a general discussion of the principle of mathematical abstraction and show how this principle can be applied to the description of the behavior of a computer. We show the correspondence between the formal model of computation and the formal semantics of a programming language. We conclude with an overview of the major approaches to formal semantics.

2.2 ABSTRACTION

Abstraction is the process of paying strict attention to the aspects of a phenomenon that are important and paying no attention to those that are not. This involves making judgments that are influenced by the purpose of the model we are trying to build. In the context of correctness proofs, our model is intended to demonstrate the correct behavior of a program with respect to functional specifications. We begin with the bewildering multitude of phenomena that occur when a program executes on a real machine—for example, magnetic, electrical, and electromechanical motion and change. We then selectively ignore those phenomena (however interesting they may be to the physicist, engineer, or business person) that do not influence our definition of correct behavior. Correct behavior is defined, at this state of our exposition, as conformance to the unambiguous functional specification. To establish this correspondence—that is, to construct program verification methods—we must develop an abstract and formal statement of the semantics of programming language constructs.

2.3 PROGRAM SEMANTICS AND ABSTRACT MACHINES

The relationship between a computer program and the computer upon which it executes is subtle and sometimes obscure. Much of the obscurity results from imprecise descriptive usage; programmers will often say "the program adds one to the counter" interchangeably with "the machine adds one to the counter." A more precise description would be that "the machine recognizes the program and performs the actions the program defines, the result of which is to add one to the counter." The imprecise usage, however, does imply an important point—that the meaning or the semantics of a program are precisely equivalent to what the program causes a machine to do.

We intend to exploit this equivalence between machine behavior and program semantics in order to ignore, or "abstract out" of our model of program execution, the vast bulk of the specific engineering details of a computer. This high degree of abstraction will have two important consequences: (1) it will make the resulting formal methods general, because they will not be influenced by any of the aspects that serve to differentiate specific machines, and (2) it will bring the formal methods closer to mathematical concepts of proof. The formal methods will accomplish this abstraction by basing the proof on the formal functional specification and a formal model of program semantics.

We begin this task of constructing an appropriate abstract model of program semantics by considering the effect of executing a program. We observe, however, that the effects of executing a program have their source in some computer system, and each of these systems has some form of memory for information storage. Moreover, we can trace each of these disparate effects to a specific value in the memory of the system. Our first step of abstraction, then, is to consider a value in memory to be equivalent to an external effect. This step abstracts out all the diversity of peripherals, displays, and actuators. We then consider the most general form of a representation of a program's data objects in memory in order to eliminate the unnecessary details of word size, storage media, and encoding techniques. The representation we choose (for reasons that will later become clear) is that of a state space—that is, a collection of named abstract objects, each capable of holding a value taken from a predefined set of legitimate values.

So far our steps have carried us toward the definition of an abstract machine, as defined by abstract objects and abstract operations on these objects. We will now consider the definition of abstract operations. Abstract operations can be defined in two ways. The first way is via an abstract definition of a machine's instructions. The consequence of this approach is that the meaning of programming language constructs needs to be associated with these abstract instructions. Thus, establishing the meaning of a program is a two-stage process. The second way is to directly give abstract definitions of the meaning of the programming language constructs themselves. This approach eliminates the computer system altogether and allows us to treat programs as linguistic entities, with syntax and semantics. Thus, we associate the state space with the program instead of with an abstract view of the computer system. Before we proceed to a discussion of approaches to the definition of program semantics, we formally introduce the notions of abstract machines and abstract programs.

2.4 ABSTRACT MACHINES

An abstract machine M is defined by a pair

$$M = (d, F),$$

where d is the *state* of M, and F is a *set of transformations* for effecting state changes. The transformations $f_i \in F$ act upon a set of data objects $\{O_1, \ldots, O_n\}$; the state d is given by the states of the data objects O_j.

A data object O is defined by a triple

$$O = (n, v, t),$$

where n is its *name*, v is its *value*, and t is its *type*. The name of a data object may be used to reference the object in a transformation description. The value of a data object defines the state of the object. The type of a data object defines the form of its value (for example, integer, real) and the operations that may legitimately be performed upon it.

The set of transformations F of an abstract machine M may be embedded into an *abstract programming language*. Then the state d of an abstract machine M is given by the values of data objects that can be created (that is, given a legitimate type), given a name, and assigned a value, using this abstract programming language. That is, the state d at a specific instant is given by the values v_i of the objects of a program written in the abstract programming language; that is,

$$d = (v_1, \ldots, v_n).$$

It is convenient for the treatment of verification to associate a state with an *abstract program*, rather than with the appropriate abstract machine. Then, the state defines the effect of executing a program up to a certain point for a specific set of input values. In addition, the *state space D* of a program may be defined as the Cartesian product

$$D = D_1 \times \ldots \times D_n$$

of the sets D_i of the legitimate states (value ranges) of all the data objects O_i referenced by that program. Legitimate input-output values may then be identified by defining subspaces of the state space D. Thus, the effect of executing a program to a certain point may be expressed in terms of a legitimate input subspace for that program and a relation on the input subspace and an output subspace of D that defines all states that might legitimately be reached by executing the program to that point. Note that this approach is independent of specific sets of input values.

2.5 APPROACHES TO DEFINING PROGRAM SEMANTICS

Having realized that our concern is with program semantics, we must now review the various approaches to the formal definition of the semantics of programming language constructs. Work in this field fits into one of three major catagories referred to [6] as the operational, denotational, and axiomatic approaches.

2.5.1 The Operational Approach

With the operational approach, the sematics of programming constructs of an abstract programming language are defined in terms of a more primitive (lower-level) abstract machine, on the assumption that the state space and operational transformations defining the primitive abstract machine are so simple that their meaning or effect cannot possibly be misunderstood. Specifically, the semantics of the abstract programming language constructs are defined in terms of the state space and operational transformations of the primitive abstract machine. Usually this is done for each programming construct, by providing a "program" that translates the construct into, perhaps, a series of primitive transformations, so that for each programming construct of the abstract programming language there exists a "defining" program in the primitive abstract programming language. To determine the semantics of a programming construct, one must trace through its associated (defining) primitive program. Consequently, to determine the semantics of a program written in the abstract programming language, one must trace through the "translated" program step by step, in order to establish its precise meaning. Definitions of programming language constructs that are oriented toward this approach are provided for PL/I (by the Vienna definition method) [7] and Algol 68 [8].

To verify programs defined by the operational approach requires the execution of (a trace through) the program written in the primitive programming language. The effect of program execution may then be determined by the individual transformations. Obviously, this method is applicable only to specific input values. Hence, a program is verified by observing the results of program executions and demonstrating that those results are in accord with the specification of expected results. The concept underlying this verification method, which maps one input state into one output state, is the common one of *program testing*. The specification of the particular set of input states and the corresponding set of output states constitutes the definition of the test cases—that is, of the test data selection.

The operational approach characterizes the actual effect of program execution by relating it to executions of a separate, lower (more primitive) level. The approach does not solve the original problem of rigorously defining the semantics of programs and programming constructs but merely pushes the problem to the lower level. More importantly, however, the operational approach tends to define the semantics of a program only for specific computations of that program, rather than for the class of all computations that it can perform. In particular, its use to define semantics of a programming language forces us to consider all programs that could possibly be written in the language. Thus, instead of giving "functions" from which the semantics of any program written in the language can be derived, the operational approach tends to suggest implementations of the language.

2.5.2 The Denotational Approach

With the denotational approach, the semantics of programming constructs of an abstract programming language are defined by so-called *semantic valuation functions* [6]. Semantic valuation functions map programming constructs to values (numbers, truth values, functions, and so on) that they denote. These valuation functions are usually defined recursively: the value denoted by a construct is given in terms of the values of its constituent parts, and an emphasis on the values *denoted* by the constituent parts gives the approach its name.

Two things are therefore necessary to the denotational approach to semantics. First, a state space must be given, and with the denotational approach the state space may include functions in addition to "normal" data objects. Second, a technique for defining semantic valuation functions must be given. (The λ-calculus [6, 9] may, for example, be used to model the concepts of function and functional abstraction, and conversion rules exist for syntactic transformations on λ-expressions. Hence, if the class of functions representable by λ-expressions are used to represent valuation functions, then the λ-calculus transformation may be used to manipulate valuation functions.)

The denotational approach to semantic definitions allow us to talk about construct and program *equality* in the sense that two constructs or programs are equal if they both denote the same value in the selected value (state) space.

Verification based on the approach proceeds by constructing the valuation functions for the program constructs and then combining them and the valuation function representing the input conditions by (algebraic) transformation rules to arrive at a valuation function for the program. Via further transformation-rule applications the valuation function for the program is mapped to the valuation function that represents the program final or output condition.

The denotational approach, in contrast to the operational approach, is independent of specific input values. It permits us to define the semantics of the class of all computations that can be performed by a program written in a denotationally defined abstract programming language.

2.5.3 The Axiomatic Approach

The idea of the axiomatic approach is to associate semantics of programming language constructs (and, hence, programs) with logical assertions of two kinds. The first, an input assertion, is assumed true prior to execution of a programming language construct, and from it and the nature of the language construct (program) a second assertion, the output assertion, is derived that is true after execution of the construct (program). The pair of assertions thus characterize legitimate construct (program) input and output states and hence the effect (semantics) of the construct (program). Assertions are derived from the construct (program) state space and the construct. This being the case, program verification based on this approach to characterizing semantics is independent of particular executions—that is, of particular input-output pairs—and proceeds for a construct in a given program by *deriving* output assertions from previously obtained input assertions, with the derivation guided by both the input assertion and the construct (program). The output assertion of one programming construct may be used as the input assertion to a subsequent programming construct, so that program verification proceeds in an *inductive manner*. The process begins with an assertion about program input and concludes when an assertion about the program as a whole has been reached (derived).

2.5.4 A Summary of Three Verification Approaches

The three approaches are contrasted in Figure 2.1, where P denotes a program written in an abstract programming language and D denotes the state space of that program.

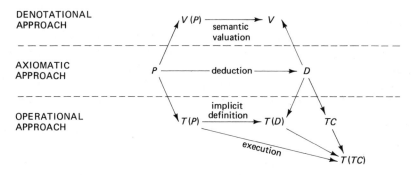

DENOTATIONAL
APPROACH

AXIOMATIC
APPROACH

OPERATIONAL
APPROACH

Figure 2.1 Comparison of Approaches

With the *operational approach*, a program P is translated into a program $T(P)$ written in the abstract programming language of a more primitive abstract machine. As a consequence, the program state space D is mapped onto the state space $T(D)$ of the program $T(P)$. Program $T(P)$ semantics are implicitly defined by the semantics of the programming constructs in $T(P)$, which are assumed to be unambiguous and obvious. In order to explicitly define the semantics of P, test cases TC for program P are defined. These test cases are mapped into the state space $T(D)$, thus yielding a set of test cases $T(TC)$ that are based on $T(D)$. The semantics of program P can then be defined explicitly by executing program $T(P)$ for the test cases $T(TC)$.

With the *denotational approach*, an appropriate value space V must be defined onto which the state space D can be mapped. The program P is then transformed into a program $V(P)$ in a programming language that allows an association between programming constructs and values in V to be established. Finally, semantic valuation functions are defined that associate the programming constructs in $V(P)$, and $V(P)$ itself, with the appropriate subspaces of the value space V (with the λ-calculus, the subspaces of V correspond to members of the class of functions representable by λ-expressions). Hence, the semantics of the program $V(P)$ are explicitly defined. The semantics of program P are indirectly defined by virtue of the conversion of program P to program $V(P)$.

The *axiomatic approach* is the most straightforward. With it the programming constructs in a program P are directly mapped onto a state space D by the explicitly defined semantics of the program P.

We summarize the developments associated with the three fundamental approaches by means of the taxonomy shown in Figure 2.2. The boxes refer to developments. The arcs show the box from which each development primarily emanates. For reference, the attached numbers refer to sections in chapters of this book where a more detailed treatment of each development can be found. The names attached to the arcs are those of at least some of the authors primarily responsible for the development to which the arc leads. As this treatise is concerned with formal methods, we shall not elaborate further on

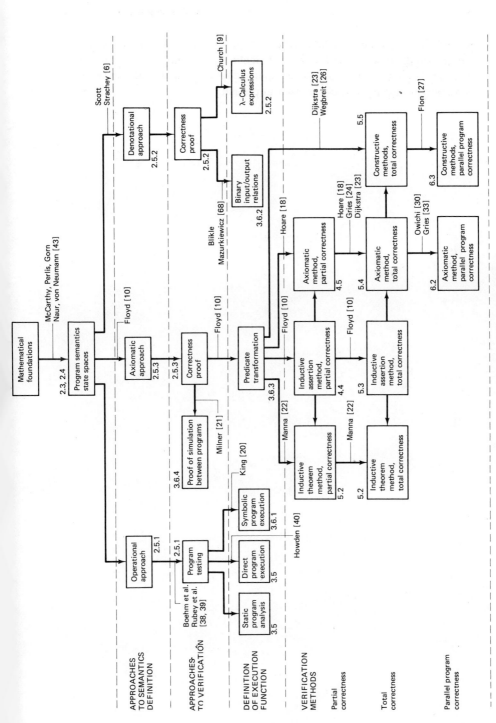

Figure 2.2 Taxonomy of verification methods

15

the different methods for program testing, although we shall include some material on the formal aspects of testing methods. Furthermore, as the axiomatic approach is the most relevant of the approaches to formal program verification, we shall concentrate entirely on that approach.

3

VERIFICATION METHODS

3.1 TERMINOLOGY AND NOTATION

In this chapter we define programs in the most general possible way, in order to show how their semantics can be formally defined. We begin by decomposing a given program into *syntactic units*, or *s-units*. These units can be thought of as corresponding to "statements" in a program. An s-unit must be unambiguously recognizable, other than that it may assume any symbolic form.

Each s-unit defines an *operation* upon some *object*. As defined in Section 2.4, objects are characterized by three attributes: name, value, and type. The name of an object is used to reference the object in an s-unit, thus providing access to the specific value and type the object has for that operation. The value of the object is used to carry out the operation—that is, to determine the results of the operation. The type of the object determines the form its value may assume (integer, real, integer array, and so on) and the operations that may legitmately be performed upon it.

We defend the generality of this representation by examining the consequences of eliminating any of its constituent parts. If we eliminate the concept of s-units, then we must examine and draw conclusions about programs as indivisible entities, a clear impossibility for programs of any size and complexity. If the s-units do not define operations, then the program does nothing and there is nothing to prove. If objects are not named, then a program could have but a single object and the scope of the program is correspondingly restricted. If the data objects do not have values, then programs do not possess a defined state, and our abstract model of program semantics is invalidated. If the values are not permitted a diversity of forms, then all objects must have the most primitive possible form; if the values of an object are not restricted to a predefined set of legitimate values, then all objects have a universal value range. Hence, programs that perform basic operations on complex objects (such as matrix multiplication) must reflect these operations in the maximum richness of the state space defined by this universal value range. This requirement complicates the program, its proof, and hence believability in its effectiveness.

The defense for each of the above attributes of a generalized program is obvious; less obvious is the reason why the type of a data object should include a definition of the operations allowed upon that object. Indeed, this concept of type is relatively new to computer science [17]. The concept arose from the realization that establishing the form that the value of an object may assume implicitly defines the operations allowable upon that object. The definition of addition, for example, is different for objects whose values are integers and those whose values are integer arrays; addition may have no meaningful definition at all for values in the form of character strings. As long as the forms of object values correspond to those of traditional mathematics, the set of meaningful operations can be readily derived from the form. Many useful and interesting programs, however, perform operations upon complex objects such as queues and multiply linked lists, for which there exist other obvious sets of allowable operations. As a result, it is necessary to allow the programmer to specify the form of value and the allowable operations separately; the two together constitute the type of the object.

The relationship between the state of the objects in a program's environment and the semantics of the program may be characterized as follows. The state of the objects is given by the collection of their current values. The state of the objects at any instant of program execution therefore is the result of all changes in the initial values that have occurred up to that instant. The changes, however, are the consequence of performing operations defined by the program. The state of the objects referenced by a program, at any point in that program's execution, is, therefore, the *effect* of executing the program up to that point.

The overall effect of a program may be given by describing the difference between an initial state, d_0, and a final state, d_f. Following Hoare [18], we adopt the notation

$$\vdash \{d_0\}\, P\, \{d_f\},$$

to mean that "if the initial program state is d_0, then execution of program P will result in the final program state d_f." Since P defines, in effect, a function that maps a program state into another program state, there exist a *domain* and a *range* for P. The domain consists of a set of initial states for which the execution of the program will result in a final state—that is, for which the function embodied by P is defined. Note that P may not be definable as a function if, for instance, it does not terminate. The range consists of a set of final states that can be reached by executing P starting from any legitimate initial state.

Rather than explicitly listing all the states that constitute the domain, we use a condition Φ to define the domain. This condition usually expresses some requirement that the states of the data objects must satisfy in order to be included in the domain. For instance, a program that computes the square root of some object of type "real" may have a restricted domain described by the condition that the initial value of the object be nonnegative. The conditions are generally specified in terms of the names of the data objects and define requirements on their associated values, hence we may say that the conditions define a subspace of a program's state space (as given by the object type definitions). Hence when we write

$$\Phi\colon n \geq 0,$$

we are using the symbol Φ to denote the condition that the value of n be nonnegative, and thereby we define a subspace of the state space as defined by the type "real."

The semantics of a particular program (or the set of legitimate final states or "range") may be specified by a condition Ψ that must be satisfied by the final state, d_f, of that program. For example, if our square-root program resulted in the assignment of the value "square root of the initial value of n" to the object named "n", we could express, very generally, the semantics of executing P by giving the condition

$$\Psi\colon n' = \mathrm{SQRT}(n)$$

as a relation between initial and final states. We designate the value of a data object at the *end* of program execution by affixing a prime to the name of that object, and we allow the unprimed name to refer to the value of that object at the outset of execution.

By using conditions to describe domains and ranges of programs, we may compactly describe the semantics of a particular program by

$$\vdash \{\Phi\}\, P\, \{\Psi\},$$

which reads: "If the initial state d_0 satisfies condition Φ, then the program terminates and the final d_f will satisfy the condition given by Ψ." Thus, we might describe the semantics of our square-root program by

$$\vdash \{n \geq 0\}\ \text{SQUARE-ROOT PROGRAM}\ \{n' = \mathrm{SQRT}(n)\},$$

which reads: "If the data object n initially has a value greater than or equal to zero, then the square-root program terminates with a value equal to the square root of that initial value."

3.2 PROGRAM CORRECTNESS

A program is a description of an algorithm for a transformation from an initial state to a final state. The actual transformation described by the program is carried out by an abstract machine, as discussed in Chapter 2. The process of transformation is referred to as the *execution* of the program.

The execution of a program P, then, can be thought of as a *function E*, whose domain is the set of legitimate initial states of P and whose range is the set of legitimate final states of P.

We call the function E the *execution function* and (as stated above) denote the condition defining the *set of legitimate initial states* of program P by Φ and the condition defining the *set of legitimate final states* of program P by Ψ. Note that Φ and Ψ state conditions that define subspaces of the state space, $D = D_1 \times \cdots \times D_n$, of the program P, which is defined by the value ranges D_i of the data objects O_i referenced by program P (see Section 2.4). Then the *final state* d_f resulting from the execution of the program P for an initial state d_0 is

$$d_f = E(P, d_0),$$

if $E(P, d_0)$ is defined.

For initial state d_0, we have

$E(P, d_0)$ is undefined, if P does not terminate for d_0

an d

$E(P, d_0)$ is the final state, if P does terminate for d_0.

A program may fail to terminate as a result of addressing errors, illegal instructions, arithmetic faults, infinite loops, and so on. $E(P, d_0)$ is thus a partial function, since it may not be defined for some initial states d_0.

The effect of program execution—that is, the program semantics—can be defined in terms of differences between initial and final states. Statements of semantic properties of program execution usually describe the execution function E over some large set of legitimate initial states.

As noted in the preceding section, we use the notation $\vdash \{\Phi\}\, P\, \{\Psi\}$ (after Hoare [18]) to denote the fact that "If the initial state d_0 satisfies Φ [that is, if $\vdash \Phi(d_0)$], then the program P will terminate with the final state satisfying Ψ [that is, then $\vdash \Psi(d_f)$]. Since the final state $d_f = E(P, d_0)$, we may now more compactly define $\vdash \{\Phi\}\, P\, \{\Psi\}$ by the equivalence:

$$\vdash \{\Phi\}\, P\, \{\Psi\} \qquad \text{(program correctness)} \tag{3.1}$$

iff

$$(\forall d_0)(\vdash \Phi(d_0) \longrightarrow \vdash (P \text{ terminates}) \underline{\text{ and }} \vdash \Psi(E(P, d_0))).$$

As we shall see, it is often convenient to consider the "conditional" or *partial* correctness of a program [as opposed to the total correctness of (3.1)] under the *assumption* that it terminates. We use the notation $\vdash \{\Phi\}\, P\, \{\Psi\}^+$ to denote the fact that if the initial state d_0 satisfies Φ *and P* terminates, then the final state d_f will satisfy Ψ; that is,

$$\vdash \{\Phi\}\, P\, \{\Psi\}^+ \qquad \text{(program partial correctness)} \qquad (3.2)$$

<u>iff</u>

$$(\forall\, d_0)((\vdash \Phi(d_0)\ \underline{\text{and}}\ \vdash (P\ \text{terminates})) \longrightarrow\ \vdash \Psi(E(P, d_0))).$$

Initially we shall focus our attention on partial correctness, since in general it is easier to prove than total correctness, which must include a proof that the program will indeed terminate.

Example:

Suppose program MAX finds the maximum value of three integers, a, b, and c, and leaves the result in the variable max. If, for example, MAX were executed with initial state $d_0 = \langle a, b, c, \text{max}\rangle^* = \langle 2, 3, 1, 0\rangle$, we would expect that

$$d_f = E(\text{MAX}, d_0) = \langle 2, 3, 1, 3\rangle.$$

If we chose

Φ: <u>true</u>,

Ψ: (max $= a$ <u>or</u> max $= b$ <u>or</u> max $= c$) <u>and</u>

max $\geq a$ <u>and</u> max $\geq b$ <u>and</u> max $\geq c$,

then we could specify a semantic property of the execution of MAX by $\vdash \{\Phi\}\, \text{MAX}\, \{\Psi\}$, which says that MAX is totally correct with respect to Φ and Ψ. In other words, for all initial states d_0 such that $\vdash \Phi(d_0)$ (in this case *any* initial state), we may conclude that MAX terminates and that $d_f = E(\text{MAX}, d_0)$ is such that $\vdash \Psi(d_f)$. By writing $\vdash \{\Phi\}\, \text{MAX}\, \{\Psi\}^+$, on the other hand, we claim only that the abovementioned relations hold if MAX terminates; that is, MAX is only *partially* correct with respect to Φ and Ψ.

3.3 SYNTACTIC UNIT CORRECTNESS

So far, we have dealt with programs from a *global* viewpoint of execution and semantics. If only a small, finite number of programs could exist, then program verification would be a dead subject once we had established semantic properties for those programs. What makes programming and program verification an interesting and challenging endeavor is that the number of potential programs is infinite. The reason for this variety, of course, is that programs are composed of smaller *syntactic units*, or *s-units*, which may be combined in different ways to produce different programs. At this juncture, therefore, we change our point of view from programs as "black boxes" to the more detailed

---

*For readability we use object names to identify the values of data objects.

view of programs as finite sequences of s-units:

$$\text{program } P$$

$$s_1;$$

$$s_2;$$

$$\cdot$$

$$\cdot \qquad\qquad\qquad\qquad (3.3)$$

$$\cdot$$

$$s_n;$$

$$\text{end } P.$$

The execution of a single s-unit may be viewed in exactly the same way as the execution of a program. This is not surprising, since we may choose to make our s-units as "large" as may be convenient, even to the point of viewing an entire program as a syntactic unit. The execution function E of a syntactic unit s_j with initial state d_0 is defined analogously to that of a program:

$$E(s_j, d_0) \text{ is undefined, if } s_j \textit{ does not } \text{terminate for } d_0,$$

and

$$E(s_j, d_0) \text{ is the final state, if } s_j \textit{ does } \text{terminate for } d_0.$$

The reasons why an s-unit may not terminate are identical to the reasons why a program may not terminate (see Section 3.2).

Additionally, the semantics of s-unit execution are expressed in a manner completely analogous to those of program execution. That is, using Q and R to denote the conditions that define the sets of legitimate initial and final states, we have

$$\vdash \{Q\}\, s_j\, \{R\} \qquad \text{(s-unit correctness)} \qquad\qquad (3.4)$$

$$\underline{\text{iff}}$$

$$(\forall d_0)\,(\vdash Q(d_0) \longrightarrow \vdash (s_j \text{ terminates}) \underline{\text{ and }} \vdash R(E(s_j, d_0)))$$

and

$$\vdash \{Q\}\, s_j\, \{R\}^{+} \qquad \text{(s-unit partial correctness)} \qquad\qquad (3.5)$$

$$\underline{\text{iff}}$$

$$(\forall d_0)((\vdash Q(d_0) \underline{\text{ and }} \vdash (s_j \text{ terminates})) \longrightarrow \vdash R(E(s_j, d_0))).$$

Example:

Suppose the program MAX of Section 3.2 is composed of the following s-units:

$$\text{program MAX}$$

$$s_1\text{: } max := a;$$

$$s_2\text{: } \underline{\text{if }} max \geq b \underline{\text{ then goto }} s_4;$$

$$s_3\text{: } max := b;$$

$$s_4\text{: } \underline{\text{if }} max \geq c \underline{\text{ then goto }} s_6;$$

$$s_5: \text{max} := c;$$

$$s_6: \underline{\text{stop}};$$

$$\text{end MAX}$$

If statement s_1 is executed with initial state $d_0 = \langle a, b, c, \text{max} \rangle = \langle 2, 3, 1, 0 \rangle$, then

$$E(s_1, d_0) = \langle 2, 3, 1, 2 \rangle.$$

Then, assuming that

$$Q: \underline{\text{true}}, \text{ with } Q = \Phi,$$

$$R: \text{max} = a,$$

we might characterize the semantics of s_1 by

$$\vdash \{Q\} \text{ max} := a \{R\}$$

if we can prove that s_1 terminates, or by

$$\vdash \{Q\} \text{ max} := a \{R\}^+$$

to express the *partial* correctness of s_1 with respect to Q and R. Q and R are called the *precondition* and *postcondition* of s_1, respectively.

3.4 PROGRAMS AND SYNTACTIC UNITS

The execution of a program depends upon the execution of its constituent s-units and the *order* in which those s-units are executed. Consequently, the semantic properties of a program depend upon the semantic properties of its constituent s-units and the way in which those "local" properties combine to give "global" meaning to the program.

The execution of a program results from the execution of a sequence of s-units from that program. Given a program $P = s_1; s_2; \ldots ; s_n$ and an initial state d_0, we define the *trace* T of P and d_0 to be the sequence of s-units executed. That is

$$T(P, d_0) = s_{i_1}, s_{i_2}, \ldots, \qquad (3.6)$$

where $i_1, i_2, \ldots \in 1 .. n$. That is, $s_{i_1}, s_{i_2}, \ldots$ are all s-units "drawn" from P. The trace $T(P, d_0)$ is a finite sequence if and only if $E(P, d_0)$ is defined (that is, if P terminates given initial state d_0). We will use the notation $|T(P, d_0)|$ to denote the length of the sequence $T(P, d_0)$ so that

$$E(P, d_0) \text{ is defined } \underline{\text{iff}} \ (\exists m \in Z^+)(m = |T(P, d_0)|). \qquad (3.7)$$

Since the execution of each s-unit has the potential to change the state of the objects it acts upon, it is also useful to consider the sequence of states, called the *computation* $C(P, d_0)$, arising from $T(P, d_0)$. That is,

$$C(P, d_0) = d_1, d_2, \ldots, \qquad (3.8)$$

where d_j is the state in the state space of P that is reached after the execution of s_{i_j}. The trace and computation of program execution are related by virtue of $|C(P, d_0)| = |T(P, d_0)|$. That is, there are as many new states "created" as there are s-units executed.

We relate program execution to the execution of its constituent syntactic units by noting that

$E(P, d_0) = d_m$ is defined

iff

$(\exists\, m \in Z^+)(m = |C(P, d_0)|)$,   where $C(P, d_0) = d_1, d_2, \ldots, d_m$;   (3.9)

$E(P, d_0)$ is undefined if no such m exists.

Example:

Taking the program MAX of Section 3.3 with initial state $d_0 = \langle a, b, c, \text{max} \rangle = \langle 2, 3, 1, 0 \rangle$, and applying the "usual" interpretations to the s-units comprising MAX, we arrive at

$E(\text{MAX}, d_0) = \langle 2, 3, 1, 3 \rangle$,

$T(\text{MAX}, d_0) = s_1, s_2, s_3, s_4, s_6$,

$C(\text{MAX}, d_0) = \langle 2, 3, 1, 2 \rangle, \langle 2, 3, 1, 2 \rangle, \langle 2, 3, 1, 3 \rangle, \langle 2, 3, 1, 3 \rangle, \langle 2, 3, 1, 3 \rangle$,

for the execution, trace, and computation, respectively.

3.5 THE RELATIONSHIP BETWEEN TESTING AND VERIFICATION

In Section 2.5 the two fundamentally different verification methods of testing and correctness proofs were sketched. These two methods may be contrasted in the framework established above, in which the effect of program execution is described by the difference between an initial state, d_0, and a final state, d_f. The notation used to express the effect of program execution,

$$\{d_0\}\, P\, \{d_f\},$$

may be considered as the definition of a test case for program P, where $d_0 \in \{d\ |\vdash \Phi(d)\}$. That is, it defines the condition

$$d_f = E(P, d_0)$$

that must be satisfied by a successful test of program P using the test data defined by d_0. Hence, *program testing* is concerned with the verification of test cases, $\{d_0\}\, P\, \{d_f\}$, or the verification of equivalences of the form $E(P, d_0) = d_f$.

Program testing may allow the program states d_i in the computation $C(P, d_0) = d_1, d_2, \ldots$ of a program to be observed. Consequently, test cases

$$\{d_{j-1}\}\, s_{i_j}\, \{d_j\}$$

may be verified for the individual s-units s_{i_j} in the trace $T(P, d_0) = s_{i_1}, s_{i_2}, \ldots$ of program P for initial state d_0. Successful tests for each individual s-unit s_{i_j} in the trace $T(P, d_0)$ with $E(s_{i_j}, d_{j-1}) = d_j$, $j \in 1, \ldots, |T(P, d_0)|$, and $d_{|T(P, d_0)|} = d_f$, constitute a successful test of the program P with $E(P, d_0) = d_f$. Thus, programs may be tested as entities using test cases $\{d_0\}\,P\,\{d_f\}$, or they may be tested inductively using test cases $\{d_{j-1}\}\,s_{i_j}\,\{d_j\}$, with $d_{j-1} = E(s_{i_{j-1}}, d_{j-2})$. The successful verification of test cases $\{d_0\}\,P\,\{d_f\}$ or $\{d_{j-1}\}\,s_{i_j}\,\{d_j\}$ is equivalent to the statements $\vdash \{d_0\}\,P\,\{d_f\}$ or $\vdash \{d_{j-1}\}\,s_{i_j}\,\{d_j\}$, respectively (see Section 3.1).

Program correctness as defined in (3.1) may be formulated with respect to program testing as follows:

$$(\forall\, d_0)(\vdash \Phi(d_0) \longrightarrow \vdash E(P, d_0) = d_f \text{ and } \vdash \Psi(d_f)), \qquad (3.10)$$

where d_0 and d_f are given by the definition of test cases $\{d_0\}\,P\,\{d_f\}$. Obviously, the definition of test cases requires knowledge of the sets of legitimate initial and final states as defined by Φ and Ψ, respectively.

We recognize from (3.10) that program correctness cannot readily be established by testing, as the set of legitimate initial states generally is infinite, so that an infinite set of test cases would have to be specified and conducted. Hence, testing validates programs by verifying an appropriate set of test cases.

In *correctness proofs* we are concerned with the establishment of $\vdash \{d_0\}\,P\,\{d_f\}$ for all legitimate initial states d_0—that is, all states d_0 with $\vdash \Phi(d_0)$. Rather than proving $E(P, d_0) = d_f$ for all these states separately, we strive for a single logical argument that establishes $\vdash E(P, d_0) = d_f$ for all legitimate initial states d_0. Therefore, we refer to conditions Φ and Ψ as introduced in Section 3.1 for defining the effect of program execution by $\{\Phi\}\,P\,\{\Psi\}$ rather than to test cases $\{d_0\}\,P\,\{d_f\}$. The associated statement of program correctness, $\vdash \{\Phi\}\,P\,\{\Psi\}$, as defined in (3.1), is then equivalent to the successful verification of all conceivable test cases, with $\vdash \Phi(d_0)$. It must be emphasized that the establishment of $\vdash \{\Phi\}\,P\,\{\Psi\}$ by a correctness proof is theoretically feasible, even if Φ defines an infinite set, whereas the verification of all conceivable test cases is not.

As this discussion indicates, there is interest and merit in finding a finite sample of test cases that could be used to establish program correctness by testing. This issue has been studied by Goodenough and Gerhart [89]. The Goodenough-Gerhart theory involves the notion of an *ideal test*, which is defined by a subset T of all legitimate initial states of a program—that is, of all initial states d_0, with $\vdash \Phi(d_0)$, such that

$$\vdash (\forall\, d_0 \in T)(E(P, d_0) = d_f \text{ and } \Psi(d_f))$$

$$\longrightarrow \vdash ((\forall\, d_0)(\vdash \Phi(d_0) \longrightarrow \vdash E(P, d_0) = d_f \text{ and } \vdash \Psi(d_f))).$$

That is, if from successful execution of P for all initial states $d_0 \in T$ we can conclude program correctness, then T constitutes an ideal test. The Goodenough and Gerhart theory defines the criteria for test data selections that ensure the identification of initial-state sets that constitute ideal tests. The theory is based on the following concepts.

Let T be a set of test data and let C be the criterion for selecting T. Then, the *completeness of a test data set* is defined by the predicate

$$\text{COMPLETE}(T, C),$$

which ensures that the successful execution of all test cases derived from T implies correctness of the program. The criterion C defines what properties a program must exhibit for the collection of test cases derived from T to constitute a *thorough test*. A test is *successful* if the execution of a program against all test cases defined by T conforms to the definition of the program semantics as given by the definition of the execution function, that is,

$$\text{SUCCESSFUL}(T): (\forall\, d_0 \in T)(d_f = E(P, d_0)).$$

To ensure that a successful test with a complete set of test data implies program correctness, the test-data selection criterion C must be reliable and valid. A test-data selection criterion C is *reliable*, if and only if for *every* set of test data T, $T \subseteq \{d_0 \mid\; \vdash \Phi(d_0)\}$, with $\text{COMPLETE}(T, C)$, we have $\text{SUCCESSFUL}(T)$ or not $\text{SUCCESSFUL}(T)$; that is,

$$\text{RELIABLE}(C): (\forall\, T_1, T_2)((\text{COMPLETE}(T_1, C) \underline{\text{ and }} \text{COMPLETE}(T_2, C))$$
$$\longrightarrow (\text{SUCCESSFUL}(T_1) = \text{SUCCESSFUL}(T_2))),$$

where $T_1, T_2 \subseteq \{d_0 \mid\; \vdash \Phi(d_0)\}$. A test-data selection criterion C is *valid*, if and only if for *every* error in a program there exists a set of test data T, with $\text{COMPLETE}(T, C)$, such that we have $\underline{\text{not}}$ $\text{SUCCESSFUL}(T)$; that is,

$$\text{VALID}(C): (\forall\, d_0)(\vdash \Phi(d_0) \longrightarrow\; \vdash d_f \neq E(P, d_0))$$
$$\longrightarrow (\exists\, T)(\text{COMPLETE}(T, C) \underline{\text{ and }} \underline{\text{not}}\ \text{SUCCESSFUL}(T)).$$

The Goodenough-Gerhart *theorem of testing* [89] is

$$(\exists\, T)((\exists\, C)(\vdash \text{COMPLETE}(T, C) \underline{\text{ and }} \vdash \text{RELIABLE}(C)$$
$$\underline{\text{and}} \vdash \text{VALID}(C) \underline{\text{ and }} \vdash \text{SUCCESSFUL}(T))$$
$$\longrightarrow (\forall\, d_0)(\vdash \Phi(d_0) \longrightarrow\; \vdash d_f = E(P, d_0))). \qquad (3.11)$$

This theorem states that tests using complete test-data sets, derived by reliable and valid test-data selection criteria, are thorough in the sense of ideal tests. Although the theorem may alleviate the need for exhaustive testing, it requires demonstrating the reliability and validity of test-data selection criteria. Note, however, that proving a test-data selection criterion to be reliable and valid, and then finding and successfully executing a complete test satisfying this criterion, is a way of proving programs correct, as stated in (3.10).

   Several situations can be distinguished on the basis of the theorem of testing. For example, if C is defined such that the only complete test is an exhaustive one, then we obviously have $\vdash \text{RELIABLE}(C)$ and $\vdash \text{VALID}(C)$. Additionally when C cannot be satisfied by any d_0 with $\vdash \Phi(d_0)$—that is, when T is the empty set—we obviously have $\vdash \text{RELIABLE}(C)$. However, in order to prove $\vdash \text{VALID}(C)$, we have to establish $(\forall\, d_0)(\vdash \Phi(d_0) \longrightarrow\; \vdash d_f = E(P, d_0)$—that is, the proof of $\vdash \text{VALID}(C)$ is equivalent to a correctness proof. The most common case is that for all d_0 with $\vdash \Phi(d_0)$ there exists a set T, with $d_0 \in T$ and $\text{COMPLETE}(T, C)$. In this case some testing must be performed, and the major concern is with the proof of the reliability of the test-data selection criterion C. In order to prove the reliability of a test-data selection criterion, tests must be designed not so much to "exercise" program paths as to "exercise" paths under circumstances that will detect errors if they exist. Tests based solely on the internal structure of a program as performed in static program analysis (see Figure 2.2) are likely to be unreliable. Rather, all conditions relevant to the correct operation of the program must be identified, and all possible combinations of these conditions must be exercised through direct program execution (Figure 2.2), an extremely difficult task.

It has been recognized [133] that the essence of testing is establishment of the basic propositions of an inductive correctness proof (see Section 4.3)—that is, inference that the success of one test-data set is equivalent to successful completion of an exhaustive program test. A formal correctness proof differs from this rigorous testing approach simply by removing test cases altogether while striving for the same inference. Both approaches rely on the definition of predicates that describe conditions and combinations of conditions relevant to the program's correct operation. In testing, these predicates are used to derive test data that collectively satisfy a test-data selection criterion. In correctness proofs, these predicates are used as assertions in a mathematical argument that establishes the correctness of the program independent of any particular execution of that program.

3.6 VERIFICATION TECHNIQUES

Fundamental differences between alternative correctness-proof techniques arise primarily from differences in the approaches taken to define the execution function E. This observation can be made directly from the definition of program correctness as given in (3.1), in which the execution function $E(P, d_0)$ plays a central role. Definitions of the execution function to be used in correctness proofs must be based solely on the semantic definition of the syntactic units of the (abstract) programming language used to write the program to be proven correct. Hence, according to the discussion in Section 2.5, three major approaches to the definition of the execution function may be distinguished:

1. The operational approach.
2. The denotational approach.
3. The axiomatic approach.

In this section we discuss the basic notions of the verification technique associated with each of the three approaches. The particular techniques we chose to illustrate these notions are identified in Figure 2.2.

3.6.1 Operational Definition of the Execution Function

An operational approach to the definition of the execution function E is given by *symbolic execution* [20]. The execution of a program is made symbolic by introducing symbolic object values as inputs in place of actual object values. (Note that a symbolic object value represents an unknown, yet fixed, actual value.) To demonstrate the concept of symbolic execution, we consider the following simple example.

We denote the value of a data object, X, by $v(X)$. Let the data objects A and B be assigned the symbolic values a and b, respectively. Then the symbolic execution of the assignment statement

$$C := A + 2 \times B$$

results in the symbolic value

$$v(C) = a + 2 \times b.$$

Using this symbolic value of C, the symbolic execution of the assignment statement

$$D := C - A$$

yields the symbolic value

$$v(D) = a + 2 \times b - a.$$

Using algebraic simplification rules, $v(D)$ may be reduced to

$$v(D) = 2 \times b.$$

It is readily recognized that, with symbolic execution, a program state d in the state space D is defined by an n-tuple of the form

$$d = (v(n_1), \ldots, v(n_n)),$$

where $v(n_i)$ denotes the symbolic value of the data object n_i referenced by the program. Consequently, the execution function $E(s, d)$ of an s-unit s is defined by a function $f(d)$ with

$$E(s, d) = f(d),$$

which incorporates the transformations contained in s and the symbolic values of the data objects referenced in s.

Given this definition of the execution function, the computation $C(P, d_0)$ of a program P may be defined by

$$C(P, d_0) = d_1, d_2, \ldots$$
$$= f_1(d_0), f_2(d_1), \ldots$$
$$= f_1(d_0), f_2(f_1(d_0)), \ldots,$$

hence the execution function of a program is given by

$$E(P, d_0) = f_{|C(P, d_0)|}(f_{|C(P, d_0)|-1}(\ldots (f_1(d_0)) \ldots))$$
$$= d_f.$$

Thus, program semantics are derived by symbolically executing the program P.

Note that the definition of the execution function by symbolic execution requires a trace through the given program, P. However, in contrast to the direct execution of a program as performed in testing, symbolic execution eliminates the need for specifying test cases. Rather, the program semantics are derived as a function of symbolic values that are independent of particular initial and final states, d_0 and d_f. Consequently, the desired program semantics may also be specified in terms of a function, $\Psi(v(n_1), \ldots, v(n_n))$, of symbolic values. Then, the correctness of a program P may be shown by proving equivalences of the form

$$\Psi(v(n_1), \ldots, v(n_n)) = E(P, (v(n_1), \ldots, v(n_n)))$$

$$= f_{|C(P,\,(v(n_1),\,\ldots,\,v(n_n)))|}(\ldots(f_1(v(n_1), \ldots, v(n_n)))\ldots).$$

To this end, algebraic simplification rules may be used.

The reader may have noticed that the definition of the execution function $E(P, (v(n_1), \ldots, v(n_n)))$ is implicitly dependent on the trace $T(P, d_0)$ $= T(P, (v(n_1), \ldots, v(n_n)))$ of the program P, which in turn is dependent on the value of the initial state d_0. In fact, this dependency constitutes one of the major limitations of symbolic execution. For conditional branches that depend on symbolic branch conditions, all alternative execution traces need be considered, hence there may exist several alternative definitions of the execution function $E(P, (v(n_1), \ldots, v(n_n)))$. Moreover, iterative constructs that are conditioned by symbolic values may lead to infinite execution traces. The latter difficulty may be overcome [20] by introducing inductive arguments according to the inductive assertion method [10] to be discussed in Section 4.4.

3.6.2 Denotational Definition of the Execution Function

With the denotational approach to semantic definition, the semantics of s-units are defined by *semantic valuation function* (see Section 2.5.2). An example of a denotational approach to this definition of the execution function is the *Blikle-Mazurkiewicz method* [68]; other approaches to denotational definitions of the execution function and verification using the λ-calculus are discussed in [6]. Here, the execution function $E(P, d_0)$ is defined by a binary relation, $R \subseteq D \times D$, which defines the input-output behavior of the program P. To establish this relation, the program P is split into a finite number of s-units, $s_1, \ldots, s_m$ (for example, assignment statements or tests), which are also defined by binary input-output relations, $R_1, \ldots, R_m$. The relation R is then defined by a semantic valuation function $f(R_1, \ldots, R_m)$ formulated in an algebra of binary relations:

$$R = f(R_1, \ldots, R_m).$$

The semantic valuation function f is found by an algebraic method that consists of writing and solving a set of fix-point equations (a kind of functional equations).

To prove the correctness of a program, the desired semantics may be specified in terms of a function $\Psi(v(n_1), \ldots, v(n_n))$ of symbolic values $v(n_i)$. Then the correctness of a program may be shown by proving equivalences of the form

$$\Psi(v(n_1), \ldots, v(n_n)) = E(P, (v(n_1), \ldots, v(n_n)))$$
$$= f(R_1(v(n_1), \ldots, v(n_n)), \ldots, R_m(v(n_1), \ldots, v(n_n))).$$

This proof is carried out in the algebra of binary relations.

This approach appears, at first glance, very similar to the symbolic execution approach. Both approaches specify the desired program semantics in terms of a function $\Psi(v(n_1), \ldots, v(n_n))$. However, in contrast to symbolic execution, the denotational approach does not rely on the trace $T(P, d_0)$ in order to define the execution function $E(P, (v(n_1), \ldots, v(n_n)))$. Rather, the input-output relations $R_i(v(n_1), \ldots, v(n_n))$ implicitly denote the symbolic value of the associated s-units s_i. That is, the definition of the relations R_i $(v(n_1), \ldots, v(n_n))$ corresponds to a transformation of the program P into a program $V(P)$ (see Section 2.5.4) that allows an association between s-units and symbolic values in the "symbolic" state space V of the program to be described. Therefore, the semantic valuation function $f(R_1, \ldots, R_m)$ may be derived algebraically to explicitly define the semantics of the program P.

3.6.3 Axiomatic Definition of the Execution Function

In the axiomatic approach, the execution function E is implicitly defined by predicate transformations. A *predicate transformation* is a function that maps an assertion and an s-unit into another assertion (see Section 2.5.3). Using the notation introduced in Section 3.3, Q and R denote the input assertion and the output assertion, respectively, of an s-unit s in $\{Q\} s \{R\}$. The semantics of the s-units s_i of a given language are defined by predicate transformations $TR(s_i, Q) = R$, such that for a given state d it is guaranteed that

$$\vdash Q(d) \longrightarrow \vdash R(E(s_i, d)).$$

Examples of predicate transformers are the "strongest verifiable consequent transformer" [10] and the "weakest precondition transformer" [23].

The derivation of the execution function $E(P, d_0)$ using predicate transformations may be illustrated as follows. Consider the trace of a program $T(P, d_0) = s_{i_1}, s_{i_2}, \ldots$. Let

$$TR(s_{i_j}, R_{j-1}) = R_j \text{ and } TR(s_{i_{j+1}}, R_j) = R_{j+1}.$$

Then we obtain by substitution

$$TR(s_{i_{j+1}}, R_j) = TR(s_{i_{j+1}}, TR(s_{i_j}, R_{j-1})) = R_{j+1},$$

and thus

$$\vdash R_{j-1}(d) \longrightarrow \vdash R_{j+1}(E(s_{i_j}; s_{i_{j+1}}, d)).$$

Consequently, we may define a predicate transformer for functional composition such that

$$TR(s_{i_{j+1}}, TR(s_{i_j}, R_{j-1})) = TR(s_{i_j}; s_{i_{j+1}}, R_{j-1}) = R_{j+1}.$$

Applying this predicate transformer inductively to the trace $T(P, d_0)$ of P, we may obtain the predicate transformation

$$TR(T(P, d_0), \Phi) = \Psi$$

or, equivalently,

$$\vdash \Phi(d_0) \longrightarrow \vdash \Psi(E(T(P, d_0), d_0)).$$

If Φ and Ψ are the desired input and output assertions of P, respectively, and P terminates, the *inductive* application of predicate transformations establishes the correctness of P for the trace $T(P, d_0)$.

As will be shown, it is possible to define predicate transformers for conditional and iterative s-units. Using these predicate transformers, derivation of program semantics becomes independent of particular initial states d_0, hence independent of individual traces $T(P, d_0)$. Consequently, a predicate transformer $TR(P, \Phi) = \Psi$ may be derived that encompasses all conceivable paths through P. This predicate transformer guarantees

$$(\forall d_0)(\vdash \Phi(d_0) \longrightarrow \Psi(E(P, d_0))).$$

Furthermore, predicate transformers may be defined such that $TR(P, \Phi) = \Psi$ guarantees $(\forall d_0)(\vdash \Phi(d_0) \longrightarrow \vdash (P$ terminates) $\underline{\text{and}} \vdash \Psi(E(P, d_0)))$. Note that the latter statement corresponds to the definition of program correctness given in (3.1). Thus, the axiomatic definition of the execution function $E(P, d_0)$—that is, the derivation of program semantics—includes the correctness proof, if the assertion defined by $TR(P, \Phi)$ implies Ψ, which specifies the desired program semantics.

3.6.4 Algebraic Simulation

An interesting variation of the previous techniques, proposed by Milner [21], is given by *algebraic simulation between programs*. Unlike the previous techniques, this one does not derive program semantics by combining semantic definitions of individual s-units, hence its approach to verification is somewhat indirect. The algebraic simulation technique involves, for a given program P, construction of a "more natural" program P' with the same semantics as P. For these two programs it proceeds with the proof that the "more natural" program P' is correct (using any of the techniques discussed above) and the demonstration that the original program P "simulates" the program P'.

More formally a program P simulates the program P' if there exists a mapping F,

$$F: D_{p'} \longrightarrow D_p,$$

such that

$$(\forall d_{p_0'})(\vdash \Phi_{p'}(d_{p_0'}) \longrightarrow (E_p(P, F(d_{p_0'})) = F(E_{p'}(P', d_{p_0'})))),$$

where $\Phi_{p'}$ characterizes the legitimate initial states of P' and the proof is carried out using the technique associated with the form of the execution function definition employed (see Sections 3.6.1, 3.6.2, and 3.6.3).

Although somewhat more indirect in its approach to verification, the technique's motivation is an ability to "handle" programs P containing "troublesome" control structures or data object forms by mapping them to structures and objects in P' that are more amenable to verification. This approach has been much used to verify microcode, where P' is given in a higher-level language and P is an assembly- (or machine-) oriented micro code program [71].

4

APPROACHES TO PROOFS
OF PARTIAL CORRECTNESS

Having sketched various verification approaches in Chapter 3, we now concentrate solely on the axiomatic approach, as it is the most popular. Our trace of the axiomatic approach begins with the inductive assertion method proposed by Floyd [10] and ends with methods and approaches for proving the correctness of parallel programs. The discussion spans three chapters: partial correctness (Chapter 4), total correctness (Chapter 5), and correctness of parallel programs (Chapter 6), and proceeds by presenting the methods encountered on the paths in Figure 2.2. For each method we give an algorithm for its application and discuss its strengths, weaknesses, and placement in the spectrum of methods. Our objective is to provide a readable account of each method; accordingly, we use a consistent notation throughout and illustrate related methods through similar examples. The reader may consider each approach as an application of a "deductive system" of mathematics, and while we have not included a discussion of each possible variant, we have tried to include each of the main-stream approaches.

4.1 DEDUCTIVE SYSTEMS: THE MATHEMATICAL BASIS
OF THE AXIOMATIC APPROACH

A deductive system $L = (A, I)$ is composed of axioms $A = (A_1, A_2, \ldots, A_n)$ and rules of inference $I = (I_1, I_2, \ldots, I_m)$ by which *valid* statements, or *theorems*, may be derived from the axioms and other theorems. The *axioms A* of a deductive system $L = (A, I)$ are a collection of statements that are assumed, a priori, to be valid and hence automatically are theorems in L. If a statement S has been shown to be a valid statement in a deductive system, we write

$$\vdash S \tag{4.1}$$

which is read: "It is true that S is valid" or equivalently "S is a theorem." The *rules of inference* I of L are the means whereby new theorems may be derived. Rules of inference generally take the form

$$\begin{array}{l} \text{IF } \vdash S_1 \text{ and } \vdash S_2 \text{ and } \dots \text{ and } \vdash S_k \\ \text{THEN } \vdash S_r \end{array} \tag{4.2}$$

which is read: "If $S_1, S_2, \dots, S_k$ are theorems, then S_r is also a theorem." $S_1, \dots, S_k$ are called the *antecedents*, and S_r the *consequent*, of the inference rule I given in (4.2).

It is often convenient to write inference rules in the form

$$\begin{array}{c} \vdash S_1 \\ \vdash S_2 \\ \cdot \\ \cdot \\ \cdot \\ \underline{\vdash S_k} \\ \vdash S_r \end{array} \tag{4.3}$$

which is interpreted exactly as in (4.2).

The *proof* of a theorem in a deductive system consists of a sequence of valid statements accompanied by *justifications* of why the statements are valid. A justification can be either an axiom, by which the statement is assumed to be valid, or an inference rule, by which a new valid statement is shown to follow from known valid statements.

Deductive systems have been an important part of mathematics since Euclid outlined an axiom set for plane geometry in his *Elements* [11]. Following Euclid, let us consider a deductive system for plane geometry, $L_g = (A_g, I_g)$, where the axioms, $A_g = (A_1, A_2, A_3)$, are:

A_1: $\vdash$ there exist at least two points

A_2: $\vdash$ if P and Q are distinct points, then there is only one line containing P and Q

A_3: $\vdash$ if L is a line, then there exists a point r not on L

and the rules of inference, $I_g = (I_1, I_2)$, are:

$$\begin{array}{l} I_1: \vdash P \\ \underline{\vdash \text{ if } P \text{ then } Q} \qquad \text{(modus ponens)} \\ \vdash Q \end{array} \tag{4.4}$$

$$I_2: \vdash P$$

$$\frac{\vdash Q}{\vdash (P \text{ and } Q)} \qquad \text{(identity)}$$

Within this system we can prove that "$\vdash$ there exist at least three points" by the following steps:

Theorem	*Justification*
1. $\vdash$ there exist at least two points	A_1
2. $\vdash$ there exists a line L	1, A_2, and I_1
3. $\vdash$ there is a point not on L	2, A_3, and I_1
4. $\vdash$ there exist at least three points	1, 3, and I_2

A deductive system is *consistent* if two contradictory statements cannot both be theorems and *complete* if any statement in the language of the system can be shown to be valid or invalid. Unfortunately, it is known that there do not exist algorithms for deciding if an arbitrary deductive system is complete [12]. The consequences of this fact will be explored in the next section, when we discuss the limitations of program proofs based on deductive systems.

4.2 LIMITATIONS OF THE AXIOMATIC APPROACH

To believe that a proof in a deductive system is correct, one must accept as valid a sequence of statements and accompanying justifications, which culminates in the desired theorem. On the face of it, this does not seem a very severe requirement. If the proof is in the form shown above, it is a simple matter to check each application of the axioms and inference rules. When justifications are seen to be correct, and the final result of the proof is the desired theorem, then it is difficult not to believe the proof.

Nonetheless, some proofs do seem to be more credible than others. Many observers, for example, find the recent proof of the "four-color" problem [13] to be less convincing than the standard proof of the Pythagorean theorem.

The reasons for the reluctance to accept a proof vary. In some cases the proof may be very long and the task of verifying all the steps prohibitive. In most mathematical proofs the arguments and justifications are given implicitly or informally. If the deductive system is not precisely specified, the proof may not be understood. In general, a proof is believable to a person if that person can internalize the steps of the proof [14]. This typically occurs when the proof is understood well enough to permit the recapitulation of the major arguments.

Currently, there is much controversy in the "verification community" concerning the credibility of proofs of program correctness [14, 15]. The source of this contention is rooted primarily in the length of the proofs necessary for program verification, lengths typically an order of magnitude longer than the programs whose correctness they prove. Some authors [14] argue that the proof process is long and is as error-prone as the initial program. The reader should keep these observations in mind as we review the extant mainstream verification methods.

Another limitation arises from the necessarily abstract view we take of program semantics and the corresponding distance that exists between a formally verified program and the physical manifestations of its behavior. If we had assurances that, for instance, the compiler for a programming language produced the correct assembly language program, that the assembler produced the proper machine language, that the interpretation of the machine language program by microprograms resulted in the activation of the proper hardware units, and so on, then we might have a high degree of confidence that a proven correct program would produce a correct effect. Unfortunately, we seldom have such assurances. The functioning of the hardware is a physical process, subject to the laws of nature. Ultimately, then, the confidence we have in the correctness of a program depends upon our belief that the proper physical actions will result. As a result, there is no "bottom line" at which we can show that executing a program is guaranteed to produce the desired effect. The best we can do is to show that programs are correct with respect to their execution on some abstract machine, which we model with a deductive system. The *truth*, as opposed to validity, of the theorems in the deductive system depends upon the proper implementation of the program semantics—that is, of the abstract machine—by hardware and software. If the implementation already exists, then the value of the proof depends upon our ability to correctly capture the behavior of the real machine in the definition of the abstract machine.

Two more limitations arise from the nature of deductive systems themselves; they deal with both the rules of inference and the theorems that arise when we attempt to use deductive systems to define program semantics. With respect to the rules of inference, it has been shown [16] that there exist programming constructs whose semantics cannot be completely expressed as rules of inference in a deductive system. This means that axiomatic semantics can be defined only for programs written in a subset of the possible programming languages.* With respect to theorems, Göedel's incompleteness theorem [12] shows that every deductive system will admit true theorems whose truth cannot be proven within the system; this means that any set of program semantics based on deductive systems will admit correct programs whose correctness cannot be proven.

Finally, any proof of correctness will depend upon a true definition of correctness; this definition will be embodied in some specification, whose

---

*We do not necessarily consider this fact limiting.

completeness and consistency with the goals of the programming task will have to be shown, as discussed in Section 1.5.

4.3 AXIOMATIC CORRECTNESS PROOFS

As outlined in Chapter 3, in order to prove semantic properties of a program we must rely upon the semantic properties of its s-units and their order of execution as given by $T(P, d_0)$. As discussed in Section 4.1, the proof of a theorem (here a theorem about program semantics) results from a chain of arguments leading to the desired conclusion. The links in this chain of arguments are provided by $T(P, d_0)$.

Given these thoughts, we revise our definition of partial program correctness as given in Section 3.4 to

$$\vdash \{\Phi\}\, P\, \{\Psi\}^+$$

<u>iff</u> (4.5)

$$(\forall\, d_0)(\vdash \Phi(d_0)\ \underline{\text{and}}\ \vdash (\exists\, m \in Z^+)(m = |\,C(P, d_0)\,|) \longrightarrow \vdash \Psi(d_m)).$$

Given (4.5), we see that one way to prove partial correctness of a program P with respect to Φ *and* Ψ is by constructing a sequence of *assertions* $M^1, M^2,$ $\ldots, M^{m-1}$, such that for all initial states d_0, with $\vdash \Phi(d_0)$:

$$\vdash (\Phi(d_0) \longrightarrow M^1(d_1)),$$
$$\vdash (M^1(d_1) \longrightarrow M^2(d_2)),$$
$$\cdot$$
$$\cdot \qquad\qquad\qquad (4.6)$$
$$\cdot$$
$$\vdash (M^{m-1}(d_{m-1}) \longrightarrow \Psi(d_m)),$$

where $C(P, d_0) = d_1, d_2, \ldots, d_m$. Then, since m is assumed to be finite, and we know that $\vdash \Phi(d_0)$, by m applications of *modus ponens* [see equation (4.4)] we may conclude $\vdash \Psi(d_m)$, and hence partial correctness as defined by (4.5).

The assertion M^j places a condition on the state d_j, and we require $\vdash M^j(d_j)$ following execution of s-unit s_{i_j}. The problem is to construct M^j and M^{j+1} in a manner such that $\vdash (M^j(d_j) \longrightarrow M^{j+1}(E(s_{i_{j+1}}, d_j)))$ can be shown for $\vdash M^j(d_j)$. If this can be accomplished, then we have effectively shown the partial correctness of our program.

The difficulty with such a proof lies in the fact that we do not know, a priori, either the number or order of s-units to be executed for a given initial state, nor do we know the sequence of states (that is, the computation) that will arise due to execution. In the next section we shall consider an approach that demonstrates the existence of such an assertion sequence, $M^1, M^2, \ldots,$ M^{m-1}, on the basis of the program itself, independent of any particular computation or trace.

4.4 THE INDUCTIVE ASSERTION METHOD

The seminal paper on program verification, "Assigning Meanings to Programs," was published in 1968 [10]. In that paper Floyd gives a method for proving semantic properties of programs from the program (text) itself. In this section we present Floyd's method, give an example of a proof of partial correctness, and discuss some of the limitations of the method.

4.4.1 Interpretation

The difficulty in assigning semantic properties to an individual s-unit s_j within a program, P, is that s_j may be executed in many different traces $T(P, d_0)$ as determined by d_0. In the program MAX in Section 3.3, for example, depending on the initial state d_0, any of the subsequences

$$\ldots, s_2, s_4, s_5, \ldots,$$
$$\ldots, s_2, s_4, s_6, \ldots,$$
$$\ldots, s_3, s_4, s_5, \ldots,$$
$$\ldots, s_3, s_4, s_6, \ldots, \tag{4.7}$$

may appear in $T(\text{MAX}, d_0)$, hence any semantic characterization of s_4 must somehow take account of all these possibilities.

We shall begin, therefore, by trying to assign *intermediate assertions* to the "paths" of control that "connect" one syntactic unit to another—that is, by making statements about intermediate program states whose truth is required when control passes from one syntactic unit to another. A *control path* exists between two s-units, s_j and s_k, if, for some d_0, $T(P, d_0) = \ldots, s_j, s_k, \ldots$. In (4.7) we see that, for s_4 in program MAX, four such paths exist:

$$\text{from } s_2 \text{ to } s_4,$$
$$\text{from } s_3 \text{ to } s_4,$$
$$\text{from } s_4 \text{ to } s_5,$$
$$\text{from } s_4 \text{ to } s_6. \tag{4.8}$$

In general, $A_{j,k}$ will be an intermediate assertion on the control path from s_j to s_k. Hence, the control paths in (4.8) will require four intermediate assertions: $A_{2,4}$, $A_{3,4}$, $A_{4,5}$, $A_{4,6}$. $A_{j,k}$ is required to be true of the state reached after the execution of s_j, *each* time control passes from s_j to s_k. That is, for all d_0, if

$$T(P, d_0) = \ldots, s_{i_l}, s_{i_{l+1}}, \ldots, \qquad \text{with } C(P, d_0) = \ldots, d_l, d_{l+1}, \ldots,$$

where $i_l = j$ and $i_{l+1} = k$, then $\vdash A_{j,k}(d_l)$ should hold [that is, the truth of $A_{j,k}(d_l)$ must be provable]. By representing a program as a flowgraph [10], the paths connecting s-units become readily apparent (although the same information is also available in the "text" format of programs by inspection of <u>goto</u> and other flow-control constructs). Figure 4.1 presents the program MA$\overline{X}$ in flowgraph form.

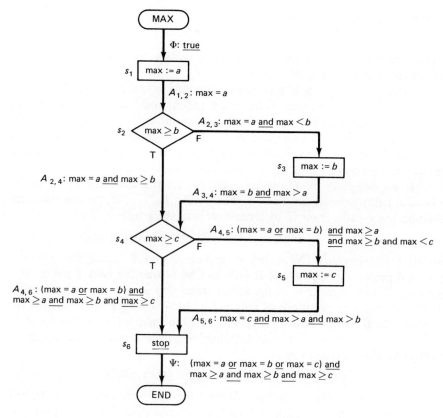

Figure 4.1   Flowgraph for program MAX

After Floyd, the assignment of intermediate assertions to the control paths in a program is called an *interpretation* of that program. Interpretations are not unique for a program but depend solely on the global semantic property to be proved. The intermediate assertions in Figure 4.1 were assigned on the basis of the global semantic property:

$$\Phi:\ \underline{\text{true}}$$

$$\Psi:\ (\text{max} = a \ \underline{\text{or}} \ \text{max} = b \ \underline{\text{or}} \ \text{max} = c) \ \underline{\text{and}}$$

$$\text{max} \geq a \ \underline{\text{and}} \ \text{max} \geq b \ \underline{\text{and}} \ \text{max} \geq c$$

for program MAX as defined in Section 3.2.

The interpretation of a program, *if* done properly, provides the sequence of assertions $M^1, M^2, \ldots, M^{m-1}$ necessary to prove partial correctness according to (4.6). Given a program P, and d_0 with

$$T(P, d_0) = s_{i_1}, s_{i_2}, \ldots, s_{i_m},$$

$$C(P, d_0) = d_1, d_2, \ldots, d_m,$$

then the interpretation provides assertions M^j, $j \in 1 \ldots m - 1$ such that

$$M^j = A_{i_j}, i_{j+1}.$$

Hence, we may *attempt* a proof of partial correctness by proving the theorems of (4.6) for the assertions $M^1, M^2, \ldots, M^{m-1}$.

Since it is not known beforehand what the actual trace will be, we do not know the particular state d_j for which the intermediate assertion M^j is to hold. Hence we face the more difficult task of showing that, for each s-unit, if that s-unit is entered by *any* of its "incoming" control paths in *any* state satisfying the intermediate assertion on that path, then after execution, control follows an "outgoing" path whose assertion holds for the new state.

If we designate by $Q_1, Q_2, \ldots, Q_r$ the intermediate assertions on the r control paths entering an s-unit s_j, and by $R_1, R_2, \ldots, R_t$ the assertions on the t outgoing paths from s_j, then our task is to show that

$$\vdash (\forall\, i \in 1 \ldots r)(\forall\, k \in 1 \ldots t)(Q_i(d) \longrightarrow R_k(E(s_j, d))) \qquad (4.9)$$

for all d with $\vdash Q_i(d)$. (Note that we include Φ and Ψ among the potential pre- and postconditions for s_j.) If (4.9) can be proven for each s-unit s_j in a program P, then regardless of the actual states that arise in any computation of P, a sequence of assertions as required by (4.6) will have been constructed. Proof of the theorems of (4.6) constitutes a proof of partial correctness of P. Furthermore, on the basis of the definition of partial s-unit correctness given in (3.5) we may rewrite (4.9) as

$$(\forall\, i \in 1 \ldots r)(\forall\, k \in 1 \ldots t)(\vdash \{Q_i\}\, s_j\, \{R_k\}) \qquad (4.10)$$

with (4.10) being called a *theorem package* for s_j. Here, then, is the desired link between program semantics and s-unit semantics. Thus, the proof of program partial correctness (3.2) depends upon the proof of individual s-unit partial correctness (3.5).

Example:

Again we take program MAX for our example. Consider the task of establishing (4.10) for s-unit s_4 in Figure 4.1. In this case, the incoming conditions Q_1 and Q_2 are given by

$$Q_1 = A_{3,4}\text{: max} = b \text{ and max} > a$$

$$Q_2 = A_{2,4}\text{: max} = a \text{ and max} \geq b$$

and the outgoing conditions R_1 and R_2 by

$$R_1 = A_{4,5}\text{: (max} = a \text{ or max} = b) \text{ and}$$

$$\text{max} \geq a \text{ and max} \geq b \text{ and max} > c$$

$$R_2 = A_{4,6}\text{: (max} = a \text{ or max} = b) \text{ and}$$

$$\text{max} \geq a \text{ and max} \geq b \text{ and max} \geq c$$

Therefore, as part of our proof of $\vdash \{\Phi\}\, \text{MAX}\, \{\Psi\}^+$ we must prove the following theorem package for s_4:

$$\vdash \{Q_1\}\, s_4\, \{R_1\},$$
$$\vdash \{Q_2\}\, s_4\, \{R_1\},$$
$$\vdash \{Q_1\}\, s_4\, \{R_2\},$$
$$\vdash \{Q_2\}\, s_4\, \{R_2\}.$$

4.4.2 Predicate Transformers and Verification Conditions

In this section we consider Floyd's method for proving the theorem-packages, associated with the s-units, emanating from a given interpretation of a program. A *verification condition* V_{s_j} is a first-order predicate calculus formula, constructed on the basis of s_j, its preconditions $Q_1, Q_2, \ldots, Q_r$ and postconditions $R_1, R_2, \ldots, R_t$. The proof of the verification condition V_{s_j} implies the truth of all members of the theorem-package for s_j. For Floyd's approach, the proof of a theorem package employs predicate transformations. Therefore, to discuss verification conditions we must first introduce the appropriate predicate (or assertion) transformers (see Section 3.6.3).

A *predicate transformer* is a function mapping an assertion and a syntactic unit to another assertion. In the study of Floyd's work, we are primarily interested in *strongest verifiable consequent* transformers. A strongest verifiable consequent,

$$\text{svc}(s_j,\, Q_i) = R_k^*,$$

is a function that, given a precondition Q_i for s-unit s_j and s_j itself, yields the "strongest" postcondition R_k^* for all outgoing paths from s_j. For R_k^* to be the strongest postcondition, we require that any postcondition R_k in a theorem package $\vdash \{Q_i\}\, s_j\, \{R_k\}$ for s_j is implied by $R_k^* = \text{svc}(s_j,\, Q_i)$; that is $\vdash (\text{svc}(s_j,\, Q_i) \rightarrow R_k)$. The determination of appropriate R_k's—that is, of the definition of an interpretation for a given s-unit—is at least partly an art. Later, when we examine the work of Dijkstra (Section 5.5.2), we will be interested in another transformation, wp, which finds the *weakest precondition* given an s-unit and a postcondition. In the case of the stop statement, the svc transformer is simply an identity mapping between assertions:

$$\text{svc}(\underline{\text{stop}},\, Q) = Q.$$

That is, since the stop statement has no effect on the program state, the same property Q holds both before and after its execution.

If s_j is an assignment statement of the form

$$s_j\!: v := e,$$

where v is some program variable (that is, a data object) and e is an expression (possibly containing v), then we have, after Floyd,

$$\text{svc}\,(v := e,\, Q) = (\exists\, x)(v = e[v \longleftarrow x]\; \underline{\text{and}}\; Q[v \longleftarrow x]),$$

where $\alpha[v \leftarrow x]$ means the systematic replacement of all occurrences of v in α (α can be an expression or an assertion) by x.

Example:

Again drawing from program MAX, suppose that we consider $svc(s_3, A_{2,3})$. Then

$svc(max := b, max = a \text{ and } max < b)$

$$= (\exists x)(max = b[max \leftarrow x] \text{ and } A_{2,3}[max \leftarrow x]) \qquad (4.11)$$

$$= (\exists x)(max = b \text{ and } x = a \text{ and } x < b).$$

That is, given that s_3 is executed beginning with a state satisfying $A_{2,3}$, statement (4.11) is the strongest verifiable consequent we may draw concerning the state after execution of s_3. That is, we can prove the theorem-package $\vdash \{A_{2,3}\} s_3 \{A_{3,4}\}$ for any $A_{3,4}$ for which $\vdash ((\exists x)(max = b \text{ and } x = a \text{ and } x < b) \rightarrow A_{3,4})$. Hence, letting $a = x$, we obtain from (4.11) $(max = b \text{ and } a = a \text{ and } a < b)$, so that

$$\vdash ((max = b \text{ and } a = a \text{ and } a < b) \longrightarrow (max = b \text{ and } max > a)),$$

which is $A_{3,4}$ given in Figure 4.1.

With svc predicate transformers in mind, we may now give the formal definition of a verification condition.

Suppose s-unit s_j has preconditions $Q_1, Q_2, \ldots, Q_r$, and postconditions $R_1, R_2, \ldots, R_t$, according to some interpretation. Then

$V_{s_j}(Q_1, Q_2, \ldots, Q_r; R_1, R_2, \ldots, R_t)$

$$= svc_1(s_j, Q_1) \text{ or } \ldots \text{ or } svc_1(s_j, Q_r) \longrightarrow R_1$$
$$\text{and}$$
$$svc_2(s_j, Q_1) \text{ or } \ldots \text{ or } svc_2(s_j, Q_r) \longrightarrow R_2 \qquad (4.12)$$
$$\text{and}$$
$$\cdot$$
$$\cdot$$
$$\cdot$$
$$\text{and}$$
$$svc_t(s_j, Q_1) \text{ or } \ldots \text{ or } svc_t(s_j, Q_r) \longrightarrow R_t.$$

By virtue of (4.12) we have

$$\vdash V_{s_j}(Q_1, \ldots, Q_r; R_1, \ldots, R_t)$$
$$\longrightarrow (\forall i \in 1 .. r)(\forall k \in 1 .. t)(\vdash \{Q_i\} s_j \{R_k\}^+). \qquad (4.13)$$

The implication (4.13) holds only if the svc's correctly capture the semantics of s-unit s_j. Thus, the ultimate correctness of a proof employing the inductive assertion method depends upon our ability to formulate an interpretation that correctly reflects semantic properties of the individual s-units.

Since the general form of a verification condition (4.12) is fixed, we need only specify the relevant svc's for each s-unit *type*. We collect together the svc's for the constructs used in program MAX. They are:

1. assignment statement:

$$\text{svc}(v := e, Q) = (\exists x)(v = e[v \longleftarrow x] \text{ and } Q[v \longleftarrow x])$$

2. branch statement:

$$\text{svc}_1(\text{if } B \text{ then goto } s_a \text{ else goto } s_b, Q) = Q \text{ and } B \qquad (4.14)$$

and

$$\text{svc}_2(\text{if } B \text{ then goto } s_a \text{ else goto } s_b, Q) = Q \text{ and not } B$$

3. stop statement:

$$\text{svc}(\text{stop}, Q) = Q$$

Example:

Employing the rules for svc's given in (4.14) and the general form for verification conditions given in (4.12), we give the verification conditions for the s-units in program MAX under the interpretation of Figure 4.1:

$$V_{s_1}(\Phi; A_{1,2}) = ((\exists x)(\text{max} = a \text{ and true}))$$
$$\longrightarrow (\text{max} = a),$$
$$V_{s_2}(A_{1,2}; A_{2,4}, A_{2,3}) = (\text{max} = a \text{ and max} \geq b)$$
$$\longrightarrow (\text{max} = a \text{ and max} \geq b)$$
$$\text{and}$$
$$(\text{max} = a \text{ and not max} \geq b)$$
$$\longrightarrow (\text{max} = a \text{ and max} < b),$$
$$V_{s_3}(A_{2,3}; A_{3,4}) = ((\exists x)(\text{max} = b \text{ and } x = a \text{ and } x < b))$$
$$\longrightarrow (\text{max} = b \text{ and max} > a),$$

$V_{s_4}(A_{3,4}, A_{2,4}; A_{4,6}, A_{4,5})$

$$= \begin{bmatrix} (\text{max} = b \text{ and max} > a \text{ and max} \geq c) \\ \text{or} \\ (\text{max} = a \text{ and max} \geq b \text{ and max} \geq c) \end{bmatrix} \longrightarrow \begin{bmatrix} (\text{max} = a \text{ or max} = b) \\ \text{and max} \geq a \text{ and} \\ \text{max} \geq b \text{ and max} \geq c \end{bmatrix}$$

$$\text{and}$$

$$\begin{bmatrix} (\text{max} = b \text{ and max} > a \text{ and not max} \geq c) \\ \text{or} \\ (\text{max} = a \text{ and max} \geq b \text{ and not max} \geq c) \end{bmatrix} \longrightarrow \begin{bmatrix} (\text{max} = a \text{ or max} = b) \\ \text{and max} \geq a \text{ and} \\ \text{max} \geq b \text{ and max} < c \end{bmatrix}$$

$V_{s_5}(A_{4,5}; A_{5,6})$

$$= \begin{bmatrix} (\exists x)(\text{max} = c \text{ and } (x = a \text{ or } x = b) \\ \text{and } x \geq a \text{ and } x \geq b \\ \text{and } x < c) \end{bmatrix} \longrightarrow (\text{max} = c \text{ and max} \geq a \text{ and max} \geq b),$$

$V_{s_6}(A_{5,6}, A_{4,6}; \Psi)$

$$= \begin{bmatrix} (\max = c \text{ and } \max > a \text{ and } \max > b) \\ \text{or} \\ ((\max = a \text{ or } \max = b) \text{ and} \\ \max \geq a \text{ and } \max \geq b \text{ and } \max \geq c) \end{bmatrix} \longrightarrow \begin{bmatrix} (\max = a \text{ or } \max = b \text{ or } \max = c) \\ \text{and } \max \geq a \\ \text{and } \max \geq b \\ \text{and } \max \geq c \end{bmatrix}$$

4.4.3 The Inductive Assertion Theorem

We now give a formal statement of the inductive assertion theorem for partial program correctness from Floyd [10].

Theorem. Let $P = s_1, \ldots ; s_n$ be a program with an interpretation such that for each $s_j, j \in 1 .. n$, $Q_i, i \in 1 .. r$, are the preconditions and $R_k, k \in 1 .. t$, are the postconditions of s_j. If

$$(\forall j \in 1 .. n)(\vdash V_{s_j}(Q_1, Q_2, \ldots, Q_r; R_1, R_2, \ldots, R_t))$$

then

$$\vdash \{\Phi\} P \{\Psi\}^+, \tag{4.15}$$

with Φ the precondition to the first executable s-unit and Ψ the postcondition for all stop s-units.

Proof. Consider any execution of P with initial state d_0, such that $\vdash \Phi(d_0)$ and P terminates with

$$T(P, d_0) = s_{i_1}, s_{i_2}, \ldots, s_{i_m},$$

$$C(P, d_0) = d_1, d_2, \ldots, d_m.$$

Then, we have

$$\vdash V_{s_{i_1}}(\Phi; R_1, \ldots, R_t) \quad \text{and} \quad (\exists k \in 1 .. t)(R_k = A_{i_1, i_2}).$$

By (4.13), we have

$$\vdash V_{s_{i_1}}(\Phi; A_{i_1, i_2}) \longrightarrow \vdash \{\Phi\} s_{i_1} \{A_{i_1, i_2}\}.$$

That is,

$$\vdash (\Phi(d_0) \longrightarrow \vdash A_{i_1, i_2}(E(s_{i_1}, d_0))) \quad \text{for all } d_0 \text{ for which } \vdash \Phi(d_0),$$

or equivalently

$$\vdash \Phi(d_0) \longrightarrow \vdash A_{i_1, i_2}(d_1).$$

By induction it follows that

$$\vdash A_{i_1, i_2}(d_1) \longrightarrow \vdash A_{i_2, i_3}(d_2)$$

$$\text{(equivalently } \vdash (A_{i_1, i_2}(d_1) \longrightarrow A_{i_2, i_3}(d_2)) \text{ for } \vdash A_{i_1, i_2}(d_1))$$

$$\vdots$$

$$\vdash A_{i_{m-1}, i_m}(d_{m-1}) \longrightarrow \vdash \Psi(d_m)$$

$$\text{(equivalently } \vdash (A_{i_{m-1}, i_m}(d_{m-1}) \longrightarrow \Psi(d_m)) \text{ for } \vdash A_{i_{m-1}, i_m}(d_{m-1})).$$

Hence, by (4.6) (that is, by induction) we may conclude: $\vdash \{\Phi\} P \{\Psi\}^+$ Q.E.D.

To conclude, we offer the following algorithm for showing the partial correctness of a program using the inductive assertion method.

1. Specify the desired semantic properties for the program P—that is, Φ and Ψ (see Section 3.1.).
2. Write the program P.
3. Assign an interpretation to P (see Section 4.4.1); that is, provide intermediate assertions.
4. For each s-unit s_j in P (see Section 4.4.2);
   a. Construct the verification condition V_{s_j}.
   b. Prove the verification condition V_{s_j}, using predicate transformations.   (4.16)
5. The interpretation can fail to yield the proof for any of several reasons:
   a. One or more of the intermediate assertions in the interpretation is incorrect; return to step 3.
   b. The program as written is in error, return to step 2.
   c. The verification condition may indeed be true but involve subtleties of reasoning beyond the skill of the "prover." In this case one might look to another source for help in proving the verification condition, or one might reformulate the program or interpretation in such a way that "manageable" verification conditions result.

Since verification conditions are predicate calculus formulas, it follows that the deductive system used in an inductive assertion proof consists of the axioms and inference rules of the predicate calculus. The validity of such a proof relies upon the transformer svc, which *links program semantics to a predicate calculus formula.*

A difficulty inherent in the inductive assertion method is the relative independence of syntactic and semantic definitions. Programs are developed, initially, without formal regard to their ultimate verification. Formal semantic definitions are then "tagged on" during program interpretation. Failure to prove the subsequent verification conditions may be due either to a fault in the program or to the occurrence of an intermediate assertion that is not implied by the corresponding svc. In the former case, there is no formal mechanism for deciding which syntactic unit(s) should be used to replace the faulty s-unit to guarantee a proof of the verification condition(s).

In the latter case, a formal mechanism—the transformer svc—does exist to help us decide which assertions hold after the execution of an s-unit. However, this mechanism is generally not applied until there is an attempt to prove a verification condition. Consequently, the proof technique cannot guide the development of the program. In Section 5.5 a method will be presented in which proof and program are developed "hand in hand" (each guiding the other) and in which the predicate transformer, wp, plays a central role in the creation of the program itself.

In itself, the use of the transformer svc causes some difficulties. One problem is that, for the assignment statement, the svc transformer introduces into the proof an "extraneous" variable that has no manifestation in terms of a program object. In fact, it refers to "a value that once existed." A further complaint about svc's is that they are, in a sense, "forward looking." That is, a given $svc(s_j, Q_i) = R_k^*$ identifies all program states d that can be reached following execution of s_j. In general, however, this information may not be helpful in deciding if progress is being made toward the final goal, Ψ. A transformer that worked "backward" might be psychologically more satisfying, in that it would tell what states must be obtained before Φ can be reached.

Finally, a few words are in order concerning the use of the inductive assertion method with "structured programming" [19]. Given a sufficiently broad view of s-units, we can construct programs in which the flow of control always proceeds from s_1 to s_n without branching among s-units. In such a case, the theorem package associated with an s-unit has only a single svc member [see (4.10)]. Hence, the verification condition associated with that s-unit is "simplified," as it has only a single precondition and postcondition for a given interpretation [see (4.12)].

Example:

A more "structured" version of program MAX eliminates the explicit goto's of our earlier version. We call this version MAX2.

> program MAX2
>
> s_1: max $:= a$;
>
> s_2: if $b >$ max then max $:= b$;   (4.17)
>
> s_3: if $c >$ max then max $:= c$;
>
> end MAX2

Since the flow of control through MAX2 is strictly sequential, an interpretation for MAX2 requires only two intermediate assertions: $A_{1,2}$ and $A_{2,3}$. But, when we allow the "nesting" of what we previously held to be "primitive" s-units [see (4.14)], the verification conditions in fact become more complex. For example:

$$V_{\text{if } B \text{ then } s_1 \text{ else } s_2}(Q; R) = V_{s_1}(Q \text{ and } B; R) \text{ and } V_{s_2}(Q \text{ and not } B; R). \qquad (4.18)$$

As the application of a complex svc transformer might become complex, the possibility for error may become large and the proof of the resultant theorem can be lengthy. Further, the specification of an svc transformer for relatively complex structures, such as the while loop, is not obvious.

4.5 THE AXIOMATIC METHOD

Based principally on the work of Floyd [10], a 1969 article by C. A. R. Hoare [18], "An Axiomatic Basis for Computer Programming," outlined an alternative to Floyd's for program verification. Most of the work that has succeeded Hoare's uses, as we do, his convenient notation. More important than the notation, however, is the "perspective" that his article provides for defining semantics.

4.5.1 Semantic Properties as Theorems

Hoare proposes that we view statements of semantic properties of syntactic units (including programs) as theorems in a deductive system (see Section 4.1). A statement such as $\vdash \{\Phi\} P \{\Psi\}^+$, then, is to be proven by the usual techniques of applying inference rules to axioms and previously proven theorems to produce the desired conclusion (a new theorem).

Theorems that are derivable from Hoare's extended deductive system are direct statements of s-unit semantics. They describe how the execution of a particular type of s-unit modifies a given program state. However, we may be required to associate different semantic properties with a single s-unit, as the meaning given to s-units is ultimately defined by the abstract machine upon which the s-units execute (see Section 2.3). Different abstract machines may in fact provide different sets of operations, hence it is necessary to construct different deductive systems for different abstract machines. This association between s-unit semantics, abstract machines, and deductive systems in Hoare's proposal is, in the inductive assertion method, given by the definition of different svc transformers for different abstract machines. In the remainder of this section we present Hoare's deductive system for an ALGOL-like abstract machine, including a discussion of the components of such a system and an example of a proof of partial correctness.

4.5.2 A Deduction System for an ALGOL-like Machine

As mentioned in Section 4.1, a deductive system L consists of two components: a set of axioms A (or basic facts that are assumed to be true), and a set of rules of inference I, from which further theorems may be deduced.

Subsequently, we construct a deductive system, $L = (A, I)$, in which the theorems are statements of semantic properties of an ALGOL-like abstract machine.

4.5.2.1 Axioms

The axioms A of the deductive system L describe the "basic facts" about the operations provided by the abstract machine. In particular, they express the effect of s-unit execution upon program state. One component of the set A then is responsible for describing the "facts" about how arithmetic and comparison take place. This component, which we label A_{AR}, typically includes axioms such as:

$$X + 0 = X \qquad \text{(additive identity)},$$
$$X + Y = Y + X \qquad \text{(additive commutativity)}, \qquad (4.19)$$
$$X * 1 = X \qquad \text{(multiplicative identity)}.$$

However, it is virtually impossible to construct a set A_{AR} that accounts for *all* imaginable abstract machines, as different machines handle various conditions in different ways. As an example, Hoare cites three ways of handling integer overflow. Namely, if we let max be the largest integer representable in an abstract machine, then we could use any of the three axioms:

(1) $\underline{\text{not}}\ (\exists x)(x = \text{max} + 1)$ (strict interpretation),

(2) $\text{max} + 1 = \text{max}$ (firm boundary),   (4.20)

(3) $\text{max} + 1 = 0$ (modular arithmetic).

Any of the axioms (1), (2), or (3) is a potential candidate for inclusion in A_{AR}, but only one may be included in A_{AR} per abstract machine, as they are mutually exclusive.

Included among—indeed central to—the operations that may be performed by the abstract machine is the *assignment* operation. Since the assignment of a new value to a data object modifies its state, it is important that this change in state be captured by an appropriate axiom. However, owing to the infinite variety of potential states and assignment statements, it is not possible to provide, in a *single* axiom, a complete description of the effect of assignment.

Instead, Hoare offers the following assignment axiom *schema:*

$$\vdash \{Q[v \longleftarrow e]\}\ v := e\ \{Q\}^+ \qquad (4.21)$$

to represent a collection A_{AS} of assignment axioms. This axiom schema is applicable to all assertions Q and s-units of the form $v := e$, where e may be any expression, and v is the name of an object. The statement (4.21) merely formalizes the fact that if Q [really $Q(v)$] is to be true after execution of the assignment $v := e$, then it must be that Q, with v replaced by the expression e, must be true before the assignment is made. That is, the condition $Q[v \longleftarrow e]$

to be satisfied by the program state before the execution of $v := e$ logically corresponds to the condition Q to be satisfied after the execution of $v := e$, but the two conditions may be defined on the basis of different sets of objects. For example, if we consider the assignment statement $v := x$, with $Q: v > 0$, we obtain $Q[v \leftarrow e]: x > 0$. Thus, the axiom schema *literally* describes the effect of assignment—that is, the assignment of the value of an expression e to a variable v that establishes the logical correspondence of $Q[v \leftarrow e]$ with Q.

Two additional points are worth considering:

1. By expressing the semantics of the assignment operation in the manner of (4.21), we truly have a semantic specification independent of any *particular* program, and clearly it says something in a direct manner about the assignment operation provided by the abstract machine.

2. The connection between (4.21) and the definition of svc for an assignment operation should now be clear: both, in effect, say the same thing. Whereas, however, owing to its "forward-looking" nature, the svc transformer necessitates the introduction of an auxiliary variable, the "backward-looking" nature of (4.21) allows a much "cleaner" view as it relates the postcondition to a modified precondition. We will explore this point further in Section 4.5.4.

The components A_{AR} and A_{AS} make up the axiom set A of the deductive system L. Having established A, we now turn our attention to the inference rules (sometimes called "proof rules") that permit us to derive more complex theorems, including theorems about the semantics of a complete program.

4.5.2.2 Inference Rules

Aside from input/output operations and parameter-passing, which we do not treat here, assignment is the only operation capable of affecting the state of objects. The control constructs in a program, however, determine the order in which modifications are made to that state. In the inductive assertion method, the separation between assignment and flow of control is not heavily emphasized. In the axiomatic approach, however, it is precisely the rules of inference that concern flow of control and that tell us how smaller semantic "chunks" may be combined to deduce program semantics. Since inference rules allow us to derive theorems from other theorems, it follows that all the inference rules in I will be of the form:

$$\vdash T_1$$
$$\vdash T_2 \qquad \text{(to be read: } \underline{\text{if }} \vdash T_1 \ \underline{\text{and }} \vdash T_2 \ldots \ \underline{\text{and }} \vdash T_n \ \underline{\text{then }} \vdash T_r \text{)}$$
$$\cdot$$
$$\cdot$$
$$\cdot$$
$$\underline{\vdash T_n}$$
$$\vdash T_r$$

where $\vdash T_r$ and $\vdash T_i$, $i \in 1 \,.\,.\, n$ are theorems (including axioms) in L. Hoare posits the following rules of inference:

1. Rules of consequence:

   (a) $\dfrac{\vdash \{Q'\}\, s\, \{R\}^+}{\vdash Q \longrightarrow \vdash Q'}$ (b) $\dfrac{\vdash \{Q\}\, s\, \{R'\}^+}{\vdash R' \longrightarrow \vdash R}$
   $$\dfrac{}{\vdash \{Q\}\, s\, \{R\}^+} \qquad \dfrac{}{\vdash \{Q\}\, s\, \{R\}^+}$$

   where (a) states that for any precondition Q' and s-unit s from which postcondition R can be deduced, Q' can be replaced by a precondition Q, whose truth implies the truth of Q', and (b) states a similar relationship for postconditions. Put differently, preconditions Q' may be replaced by "stronger" preconditions Q; postconditions R' may be replaced by "weaker" postconditions R. Generally, weak conditions are satisfied by more elements of the state space than are strong conditions.

2. Rule of composition:
   $$\dfrac{\vdash \{Q\}\, s_1\, \{R'\}^+}{\vdash \{R'\}\, s_2\, \{R\}^+} \over \vdash \{Q\}\, s_1 ; s_2\, \{R\}^+$$

   which defines the semantics of the control construct ";"—that is, the effect of successively executing the statement s_1 and then s_2.

   Hoare's third rule, the rule of iteration, will be discussed in Chapter 5.
   It should be clear that Hoare's approach permits very *direct* definitions of control-construct semantics, without the camouflage of verification conditions. For example, we could add to Hoare's set the

3. Rule of conditionals:
   $$\dfrac{\vdash \{Q \text{ and } B\}\, s\, \{R\}^+}{\vdash (Q \text{ and not } B) \longrightarrow \vdash R} \over \vdash \{Q\} \text{ if } B \text{ then } s\, \{R\}^+$$

4.5.3 Proof Procedure

Before giving an example of an axiomatic proof, we offer the following algorithm for using the axiomatic method.

1. Specify the desired semantic properties for the program P—that is, Φ and Ψ.
2. Write the program P.
3. Repeatedly apply the rules of inference of the deductive system to s-units, obtaining theorems, until the theorem $\vdash \{\Phi\}\, P\, \{\Psi\}^+$ is deduced.
4. Inability to prove the program may demand that segments of the program

be rewritten, or that there is an error in the proof. The rules of consequence can be used to mesh the semantics of the new segments with those of the remainder of the program. (*Note:* In general, this entails significantly less work than "fixing up" a proof using the inductive assertion method, as it might then be necessary to substantially alter the interpretation of the program, hence to prove a new set of verification conditions. Of course, as with the inductive assertion method, the properties that may be proved about a program depend upon the skill of the "prover.")

Example:

To make these ideas more concrete, we offer an axiomatic proof of the program MAX2 as originally given in Section 4.4.3, using the proof procedure outlined above.

1. Φ: true
   Ψ: $(\text{max} = a \text{ or max} = b \text{ or max} = c) \text{ and max} \geq a \text{ and max} \geq b \text{ and max} \geq c$

2. program MAX2
   s_1: max := a;
   s_2: if $b >$ max then max := b;
   s_3: if $c >$ max then max := c;
   end MAX2

3. *Proof:* As is often the case when using the axiomatic method, we can understand the proof more easily if we define critical assertions at the outset. Φ and Ψ are defined in step 1 above. Let us also define:

   $$P: \text{max} = a$$

   $$Q: (\text{max} = a \text{ or max} = b) \text{ and max} \geq a \text{ and max} \geq b.$$

   Our overall verification strategy will be to:

   (a) Demonstrate $\vdash \{\Phi\} \text{ max} := a \{P\}^+$.
   (b) Demonstrate $\vdash \{P\} \text{ if } b > \text{ max then max} := b \{Q\}^+$.
   (c) Demonstrate $\vdash \{Q\} \text{ if } c > \text{ max then max} := c \{\Psi\}^+$.
   (d) Conclude by two applications of the rule of composition that

   $$\vdash \{\Phi\} \text{ MAX2 } \{\Psi\}^+.$$

   Although the order of proof is irrelevant, we shall proceed sequentially to establish (a), (b), and (c).

   Demonstration of (a). Strategy:

   (1) Demonstrate $\vdash \{P[\text{max} \leftarrow a]\} \text{ max} := a \{P\}^+$.
   (2) Demonstrate $\vdash \Phi \rightarrow \vdash P[\text{max} \leftarrow a]$.
   (3) Conclude, by rule of consequence (a), $\vdash \{\Phi\} \text{ max} := a \{P\}^+$.

   Proof: (1) follows directly from A_{AS}. (2) is established by noting that:

   $$P[\text{max} \leftarrow a] = (a = a) = \underline{\text{true}}$$

   and that true is the absolutely weakest condition that is implied by any other condition.

Demonstration of (b). Strategy:

(1) Demonstrate $\vdash \{P \text{ and } b > \max\} \max := b \{Q\}^+$.
(2) Demonstrate $\vdash P \text{ and not } b > \max \longrightarrow \vdash Q$.
(3) Conclude, by rule of conditionals,

$$\vdash \{P\} \text{ if } b > \max \text{ then } b := \max \{Q\}^+.$$

To demonstrate (1): By A_{AS},

$$\vdash \{Q[\max \longleftarrow b]\} \max := b \{Q\}^+.$$

But

$$\vdash Q[\max \longleftarrow b] = (b = a \text{ or } b = b) \text{ and } b \geq a \text{ and } b \geq b = b \geq a$$

and

$$\vdash P \text{ and } b > \max = \max = a \text{ and } b > \max \longrightarrow b > a.$$

Thus,

$$\vdash P \text{ and } b > \max \longrightarrow b > a \longrightarrow b \geq a = Q[\max \longleftarrow b]$$

and by the rule of consequence (a), (1) is established.

To demonstrate (2):

$$\vdash P \text{ and not } b = \max = a \text{ and } b \leq \max$$
$$\longrightarrow \max = a \text{ and } \max \geq a \text{ and } \max \geq b$$
$$\longrightarrow (\max = a \text{ or } \max = b) \text{ and } \max \geq a \text{ and } \max \geq b = Q.$$

Demonstration of (c). Strategy:

(1) Demonstrate $\vdash \{Q \text{ and } c > \max\} \max := c \{\Psi\}^+$.
(2) Demonstrate $\vdash Q \text{ and not } c > \max \longrightarrow \vdash \Psi$.
(3) Conclude by rule of conditionals, $\vdash \{Q\} \text{ if } c > \max \text{ then } c := \max \{\Psi\}^+$.

[Our strategy here is the same as in (b), but the assertions are different.]

To demonstrate (1): By A_{AS},

$$\vdash \{\Psi[\max \longleftarrow c]\} \max := c \{\Psi\}.$$

But

$$\vdash \Psi[\max \longleftarrow c] = (c = a \text{ or } c = b \text{ or } c = c) \text{ and } c \geq a$$
$$\text{and } c \geq b \text{ and } c \geq c = c \geq a \text{ and } c \geq b.$$

and

$$\vdash Q \text{ and } c > \max = (\max = a \text{ or } \max = b)$$
$$\text{and } \max \geq a$$
$$\text{and } \max \geq b$$
$$\text{and } c > \max$$
$$\longrightarrow c \geq a \text{ and } c \geq b \text{ (transitivity)}.$$

Thus,

$$\vdash Q \text{ and } c > \max \longrightarrow c \geq a \text{ and } c \geq b = \Psi[\max \longleftarrow c]$$

and by the rule of consequence (a), (1) is established.

To demonstrate (2):

$$\vdash Q \text{ and } \underline{\text{not }} c \geq \max = (\max = a \underline{\text{ or }} \max = b)$$
$$\underline{\text{and}} \max \geq a$$
$$\underline{\text{and}} \max \geq b$$
$$\underline{\text{and}} \max \geq c$$
$$\longrightarrow (\max = a \underline{\text{ or }} \max = b \underline{\text{ or }} \max = c)$$
$$\underline{\text{and}} \max \geq a \underline{\text{ and }} \max \geq b \underline{\text{ and }} \max \geq c$$
$$= \Psi.$$

Having thus established (a), (b), and (c), we conclude

$$\vdash \{\Phi\} \text{ MAX2 } \{\Psi\}^{+} \qquad \text{Q.E.D.}$$

4.5.4 Remarks

Use of the axiomatic method does not permit stronger conclusions to be drawn than does use of the inductive assertion method. Its advantage lies in the more direct means it provides for expressing semantics. As we shall see in Chapter 5, induction remains the basis for the axiomatic method when iterative constructs are considered. It will be applied only to the local properties of iterative constructs (for example, while loops), rather than (as with the inductive assertion method) to the program as a whole. That is, induction is "built into" the inference rules governing iterative constructs. As such, the axiomatic method is more attuned to modern control constructs than is the inductive assertion method.

A proof using the inductive assertion method proceeds from analysis of individual s-unit semantics. Each verification condition is established independently of the others, and there is no "coalescing" of proof other than the final appeal to the inductive assertion theorem. In an axiomatic proof, on the other hand, program semantics are established by building larger and larger semantic "chunks" until the whole program has been assigned some meaning. There is no need for a priori assigment of intermediate assertions, as the necessary "intermediate semantics" are deduced as part of the proof in a deductive system. The connection to intermediate assertions, however, should be clear. One way to effect an axiomatic proof is to construct intermediate assertions, a la Floyd, and use them as "subgoals" in the proof. The skeptical reader should note the similarity between the intermediate assertions in Figure 4.1 and the arguments in the axiomatic proof of MAX2 in Section 4.5.3.

In each method the proof of partial correctness requires the proof of several "smaller" theorems. In the inductive assertion approach the order in which verification conditions are proved in irrelevant, owing to their relative independence of each other. In the axiomatic approach, where the order in which small s-unit "chunks" are grouped together is flexible, there is a much stronger dependence between the semantics of adjacent s-units, owing to the rules of composition and consequence. For this reason it is convenient to proceed stepwise through the program in a linear fashion. In the example in Section 4.5.3 a proof was effected by moving in a forward manner from the first s-unit to the last s-unit. At each step in the proof we had available

1. The next s-unit to be considered.
2. An assertion about the state prior to execution of that s-unit—that is, the precondition.

Armed with this information, we can "discover" via the deductive system the appropriate postcondition to be associated with that s-unit.

The distinction between the inductive assertion method and the axiomatic method may be illustrated as follows. We use the notation $\{\ \}$ to denote the fact that a postcondition or precondition need not be given a priori to verify s-unit correctness but is derived as part of the verification effort.

1. *Inductive assertion method:* given $\{Q\}\,s\,\{R\}$. To prove a verification condition,

   $$V_s(Q; R) = \text{svc}(s, Q) \longrightarrow R,$$

   requires the intermediate assertions Q and R to be prespecified for each s-unit s.

2. *Axiomatic method.* Here a "forward" and a "backward" approach can be distinguished.

   a. *Forward: given* $\{Q\}\,s\,\{\ \}$. The postcondition R is left open, to be "discovered" from the specified precondition Q and the s-unit s as part of the proof in the deductive system. To this end the appropriate postcondition to be used as a precondition in the next step of the proof can be deduced by employing part (b) of the rules of consequence. That is, any postcondition R with $\vdash T(s, Q) \longrightarrow \vdash R$, may be deduced, where $T(s, Q) = R'$ represents a deductive transformation in $L = (A, I)$. [Note that the inductive assertion method can be used analogously by choosing $T(s, Q)$ to be $\text{svc}(s, Q)$, with the additional proviso that the verifiably strongest postcondition is obtained.]

   b. *Backward: given* $\{\ \}\,s\,\{R\}$. The precondition Q is left open to be discovered from the specified postcondition R and the s-unit s as part of the proof in the deductive system. That is, we must establish a Q' that satisfies the rule of inference of the given s-unit s for the given postcondition R. From that Q' we may infer, by employing part (a) of the rules of consequence, a precondition to be used as a postcondition in the next step in the proof. Formally, the resulting precondition is any Q, such that, $\vdash Q \longrightarrow \vdash T(s, R)$, with $T(s, R) = Q'$.

The two methods require, however, that the s-unit be given at each step in the proof. Additionally, the two methods require the assertions Φ and Ψ specifying the semantic properties, $\{\Phi\}\,P\,\{\Psi\}$, of the program to be given. In the inductive assertion method $\vdash \{\Phi\}\,P\,\{\Psi\}^+$ can be established only by proving a verification condition of the form $V_s(Q;\Psi)$ for some s-unit s. In the axiomatic method $\vdash \{\Phi\}\,P\,\{\Psi\}^+$ is established by *either* deducing a postcondition R, with $\vdash R \longrightarrow \vdash \Psi$ (forward approach), or a precondition Q, with $\vdash \Phi \longrightarrow \vdash Q$ (backward approach).

In Section 5.5 on constructive methods we shall present Dijkstra's calculus for discovering not only the appropriate assertions but also the s-unit necessary at each stage in the proof.

5

APPROACHES TO PROOFS
OF TOTAL CORRECTNESS

5.1 EXECUTION TERMINATION

In Chapter 4 we omitted the question of execution termination to simplify the discussion. However, this topic plays a central role in our concern for constructing correct programs.

In Section 3.2 we offered the following definition of partial correctness of a program P with respect to Φ and Ψ:

$$\vdash \{\Phi\}\, P\, \{\Psi\}^+$$

$$\underline{\text{iff}} \tag{5.1}$$

$$(\forall\, d_0)(\vdash \Phi(d_0) \ \underline{\text{and}} \ \vdash (P \text{ terminates}) \longrightarrow \vdash \Psi(E(P, d_0))).$$

Suppose that program P is constructed such that execution may not terminate. (We ignore the execution-time limitation that might be imposed by some operating system or hardware constraint.) If P does not terminate, the condition for partial correctness (5.1) is vacuously satisfied. For instance, suppose we choose the following conditions for Φ and Ψ:

$$\Phi: \ \underline{\text{true}}$$

$$\Psi: \ (\exists a, b, c, n \in Z^+)(n \geq 2 \ \underline{\text{and}} \ a^n + b^n = c^n).$$

The reader will recognize Ψ as a statement of the converse of Fermat's last theorem. The program

$$\underline{\text{program}} \; \text{FLT}$$

$$\underline{\text{integer}} \; a, b, c, n;$$

$$\underline{\text{for all}} \; a > 0, b > 0, c > 0, n > 2$$

$$\underline{\text{if}} \; a^n + b^n = c^n \; \underline{\text{then}} \; \underline{\text{stop}}$$

$$\underline{\text{end}} \; \text{FLT}$$

is partially correct with respect to Φ and Ψ. That is, if FLT ever terminates, it will establish the falsehood of Fermat's last theorem. Clearly the concept of partial correctness does not completely answer our inquiries about program correctness. Although FLT is partially correct with respect to Φ and Ψ, mathematicians have been trying for centuries to prove whether or not FLT terminates. A program that "does the right thing *if* it terminates" may be of philosophical interest but is of little practical value if it doesn't. The recognition of this difficulty in no way invalidates the conclusions reached in Chapter 4. The versions of the program MAX presented in Chapter 4 contain no iterative constructs. As a result, we have a strong intuitive feeling that execution of MAX will indeed terminate, hence MAX will be totally correct with respect to the associated Φ and Ψ. This notion stems from the fact that *we assume* noniterative s-units to have a guaranteed finite execution time.

When we speak of execution termination, we mean to imply that termination will occur "in the normal way," that is, by the execution of a stop s-unit. Thus, "aborted" executions of an s-unit due to addressing errors, arithmetic faults, attempts to execute an illegal instruction, and so on are deemed "nonterminating" phenomena. While these phenomena are important considerations, we shall ignore them in order to discuss the more pressing concern of the nontermination of (iterative) s-units, owing to the infinite execution of perfectly valid instructions. In other words, our concern is the *infinite loop*. Discussion of the formal semantics of aborts may be found in [134]. In discussing the approaches to establishing (total) correctness, we shall assume that all nonlooping constructs terminate. Hence, the following conclusion is to be taken as axiomatic:

$$\vdash \{Q\} \, s \, \{R\}^+ \; \underline{\text{and}} \vdash (s \text{ contains no loop}) \longrightarrow \vdash \{Q\} \, s \, \{R\}. \tag{5.2}$$

Given this assumption, we see that the material presented in Chapter 4 remains viable. Since none of the versions of program MAX contain loops, and since they were all shown to be partially correct with respect to the given Φ and Ψ, we may conclude using (5.2) that they are (totally) correct with respect to that Φ and Ψ. Programming experience tells us, however, that the "loop-free" program is the exception rather than the rule and that the more "interesting" programs are those involving iteration. In this chapter we shall focus on methods for showing the conditions under which iterative constructs can be shown to terminate in a finite time.

5.2 TOTAL CORRECTNESS AND NONSATISFIABILITY

As we saw in Chapter 4, a proof of partial correctness that uses the inductive assertion method depends upon the existence of an *interpretation that satisfies* the verification conditions for that interpretation. For program $P = s_1; s_2; \ldots; s_n$, with precondition Φ and postcondition Ψ, we may express the inductive assertion theorem for partial correctness (see Section 4.4.3) in terms of the satisfiablity requirement:

$$\text{if} \vdash \{\Phi\} P \{\Psi\}^+,$$

then there exists an interpretation for P such that   (5.3)

$$(\forall d_0)(\vdash \Phi(d_0) \longrightarrow (\vdash V_{s_1} \text{ and } + V_{s_2} \text{ and} \ldots \text{ and } \vdash V_{s_n})).$$

We have already seen an application of this theorem in the proof of the program MAX, in which we explicitly gave an interpretation that allowed us to deduce the partial correctness of MAX. For such a proof, of course, the burden of finding a suitable interpretation rests with the verifier.

This view of the equivalence between partial correctness and the *satisfiability* of the verification conditions in an interpretation is due primarily to Manna [22]. The distinguishing feature of Manna's approach is that a *proof of partial correctness* is *formally reduced* to a *proof of the satisfiability of a first-order predicate calculus formula* (that is, the conjunction of the verification conditions). For Floyd's approach we first establish, for a given s_j, the pre- and postconditions Q and R and then, using the established conditions, we prove $\vdash V_{s_j}(Q; R)$. With Manna's approach, no interpretation is needed. Instead, assertions Q and R are found, as part of the proof, that guarantee $\vdash V_{s_j}(Q; R)$. Floyd's technique is analytic, whereas Manna's is synthetic.

If it can be shown that *no* interpretation exists that satisfies the verification conditions for a program, then we may conclude, on the basis of (5.3),

if not (there exists an interpretation for P such that

$$(\forall d_0)(\vdash \Phi(d_0) \longrightarrow (\vdash V_{s_1} \text{ and } \vdash V_{s_2} \text{ and} \ldots \text{ and } \vdash V_{s_n}). \quad (5.4)$$

then not $(\vdash \{\Phi\} P \{\Psi\}^+).$

Now suppose that, instead of using Ψ for the postcondition of P, we substitute its negation, not Ψ. (The original precondition Φ is retained.) According to (5.4), if there is no interpretation satisfying the verification conditions (using the postcondition not Ψ), then we may conclude:

$$\text{not } (\vdash \{\Phi\} P \{\text{not } \Psi\}^+). \quad (5.5)$$

It turns out, moreover, that there is a strong link between (5.5) and the total correctness of P with respect to Φ and Ψ, which is established as follows. Consider

$$\vdash \{\Phi\}\, P\, \{\Psi\} \; \underline{\text{or}} \vdash \{\Phi\}\, P\, \{\underline{\text{not}}\ \Psi\}^{+}$$

$$= (\forall d_0)(\vdash \Phi(d_0) \longrightarrow \vdash (P \text{ terminates}) \; \underline{\text{and}} \vdash \Psi(E(P, d_0)))$$

$$\underline{\text{or}}$$

$$(\forall d_0)(\vdash \Phi(d_0) \longrightarrow \vdash (\underline{\text{not}}\ P \text{ terminates}) \; \underline{\text{or}} \vdash \underline{\text{not}}\ \Psi(E(P, d_0)))^{*}$$

$$= (\forall d_0)(\vdash \Phi(d_0) \longrightarrow \vdash (P \text{ terminates}) \; \underline{\text{and}} \vdash \Psi(E(P, d_0))) \qquad (5.6)$$

$$\underline{\text{or}}$$

$$(\forall d_0)(\vdash \Phi(d_0) \longrightarrow \underline{\text{not}}\ (\vdash (P \text{ terminates}) \; \underline{\text{and}} \vdash \Psi(E(P, d_0))))$$

$$= (\forall d_0)(\vdash \Phi(d_0) \longrightarrow \underline{\text{true}})$$

$$= \underline{\text{true}}.$$

Hence, taking the first and last expressions of (5.6), we may obtain

$$\vdash \{\Phi\}\, P\, \{\Psi\} \; \underline{\text{or}} \vdash \{\Phi\}\, P\, \{\underline{\text{not}}\ \Psi\}^{+} = \underline{\text{true}}$$

and therefore

$$\vdash (\underline{\text{not}}\ (\vdash \{\Phi\}\, P\, \{\underline{\text{not}}\ \Psi\}^{+})) \longrightarrow \vdash \{\Phi\}\, P\, \{\Psi\}. \qquad (5.7)$$

The nonexistence of an interpretation for P using conditions Φ and $\underline{\text{not}}\ \Psi$ implies the total correctness of P with respect to Φ and Ψ. Thus, whereas partial correctness may be established by showing the *existence* of an interpretation, total correctness may be demonstrated by proving the nonexistence of an interpretation.

In general, a proof of nonsatisfiability is significantly more difficult than a proof of satisfiability, in which the verifier need only find a single interpretation that will work. To establish nonsatisfiability, one must show that there is not a single interpretation that will satisfy all the verification conditions associated with the program in question.

To further complicate matters, it is well known (see [12]) that satisfiability is, in general, undecidable for the first- (and higher-) order predicate calculus. Hence, there is no automatic algorithm that can be applied to a program to see if an appropriate interpretation does or does not exist.

Example:

While formal applications of (5.7) tend to be quite long and involved, we will present a rather informal argument that makes use of the nonsatisfiability method to show the correctness of the program AMAX in Figure 5.1 (cf. Section 5.3.1):

---

*We have used the following definition of partial correctness, which is equivalent to (3.2): $\vdash \{\Phi\}\, P\, \{\Psi\}^{+}$ iff $(\forall d_0)\, (\vdash \Phi(d_0) \longrightarrow \vdash (\underline{\text{not}}\ P \text{ terminates}) \; \underline{\text{or}} \; (\vdash (P \text{ terminates}) \; \underline{\text{and}} \vdash \Psi(E(P, d_0)))$. Additionally we used the equivalence: $(\underline{\text{not}}\ b \; \underline{\text{or}} \; \underline{\text{not}}\ c) = \underline{\text{not}}\ (b \; \underline{\text{and}}\ c)$.

Given: program AMAX in Figure 5.1, and

Φ: $\underline{\text{true}}$

Ψ: $(\exists j \in 1 \ldots 100)(\text{max} = A[j])$ $\underline{\text{and}}$ $(\forall k \in 1 \ldots 100)(\text{max} \geq A[k])$

Prove: $\vdash \{\Phi\} \text{AMAX} \{\Psi\}$

Proof: Suppose that there exists an interpretation for AMAX such that $\vdash \{\Phi\} \text{AMAX} \{\underline{\text{not}} \ \Psi\}^{+}$. For $\underline{\text{not}} \ \Psi$ to be true at the end of execution of AMAX, the following conditions must hold:

$\underline{\text{not}} \ \Psi$:

(1) $(\forall j \in 1 \ldots 100)(\text{max} \neq A[j])$

$\underline{\text{or}}$

(2) $(\exists k \in 1 \ldots 100)(\text{max} < A[k])$.   (5.8)

Consider condition (1). Clearly, the array A is left intact by execution of AMAX, and the variable max is assigned values only during execution from those found in A. Hence, (1) could be satisfied only if max were never assigned a value from A. Since the second s-unit of AMAX is "max := $A[1]$," it follows that (1) cannot be true. That is, there is no interpretation of AMAX that would allow us to conclude that (1) is true. Since condition (1) does not hold, condition (2) must be true for (5.8) to be true. Let us pick k such that $A[k]$ is the first occurrence of the "actual" maximum value in the array A. As max $< A[k]$, it follows that max $\neq A[k]$. This can be the case only if (a) max was never assigned the value of $A[k]$ *or* (b) max was assigned the value of $A[k]$ but subsequently assigned some other value from the array A. As $A[k]$ is the occurrence of the actual maximum value, (a) cannot hold. Hence, (b) must be true. That is, at some point max took on the value of $A[k]$. For max to be assigned some other value during the course of execution, the condition max $< A[i]$ must have been true for some $i \in k \ldots 100$. But since, at that point, max $= A[k]$, it follows that $A[k] < A[i]$. This violates our assumption that $A[k]$ is the "true" maximum of the array A. Thus, no such k exists.

Consequently, neither condition (1) nor condition (2) could hold for the final state after execution of AMAX. Hence, no interpretation could exist for conditions Φ and $\underline{\text{not}} \ \Psi$. Therefore, by (5.7), since $\vdash (\underline{\text{not}} (\vdash \{\Phi\} \text{AMAX} \{\underline{\text{not}} \ \Psi\}^{+}))$, we may conclude $\vdash \{\Phi\} \text{AMAX} \{\Psi\}$.   Q.E.D.

5.3 TOTAL CORRECTNESS AND THE INDUCTIVE ASSERTION METHOD

5.3.1 Well-Ordered Sets

The method proposed by Floyd [10] for establishing termination rests on the notion of a well-ordered set. We say that a set C is *ordered* with respect to ">" if, for $x, y, z \in C$:

(1) if $x \neq y$, then either $x > y$ <u>or</u> $y > x$ (asymmetric property),

(2) if $x > y$, then $x \neq y$ (irreflexive property),

(3) if $x > y$ <u>and</u> $y > z$, then $x > z$ (transitive property).

If, in addition, every nonempty subset of C can be shown to have a "least" member, then C is said to be *well ordered*. That is, given a set C, x is the least member of C if

$$(\forall \, y \in C)(y \neq x \longrightarrow y > x).$$

In particular, C must have a least element.

Consider program $P = s_1 ; s_2 ; \ldots ; s_n$ and an initial state, d_0 such that

$$T(P, d_0) = s_{i_1}, s_{i_2}, \ldots \quad \text{and} \quad C(P, d_0) = d_1, d_2, \ldots.$$

Suppose that there exists a sequence

$$F(P, d_0) = f^1(d_1), f^2(d_2), \ldots$$

of functions from states into a well-ordered set C. We call f^j a *selection function*, which, based on the data state d_j, selects some member of the well-ordered set C. If we designate

$$f^1(d_1) = c_{i_1}, \quad f^2(d_2) = c_{i_2}, \quad \ldots,$$

and impose the condition that

$$c_{i_1} > c_{i_2} > \cdots > c_{i_j} > c_{i_{j+1}} > \cdots,$$

where "$>$" is the well-ordering relation in the set C, then, since the sequence $c_{i_1}, c_{i_2}, \ldots$ is strictly decreasing, and C has a least element, it follows that the execution of program P must eventually terminate.

The proof of the existence of a sequence of selection functions $f^1, f^2, \ldots$ is handled in the same way as our demonstration of the existence of a sequence of intermediate assertions $M^1, M^2, \ldots$ in Section 4.3. That is, we define an *interpretation* of a program in which a selection function $w_{i,j}$ is associated with the control path from s-unit s_i to s-unit s_j. For a given trace $T(P, d_0) = s_{i_1}$, $s_{i_2}, \ldots, s_{i_j}, s_{i_{j+1}}, \ldots$ the strictly decreasing sequence $f^1(d_1), f^2(d_2), \ldots$ is then demonstrated by showing that the association $f^j(d_j) = w_{i_j, i_{j+1}}$ holds. As in the case of intermediate assertions, we use *local* information (the $w_{i,j}$'s) to deduce *global* (termination) properties of the program.

A common choice for the well-ordered set C is the set of nonnegative integers Z^+. In Figure 5.1 we present program AMAX, which finds the maximum element in an integer array A of length 100. The selection functions (the w-functions) for this program are mappings from the program state into the set of nonnegative integers. Some of the $w_{i,j}$'s, such as $w_{1,2}, w_{2,3},$ and $w_{3,7}$, are constant functions, whereas the remainder depend upon the current value of the program variable i. As there are four statements in the loop and $i \in 1 \,..\, 100$, we choose w-functions of the form $(400 + x) - 4i$, $x \in 2 \,..\, 5$. In order to prove that program AMAX terminates, we must show that if an s-unit is entered

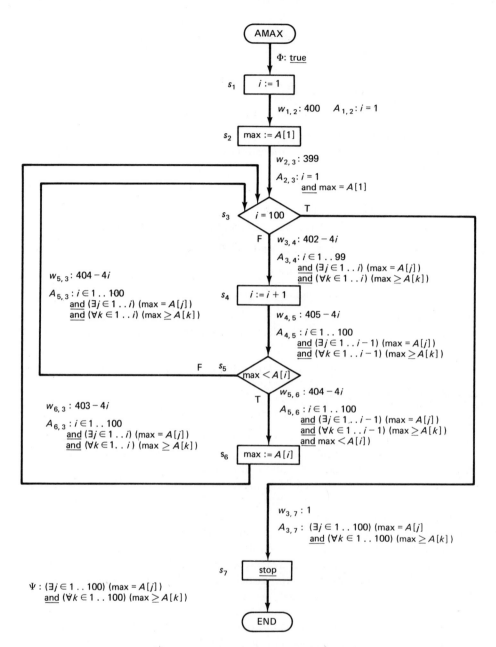

Figure 5.1 Flowgraph for program AMAX

from some control path with w-function having value α, then control will exit along some control path whose associated w-function value is *strictly less* than α. The inductive assertion theorem for total correctness given in the next section is the basis for this proof.

5.3.2 The Inductive Assertion Theorem
for Total Correctness

The establishment of program termination depends upon the intermediate assertions in the interpretation for the program. Termination is *not* shown independent of partial correctness; rather, the means for establishing total correctness are provided by extending the verification conditions to include conditions on the w-functions that ensure program termination. With this observation as a basis, we present a formal statement of the inductive assertion theorem for establishing total correctness.

Theorem.   Let $P = s_1; \ldots ; s_n$ be a program with an interpretation, including w-functions, such that for each $s_j, j \in 1 .. n$, with Q_i and $g_i, i \in 1 .. r$ being the preconditions and associated w-functions, respectively, and R_k and $h_k, k \in 1 .. t$ being the postconditions and associated w-functions, respectively, we define

$$Q_i' = Q_i \text{ and } (\exists \alpha)(\alpha = g_i), \qquad i \in 1, .. r,$$
$$R_k' = R_k \text{ and } \alpha > h_k, \qquad k \in 1, .. t. \tag{5.9}$$

If $(\forall j \in 1 .. n)(\vdash V_{s_j}(Q_1', Q_2', \ldots , Q_r'; R_1', R_2', \ldots , R_t'))$, then

$$\vdash \{\Phi\} P \{\Psi\},$$

where Φ is the precondition to the first executable s-unit, and Ψ the postcondition for all stop s-units.

Proof. By the inductive assertion theorem for partial correctness (see Section 4.4.3) we know: if $(\forall j 1 .. n)(\vdash V_{s_j}(Q_1, Q_2, \ldots , Q_r; R_1, R_2, \ldots, R_t))$, then $\vdash \{\Phi\} P \{\Psi\}^+$. Execution of each s-unit results in the selection of a member of a well-ordered set C. By (5.9) we know that each member selected is strictly less than the previously selected member. Since C has a least member, there can be no infinitely decreasing sequence of members drawn from C. Thus, P must terminate, and we may conclude $\vdash \{\Phi\} P \{\Psi\}$.   Q.E.D.

Example:

We will now give a proof of total correctness for s-unit s_4 in program AMAX (see Figure 5.1). For s-unit s_4 we have:

precondition

$$A_{3,4}: (i \in 1 .. 99) \text{ and}$$
$$(\exists j \in 1 .. i)(\max = A[j]) \text{ and}$$
$$(\forall k \in 1 .. i)(\max \geq A[k])$$

with associated w-function

$$w_{3,4}: 402 - 4i,$$

and postcondition

$$A_{4,5}: (i \in 1 .. 100) \text{ and}$$
$$(\exists j \in 1 .. i - 1)(\max = A[j]) \text{ and}$$
$$(\forall k \in 1 .. i - 1)(\max \geq A[k])$$

with associated w-function,

$$w_{4,5}: 405 - 4i.$$

Then

$$Q' = A_{3,4} \text{ and } (\exists \alpha)(\alpha = 402 - 4i)$$

and

$$R' = A_{4,5} \text{ and } \alpha > 405 - 4i.$$

According to the rules for constructing verification conditions given in Section 4.4.2, we have

$$V_{i:=i+1}(Q'; R') = (\exists x)(i = x + 1 \text{ and } Q'[i \longleftarrow x]) \longrightarrow R'$$

$$= \begin{array}{c} (1) \\ (2) \\ (3) \\ (4) \end{array} \begin{bmatrix} (\exists x)(i = x + 1 \text{ and} \\ x \in 1 .. 99 \text{ and} \\ (\exists j \in 1 .. x)(\max = A[j]) \text{ and} \\ (\forall k \in 1 .. x)(\max \geq A[k]) \text{ and} \\ (\exists \alpha)(\alpha = 402 - 4x)) \end{bmatrix} \longrightarrow \begin{bmatrix} (i \in 1 .. 100) \text{ and} \\ (\exists j \in 1 .. i - 1)(\max = A[j]) \text{ and} \\ (\forall k \in 1 .. i - 1)(\max \geq A[k]) \text{ and} \\ \alpha > 405 - 4i \end{bmatrix}.$$

Proof of $V_{s_4}(Q'; R')$:

1. $i = x + 1 \text{ and } x \in 1 .. 99 \longrightarrow i \in 2 .. 100$
   $$\longrightarrow i \in 1 .. 100.$$

2. $i = x + 1 \text{ and } (\exists j \in 1 .. x)(\max = A[j])$
   $$\longrightarrow (\exists j \in 1 .. i - 1)(\max = A[j]).$$

3. $i = x + 1 \text{ and } (\forall k \in 1 .. x)(\max \geq A[k])$
   $$\longrightarrow (\forall k \in 1 .. i - 1)(\max \geq A[k]).$$

4. $i = x + 1 \text{ and } (\exists \alpha)(\alpha = 402 - 4x) \longrightarrow \alpha = 402 - 4i + 4$
   $$\longrightarrow \alpha = 406 - 4i$$
   $$\longrightarrow \alpha > 405 - 4i. \quad \text{Q.E.D.}$$

Hence, by (1) through (4), $\vdash V_{s_4}(Q'; R')$. In a proof of partial correctness, only points (1), (2), and (3) would need to be established. The stronger claim of total correctness, however, requires the additional step (4) to show that a strictly decreasing sequence from $Z^+(Z^+$ being the well-ordered set C utilized) arises for any possible trace $T(\text{AMAX}, d_0)$ through program AMAX.

5.4 TOTAL CORRECTNESS AND THE AXIOMATIC METHOD

In Section 4.5 we considered Hoare's axiomatic method for establishing the partial correctness of programs. Using the deductive system outlined in Section 4.5.2, a partial correctness proof was given for the simple nonlooping program,

MAX2. Under the assumption that all nonlooping s-units terminate (see Section 5.1) we may also infer the total correctness of MAX2 with respect to the given Φ and Ψ. With the introduction of iterative constructs such as those used in program AMAX, we find that we must extend the axiomatic approach to allow proofs of total correctness. We proceed by considering iterative constructs as single s-units, and we begin by discussing partial correctness for such s-units.

5.4.1 Iterative Constructs and Partial Correctness

The deductive system outlined in Section 4.5.2 did not contain inference rules defining the semantics of iterative constructs. Hence, to obtain a partial correctness proof for a program, such as AMAX2 given below, we shall have to augment the inference rules of that deductive system.

$$
\begin{aligned}
&\text{program AMAX2} \\
&\quad i := l; \\
&\quad \text{max} := A[1]; \\
&\quad \text{while } i < 100 \text{ do} \\
&\qquad \text{begin} \\
&\qquad\quad i := i + 1; \\
&\qquad\quad \text{if max} < A[i] \text{ then max} := A[i] \\
&\qquad \text{end} \\
&\text{end AMAX2}
\end{aligned}
$$

In particular, for AMAX2, we shall need an inference rule that describes the semantics of the while construct. Hoare [18] provides the rule:

while rule

$$\frac{\vdash \{Q \text{ and } B\}\, s\, \{Q\}^+}{\vdash \{Q\}\, \text{while } B \text{ do } s\, \{Q \text{ and not } B\}^+.} \tag{5.10}$$

The while rule relates the partial correctness of s-unit s with respect to precondition Q and B and postcondition Q, to the partial correctness of the while construct with respect to precondition Q and postcondition Q and not B.

The condition Q in (5.10) is usually referred to as the "loop invariant." In order to use the while rule, one must find a loop invariant that is true on each entry to, and final exit from, the loop in question. It is not necessary, nor even likely, that the loop invariant hold at every point within the body of the loop. Hence, loop invariants are best viewed as descriptions of the action of the loop taken as an "indivisible" syntactic unit.

Loop invariants are sometimes misinterpreted as being necessarily "fixed" statements in the predicate calculus. In fact, the "meaning" of the invariant can change with each pass through the loop. For example, in our verification of program AMAX2 we use the loop invariant I:

$$
\begin{aligned}
I: \; & i \in 1 \ldots 100 \text{ and } (\exists j \in 1 \ldots i)(\text{max} = A[j]) \\
& \text{and } (\forall k \in 1 \ldots i)(\text{max} \geq A[k])
\end{aligned}
$$

which describes a collection of assertions, dependent on the value of the program variable i. Hence it is the "parameterized" condition I that must be shown to hold upon each entry to, and final exit from, the <u>while</u> loop in AMAX2

Example

Armed with the loop invariant I, we now use the <u>while</u> rule (5.10) to establish the partial correctness of program AMAX2 with respect to the pre- and postconditions Φ and Ψ, given below:

> Φ: <u>true</u>
>
> Ψ: $(\exists j \in 1 .. 100)(max = A[j])$ <u>and</u> $(\forall k \in 1 .. 100)(max \geq A[k])$.

Proof: Our goal is to establish $\vdash \{\Phi\}$ AMAX2 $\{\Psi\}^+$.

Overall strategy:

(a) Demonstrate

$$\begin{aligned}
&\vdash \{\Phi\} \\
&i := 1; \\
&max := A[1] \\
&\quad \{I\}^+.
\end{aligned}$$

(b) Demonstrate

$$\begin{aligned}
&\vdash \{I\} \\
&\quad \text{while } i < 100 \text{ do} \\
&\qquad \text{begin} \\
&\qquad\quad i := i + 1; \\
&\qquad\quad \text{if } max < A[i] \text{ then } max := A[i] \\
&\qquad \text{end} \\
&\quad \{I \text{ and } i \geq 100\}^+.
\end{aligned}$$

(c) Demonstrate

$$\vdash (I \text{ and } i \geq 100) \longrightarrow \vdash \Psi.$$

(d) Conclude, by the rule of composition, and by rule of consequence (a),

$$\vdash \{\Phi\} \text{ AMAX2 } \{\Psi\}^+.$$

Demonstration of (a).

By simple application of A_{AS}, (4.21), the rule of consequence (a), and the rule of composition, it can be seen that

$$\begin{aligned}
&\vdash \{\Phi\} \\
&i := 1; \\
&max := A[1] \\
&\quad \{i = 1 \text{ and } max = A[1]\}^+.
\end{aligned}$$

Further, since

$$\vdash i = 1 \longrightarrow \vdash i \in 1 \, .. \, 100, \text{ and}$$
$$\vdash \text{max} = A[1] \longrightarrow \vdash (\exists j \in 1 \, .. \, 1)(\text{max} = A[j]), \text{ and}$$
$$\vdash \text{max} = A[1] \longrightarrow \vdash (\forall k \in 1 \, .. \, 1)(\text{max} \geq A[k])$$

follow from A_{AR} (see Section 4.5.2.1), we may conclude from the rule of consequence (b) that

$$\vdash \{\Phi\}$$
$$i := 1;$$
$$\text{max} := A[1]$$
$$\{I\}^+.$$

Thus, (a) is established.

Demonstration of (b).

An examination of the while rule tells us that (b) follows immediately if we can establish the theorem:

$$\vdash \{I \text{ and } i < 100\}$$
$$i := i + 1;$$
$$\text{if max} < A[i] \text{ then max} := A[i] \qquad\qquad (5.11)$$
$$\{I\}^+.$$

In order to establish theorem (5.11), we need to find an assertion which holds following the assignment statement and preceding the conditional. By an application of A_{AS}, we can see

$$\vdash \{I \text{ and } 1 < 100\} \, i := i + 1 \, \{I[i \longleftarrow i - 1] \text{ and } i < 101\}^+,$$

so our proof of (b) reduces to a proof of the following theorem:

$$\vdash \{I[i \longleftarrow i - 1] \text{ and } i < 101\}$$
$$\text{if max} < A[i] \text{ then max} := A[i] \qquad\qquad (5.12)$$
$$\{I\}^+.$$

To prove (5.12), we must turn to the rule of conditionals, which requires us in turn to establish the theorems:

(1) $\vdash \{I[i \longleftarrow i - 1] \text{ and } i < 101 \text{ and max} < A[i]\} \, \text{max} := A[i] \, \{I\}^+,$

(2) $\vdash I[i \longleftarrow i - 1] \text{ and } i < 101 \text{ and max} \geq A[i] \longrightarrow \vdash I.$

Demonstration of (1). By A_{AS}, we have

$$\vdash \{I[\text{max} \longleftarrow A[i]]\} \, \text{max} := A[i] \, \{I\}^+. \qquad\qquad (5.13)$$

Our strategy, then, will be to demonstrate that the precondition in (1) guarantees the precondition in (5.13), from which we may conclude, using the rule of consequence (a), that (1) is a valid theorem.

Expanding the two expressions, we are left with establishment of the following theorem:

$$\vdash \begin{bmatrix} (i \in 2 .. 101) \text{ and} \\ (\exists j \in 1 .. i - 1)(\max = A[j]) \text{ and} \\ (\forall k \in 1 .. i - 1)(\max \geq A[k]) \text{ and} \\ i < 101 \text{ and} \\ \max < A[i] \end{bmatrix}$$

$$\longrightarrow \vdash \begin{bmatrix} i \in 1 .. 100 \text{ and} \\ (\exists j \in 1 .. i)(A[i] = A[j]) \text{ and} \\ (\forall k \in 1 .. i)(A[i] \geq A[k]) \end{bmatrix} \cdot \quad (5.14)$$

We proceed by demonstrating that each conjunct in the consequent of (5.14) can be established from the antecedent:

$$\vdash (i \in 2 .. 101) \text{ and } i < 101 \longrightarrow \vdash i \in 2 .. 100 \longrightarrow \vdash i \in 1 .. 100,$$

by A_{AR};

$$\vdash (\exists j \in 1 .. i)(A[i] = A[j]),$$

by A_{AR}, noting the identity $A[i] = A[i]$;

$$\vdash (\max < A[i]) \text{ and } (\forall k \in 1 .. i - 1)(\max \geq A[k])$$
$$\longrightarrow \vdash (\forall k \in 1 .. i)(A[i] \geq A[k]),$$

by A_{AR} (transitivity). With each part of (5.14) established, we can assert the validity of (1).

Demonstration of (2). Expanding the antecedent and consequent of (2), we find that we must now prove the following theorem:

$$\vdash \begin{bmatrix} i \in 2 .. 101 \text{ and} \\ (\exists j \in 1 .. i - 1)(\max = A[j]) \text{ and} \\ (\forall k \in 1 .. i - 1)(\max \geq A[j]) \text{ and} \\ i < 101 \text{ and} \\ \max \geq A[i] \end{bmatrix}$$

$$\longrightarrow \vdash \begin{bmatrix} i \in 1 .. 100 \text{ and} \\ (\exists j \in 1 .. 1)(\max = A[j]) \text{ and} \\ (\forall k \in 1 .. i)(\max \geq A[k]) \end{bmatrix} \quad (5.15)$$

Again, it easily follows that

$$\vdash (i \in 2 .. 101) \text{ and } (i < 101) \longrightarrow \vdash i \in 1 .. 100,$$

and by simple application of A_{AR},

$$\vdash (\exists j \in 1 .. i - 1)(\max = A[j]) \longrightarrow \vdash (\exists j \in 1 .. i)(\max = A[j]).$$

And finally, again by A_{AR},

$$\vdash (\forall k \in 1 .. i - 1)(\max \geq A[k]) \text{ and } \max > A[i]$$
$$\longrightarrow \vdash (\forall k \in 1 .. i)(\max \geq A[k]).$$

Hence, (2) is established.

With (1) and (2) shown to be valid, we may conclude from the rule of conditionals that (b) also holds.

Demonstration of (c).

Again, by expanding (c), we see that we must prove the theorem:

$$\vdash \begin{bmatrix} i \in 1 .. 100 \text{ and} \\ (\exists j \in 1 .. i)(\max = A[j]) \text{ and} \\ (\forall k \in 1 .. i)(\max \geq A[k]) \text{ and} \\ i \geq 100 \end{bmatrix}$$
$$\longrightarrow \vdash \begin{bmatrix} (\exists j \in i .. 100)(\max = A[j]) \text{ and} \\ (\forall k \in 1 .. 100)(\max \geq A[k]) \end{bmatrix}. \quad (5.16)$$

This is easily established by noting

$$\vdash (i \in 1 .. 100) \text{ and } i \geq 100 \longrightarrow \vdash i = 100,$$

and by two simple substitutions in the quantified conjuncts of the antecedent of (5.16) the consequent is established.

Thus, (a), (b), and (c) are valid theorems, and we may finally conclude:

$$\vdash \{\Phi\} \text{ AMAX2 } \{\Psi\}^+. \quad \text{Q.E.D.}$$

5.4.2 Iterative Constructs and Total Correctness

Ultimately, program AMAX2 terminates if and only if its embedded while loop terminates. The next logical step, then, is to consider the conditions under which such a construct does terminate. Several authors, notably Manna [22] and Dijkstra [23], have proposed while inference rules that permit the conclusion of *total loop correctness*. The implication of such rules is that if each iterative construct can be shown to terminate, then we can be assured that the entire program terminates. In reality iterative constructs are apt to be compound s-units, hence it becomes necessary for the loop invariant, Q, to capture the "essence" of the semantics of the contained primitive s-units. The semantic properties of the contained s-units need be reflected by Q, since the axiomatic approach to proving total correctness still relies on the notion of well-ordered sets (see Section 5.3.1). Inference rules for iterative constructs are applied by selecting a single element from the well-ordered set for each pass through the entire loop. This technique contrasts with the inductive assertion approach to proving total correctness in that the selection of members from a well-ordered set for each s-unit in the program is reduced to only the compound s-units representing the body of iterative constructs.

In a variant of Dijkstra's work [23], Gries [24] offers the while rule for total correctness:

$$\vdash \{Q \text{ and } B\} s \{Q\}^+$$
$$\vdash \{Q \text{ and } B \text{ and } t \leq t_0 + 1\} s \{t \leq t_0\}^+$$
$$\vdash (Q \text{ and } B) \longrightarrow \vdash t > 0 \tag{5.17}$$
$$\overline{\vdash \{Q\} \text{ while } B \text{ do } s \{Q \text{ and not } B\},}$$

where t and t_0 denote an integer *function* of the program state and an integer constant, respectively. The first line of the antecedent is drawn from Hoare's while rule (5.10). The second line requires that a function, t, be found that selects a member from a *decreasing* sequence of values from a (lower) bounded well-ordered set for each pass through the loop. The set assumed by the rule is Z^+. The third line ensures that when the least member is reached, the iteration terminates. Note that the first two lines are only statements concerning partial correctness and that the additional requirement for total correctness is given by the third line.

Gries owes a debt to Floyd for the second and third lines of the antecedent. Whereas, however, Floyd's w-functions (see Section 5.3.1) refer to each primitive s-unit in an iterative construct, the *selection function t* applies to the compound s-unit included in the while construct.

Example
Returning to the example program AMAX2 (see Section 5.4.1), we now show that it is *totally* correct with respect to Φ and Ψ as given in Figure 5.1. As we have already seen a proof of partial correctness, we need only establish the termination of the while loop in order to conclude total correctness.

Proof. In Section 5.4.1 we established $\vdash \{\Phi\} \text{ AMAX2 } \{\Psi\}^+$. In order to establish termination of the while loop, we choose as our function t:

$$t(i) = 101 - i.$$

The first line of the antecedent in (5.17) has already been established for Q given by:

Q: $i \in 1 .. 100$ and $(\exists j \in 1 .. i)(\max = A[j])$ and $(\forall k \in 1 .. i)(\max \geq A[k])$.

Since $(i \in 1 .. 100) \rightarrow (t(i) > 0)$, we have that $\vdash (Q \text{ and } B) \rightarrow \vdash t > 0$.

To show the second part of the antecedent of (5.17), we observe that

$$\vdash \{t(i + 1) \leq t_0\} i := i + 1 \{t(i) \leq t_0\}^+, \qquad \text{by } A_{AS}.$$

Further,

$$t(i + 1) \leq t_0 = 101 - (i + 1) \leq t_0$$
$$= 101 - i \leq t_0 + 1$$
$$= t(i) \leq t_0 + 1, \qquad \text{by } A_{AR}.$$

Hence, it follows that

$$\vdash \{t \leq t_0 + 1\}\, i := i + 1\, \{t \leq t_0\}^+.$$

Since the assignment $i := i + 1$ is the only primitive s-unit affecting the value of the function t, we may conclude:

$$\vdash \{t \leq t_0 + 1\}\, i := i + 1;\ \underline{\text{if}}\ \max < A[i]\ \underline{\text{then}}\ \max := A[i]\, \{t \leq t_0\}^+.$$

Then, by appealing to the rules of consequence (a), we have

$$\vdash \{Q\ \underline{\text{and}}\ i < 100\ \underline{\text{and}}\ t \leq t_0 + 1\}$$
$$i := i + 1;$$
$$\underline{\text{if}}\ \max < A[i]\ \underline{\text{then}}\ \max := A[i]$$
$$\{t \leq t_0\}^+,$$

and finally, by (5.17), we establish the theorem:

$$\vdash \{i \in 1 .. 100\ \underline{\text{and}}\ (\exists j \in 1 .. i)(\max = A[j])\ \underline{\text{and}}\ (\forall k \in 1 .. i)(\max \geq A[k])\}$$
$$\underline{\text{while}}\ i < 100\ \underline{\text{do}}$$
$$\quad \underline{\text{begin}}$$
$$\qquad i := i + 1;$$
$$\qquad \underline{\text{if}}\ \max < A[i]\ \underline{\text{then}}\ \max := A[i]$$
$$\quad \underline{\text{end}}$$
$$\{(\exists j \in 1 .. 100)(\max = A[j])\ \underline{\text{and}}\ (\forall k \in 1 .. 100)(\max \geq A[k])\}.$$

With the addition of this theorem to the partial correctness proof given in 5.4.1, we may conclude $\vdash \{Q\}\ \text{AMAX2}\ \{\Psi\}$.   Q.E.D.

5.4.3 Remarks

While the approach to total correctness using the axiomatic method draws heavily upon the work of Floyd, its advantage lies in the fact that termination conditions may be given explicitly for various iterative constructs, *independent* of their context within a particular program. By contrast with Floyd's approach, the axiomatic approach is more direct in expressing the semantic properties of iterative constructs. Manna and Pnueli [25] have presented a fairly complete deductive system for an ALGOL-like language which includes several additional versions of the while rule presented in this section, and their inference rules are geared solely toward the establishment of theorems concerning *total* program correctness.

5.5 CONSTRUCTIVE METHODS

The verification methods discussed thus far involve "a posteriori" analyses; that is, the program is given as a fait accompli, and verification proceeds by examination of the program. As a result, the task of proving a program correct may be difficult and time consuming, especially if the program is written without regard to how the subsequent proof must proceed. This is particularly true as regards total correctness, as the discrepancy between the generation of program code and the construction of assertions may cause problems in the practical application of program verification techniques. These difficulties are exemplified by the need to provide the specification of a loop invariant Q for a given loop body and termination condition B, as demonstrated in Section 5.4.2. More specifically, the loop invariant should permit the conclusion of total loop correctness and capture the "essence" of the semantics of the primitive s-units (see Section 5.4.2) contained in the compound s-unit that constitutes the body of the iterative construct. As a consequence, it is often easier to derive the proper "terminating conditions," and eventually the "body" of a loop, when the intended invariant Q is specified *before* the loop itself is constructed.

The objective of "constructive" methods is the development of program verification disciplines that overcome the above problem by interweaving program generation and the construction of assertions. These constructive methods are concerned primarily with total correctness, as the major problems associated with *analytic* verification methods (which synthetic verification methods attempt to overcome) tend to be those associated with compound s-units, which constitute the body of iterative constructs.

5.5.1 Interweaving of Program Construction and Correctness Proof

A constructive method for program verification that extends Floyd's analytic method into a partially synthetic one has been proposed by Wegbreit [26]. With his approach, correctness proofs are established constructively by interweaving the generation of program statements and their accompanying assertions with *proof justifications*, which establish in a precise algorithmic notation the *reasoning* (or steps taken) to establish the validity of the assertions. Furthermore, the reasoning employed to establish the validity of the assertions is similar to the reasoning employed to construct the program statements them-selves. The truth of this statement is based on the fact that the execution of the program statements results in program states that are formally described by the assertions. In review of the previous section, proof justifications establish a connection between the program statements and their associated assertions by documenting, for all s-units, the reasoning that establishes the correctness of the relationship between them, Therefore, it is appropriate that the correctness proof proceeds constructively by exhibiting, via proof justifications, the values of dependent variables for which the truth of the assertions can be guaranteed. As a result, the proof of assertions in the framework of first-order predicate calculus, which is not decidable, is reduced to the decidable task of proving quantifier-free formulas—that is, formulas without occurrences of $\exists$ or $\forall$. The major objective of interweaving proof justifications with program text and assertions is to shift part of the task of proving programs correct from the formal proof of assertions to the design of precise algorithmic notations for these proofs.

On the one hand, this discipline makes correctness proofs constructive, as they are explicitly considered as part of the programming process. On the other hand, the instantiation of quantifier formulas (that is, assertions) through justifications aids the construction of assertions that are strong enough to be decidable in the deductive system employed.

Dijkstra [23] further develops constructive methods (methods that interweave program development and proof of correctness) by proposing a fully synthetic method for program verification. He proposes that entire programs be constructed hand-in-hand with their proof of correctness. The basic procedure involves deciding on the assertion to be satisfied and then discovering the proper program construct that will guarantee the truth of that assertion. The end product is a verified program, with program and proof the dual reward of the effort. In comparison to Wegbreit's approach, Dijkstra's internalizes the specification of proof justifications into the construction of the s-units that affect the truth of the derived assertions. That is, justifications are not based on the constructed s-units and their associated assertions, as in Wegbreit's approach, but are applied by employing the deductive system in the "construction" of s-units. When this view is taken, programming becomes a deductive discipline, with less emphasis on experience in traditional programming and considerably more emphasis on the ability to work within a deductive system. Thus, we "discover" programs by considering the formal statement of the assertions we wish to guarantee. Ideally, such an approach would allow us to create programs to solve problems for which we have no "intuitive" feeling. In the remainder of this section we concentrate on Dijkstra's constructive method.

5.5.2 Weakest Preconditions

A predicate transformer, as outlined in Section 4.4.2, is a function mapping an assertion and a syntactic unit to another assertion. In constructing verification conditions Floyd makes use of the idea of the *strongest verifiable consequent* (svc) transformer:

$$R^* = \text{svc}(s, Q), \qquad \text{with } (\forall R)(\vdash \{Q\} \, s \, \{R\} \longrightarrow \vdash (R^* \longrightarrow R)).$$

In Floyd's terminology, R^* is the strongest verifiable consequent for Q and s in the sense that it implies any other consequent R that may be inferred, given the execution of s-unit s on a program state satisfying Q.

Analogous to the strongest verifiable consequent is the idea of a *weakest precondition* [23], wp, defined by

$$Q^* = \text{wp}(s,R), \qquad \text{with } (\forall Q)(\vdash \{Q\} \, s \, \{R\} \longrightarrow \vdash (Q \longrightarrow Q^*)). \qquad (5.18)$$

Q^* is the *weakest* precondition for s and R in the sense that it is implied by any other precondition Q that, when true for a given program state subject to the subsequent execution of s, results in a state satisfying R. Whereas the svc transformer works "forward," allowing postconditions to be derived from preconditions and s-units, the wp transformer works "backward," allowing preconditions to be derived from s-units and their postconditions.

Of course, the wp transformer is dependent upon the types of s-units used to construct programs. For some of the s-unit types, the specification of wp is quite straightforward. For example, we have trivially:

$$\text{wp}(\underline{\text{stop}}, R) = R = Q^*, \quad \text{for any postcondition } R.$$

That is, whatever is true of the state following the execution of a stop must also have been true just prior to its execution.

For an assignment statement, $v := e$ (where e is some arbitrary expression resulting in a value of the same type as v), we have

$$\text{wp}(v := e, R) = R[v \longleftarrow e] = Q^*, \quad \text{for any postcondition } R.$$

Note the similarity between this statement and Hoare's "axiom of assignment" given in Section 4.5.2.1.

The wp for the "functional composition" of two s-units—that is, the wp of the operator ";"—is defined by

$$\text{wp}(s_1; s_2, R) = \text{wp}(s_1, \text{wp}(s_2, R)). \tag{5.19}$$

The semantics of the composition $s_1; s_2$ are intuitively understood to be that s-unit s_1 is *first* executed and, upon termination, s-unit s_2 is executed. For the semantic definition given by (5.19), postcondition R is supplied to the predicate transformer, $\text{wp}(s_2, R)$, hence the execution of $s_1; s_2$ ends with the execution of s_2. As $\text{wp}(s_2, R) = Q^*$ is supplied as postcondition to the wp for s_1, we identify the precondition Q^* for s_2 with the postcondition for s_1. This relationship establishes that the execution of s_1 is followed by the execution of s_2.

For the alternative construct, if B then s, we find

$$\text{wp}(\underline{\text{if}}\ B\ \underline{\text{then}}\ s, R) = (\vdash B \longrightarrow \vdash \text{wp}(s, R)).$$

The semantics defined by the wp for the "if statement" state that the weakest precondition $\text{wp}(s, R)$ must be true for *any* program state for which the condition B is true and whose transformation by the execution of s results in a state satisfying R.

In the case of the iterative construct, while B do s, the specification of wp is more complex. Dijkstra offers the following definition:

if $H_0(R) = R$ and not B

and $(\forall k > 0)(\text{wp}(\underline{\text{if}}\ B\ \underline{\text{then}}\ s, H_{k-1}(R))$ or $H_0(R) = H_k(R))$

then $\text{wp}(\underline{\text{while}}\ B\ \underline{\text{do}}\ s, R) = (\exists k > 0)(H_k(R))$.

The first line of the definition expresses the fact that if the condition B is not satisfied, the truth of R before the execution of the while construct if necessary and sufficient to guarantee the truth of R at exit from the while construct. The second line ensures that there exist weakest preconditions H_k, such that the while construct will terminate after exactly k iterations with the program state satisfying the postcondition R. The third line requires the existence of the integer value k, such that at most k iterations will be needed before the while construct terminates.

In comparison with the definition of the while rule for total correctness as given in Section 5.4.2, we here recognize the correspondence of R to the loop invariant Q. Furthermore, the index k implicitly defines the integer function t that, for each pass through the loop, selects a member from a strictly decreasing sequence of values from the set Z^+. The conceptual difference between the two while rules (as given in Section 5.4.2 and here) can be stated as follows. The rule given above gives a "measure" for the *construction* of the compound s-unit s that constitutes the loop body, such that the loop invariant (the given post-condition R) remains true for *exactly* k passes through the loop. The while rule as given in Section 5.4.2, on the other hand, allows us to prove in a deductive system that the loop invariant (the given precondition Q) remains true for each pass through the *given* loop and that after a finite number of iterations an exit is taken from the *given* loop.

The wp transformers presented in this section correspond to the axioms and inference rules discussed in Sections 4.5.2 and 5.4.2. The programming constructs defined by these transformers are deterministic in the sense that, for any state d satisfying the precondition of such a construct in a program, there exists a unique trace through the constituent s-units by which this state is transformed into a state satisfying the postcondition. Dijkstra extended the notion of wp transformers to a class of nondeterministic constructs called "guarded commands" [23]. For this class of programming constructs there may exist more than a single trace through the constituent s-units for any given state d satisfying the precondition. However, the definition of the wp transformer guarantees that, independent of the particular trace, the execution of the guarded command for an input state satisfying the weakest precondition will result in a state satisfying the postcondition used to deduce that weakest precondition.

We may think of wp transformers as a calculus of programming or program construction. This calculus allows programs to be constructed from s-units, which can be selected on the basis of a deductive argument determining their "semantic contribution" to the establishment of their postcondition and ultimately to the establishment of the postcondition of the entire program. The calculus suggests a backward approach to program construction, which starts from the program's postcondition and ends when a program precondition is found that can be satisfied by the input data of that program. It has been shown [69] that any program that is specified by a precondition and post-condition has a unique wp transformer from which the weakest program precondition can be derived. Thus, backward program construction as suggested by Dijkstra's calculus can end for any program precondition that implies this unique weakest precondition. Dijkstra's calculus of programming for the wp transformers discussed in this section is presented below.

5.5.3 A Calculus of Programming

Ultimately, the objective of defining wp transformers on the basis of a given postcondition R and a selected s-unit type is a discipline for the construction of correct programs. That is, the wp transformers discussed above are part of a *calculus* (a deductive system) that can be used to discover the s-unit (and precondition) necessary to ensure a particular postcondition. For example, given a postcondition Ψ, we might find

$$\begin{aligned}
\text{wp}(s_3, \Psi) &= Q_3^*, \\
\text{wp}(s_2, Q_3^*) &= Q_2^*, \\
\text{wp}(s_1, Q_2^*) &= Q_1^* = \Phi,
\end{aligned} \tag{5.20}$$

whereby we conclude $\vdash \{\Phi\}\, s_1 \,;\, s_2 \,;\, s_3 \,\{\Psi\}$, using the definition of the wp transformer (5.19) for functional composition. The "discovery" of the s-units s_1, s_2, and s_3 is presumably the result of a trial-and-error process in which several s-units are examined until the "proper" ones are discovered.

Unfortunately, the examination of s-units using the deductive system of wp transformers is not always a straightforward process in which the wp transformer for functional composition is inductively applied. For more complex (and interesting) constructs (such as the while construct) it is often the case that we cannot find an explicit formulation of a weakest precondition. However, by the definition of the weakest precondition (5.18) it is sufficient to find *some* condition that implies the desired wp. Hence, instead of the paradigm given in (5.20), the construction of correct programs is more likely to proceed along the following lines.

Given a postcondition Ψ we might construct an s-unit s_3 with

$$\text{wp}(s_3, \Psi) = Q_3^*$$

and then find a precondition Q_3 with

$$\vdash Q_3 \longrightarrow \vdash Q_3^*.$$

Analogously, we then construct s-unit s_2 such that

$$\text{wp}(s_2, Q_3) = Q_2^*,$$

and then find a Q_2 such that

$$\vdash Q_2 \longrightarrow \vdash Q_2^*.$$

Finally we find

$$\text{wp}(s_1, Q_2) = Q_1^*.$$

and then find a $Q_1 = \Phi$, with

$$\vdash \Phi \longrightarrow \vdash Q_1^*,$$

which completes program construction and proof by the inductive application of (5.19). In essence, this *modified construction principle* repeatedly employs the definition of the wp transformer (5.18) to establish preconditions Q that are more suitable to the use of the wp transformer associated with the s-unit that we choose to employ in the next constructive step.

Dijkstra offers inference rules to guide the application of the modified construction principle. For example, for the if-construct we are offered: alternative construct theorem:

$$\vdash (Q \text{ and } B) \longrightarrow \vdash \text{wp}(s, R)$$
$$\vdash (Q \text{ and not } B) \longrightarrow \vdash R \qquad (5.21)$$
$$\overline{\vdash Q \longrightarrow \vdash \text{wp}(\text{if } B \text{ then } s, R).}$$

This rule gives us a "measure" for the selection of an appropriate precondition Q for the if construct that is a suitable postcondition for the application of the wp transformer in the next constructive step.

Analogously, for the while construct we are offered:

invariant iterative construct theorem:

$$\vdash (Q \text{ and } B) \longrightarrow \vdash \text{wp}(s, Q)$$
$$\vdash (Q \text{ and } B) \longrightarrow \vdash t > 0$$
$$\vdash (Q \text{ and } B \text{ and } t \leq t_0 + 1) \longrightarrow \vdash \text{wp}(s, t \leq t_0) \qquad (5.22)$$
$$\overline{\vdash Q \longrightarrow \vdash \text{wp}(\text{while } B \text{ do } s, Q \text{ and not } B),}$$

where t is some integer function of the program state, and t_0 is some arbitrary positive integer constant. While (5.21) and (5.22) do not give explicit formulations for weakest preconditions, they do provide a calculus by which we may construct programs using the modified construction principle. The reader should note the close connection between (5.21) and (5.22) and the rule of conditionals in Section 4.5.2.2 and the while rule of Section 5.4.2, respectively. This connection stems from the fact that the rules (5.21) and (5.21) assume the *previous* construction of the s-unit s, and this assumption is also implicit to the axiomatic method.

Before proceeding to an example, we give the algorithm for developing a totally correct program P, using Dijkstra's calculus of programming consisting of the wp transformers and the modified construction principle.

1. Specify the precondition Φ and postcondition Ψ for program P.
2. Starting from Ψ, select an s-unit s, guaranteeing $\vdash \{Q\} s \{R\}$, where $\vdash R \to \vdash \Psi$. The s-unit should be selected such that the resulting precondition is semantically "closer" to Φ than the original postcondition Ψ. The selection is guided by the calculus of wp transformers.
3. If $\vdash \Phi \to \vdash Q$, the program and proof are complete. Otherwise, begin again at step 2, choosing as the new postcondition the precondition Q from the previous pass through step 2.
4. We will fail to complete the program if we cannot find a Q (applying the calculus) such that $\vdash \Phi \to \vdash Q$. If this is the case, it may be nec-

essary to backtrack to some point "further down" in the program and begin anew from that point.

5.5.4 An Example of the Programming Calculus

Using the subset of Dijkstra's calculus of programming, we illustrate its application by constructing a program, AMAX3, to find the maximum value, max, in an array $A[1 .. 100]$ of integers. We choose as our postcondition

Ψ: $(\exists j \in 1 .. 100)(\text{max} = A[j])$ and $(\forall k \in 1 .. 100)(\text{max} \geq A[k])$.

We proceed backward by initially observing that in order to satisfy the first part of Ψ, we must in some way ensure that max has a final value equal to the value of some element of A. One way to accomplish this is via an assignment statement. Applying the predicate transformer wp for the assignment statement to max := $A[1]$, we obtain

wp(max := $A[1]$, Ψ)

$= (\exists j \in 1 .. 100)(A[1] = A[j])$ and $(\forall k \in 1 .. 100)(A[1] \geq A[k])$ (5.23)

$= (\forall k \in 2 .. 100)(A[1] \geq A[k])$.

If at the beginning of execution of AMAX3 we were assured that the array A was sorted into nonincreasing order, then our objective for construction of AMAX3 would be to arrive at the precondition

Φ: $(\forall j \in 1 .. 99)(A[j] \geq A[j + 1])$,

from which we could conclude

$\vdash \Phi \longrightarrow \vdash$ wp(max := $A[1]$, Ψ)

and hence, according to (5.18),

$\vdash \{\Phi\}$ AMAX3 $\{\Psi\}$.

If, however, we place no such restriction upon the original arrangement of values within A, and we select the assignment max := $A[1]$ as the final s-unit of our program, then the s-units preceding max := $A[1]$ must somehow ensure condition (5.23). Programming experience tells us that this will likely lead to the need for the sorting of A. Therefore, we begin anew by recognizing that any suitable algorithm will likely include an iteration. Intuitively, given no constraints upon A, we believe that to find the maximum value in A we will need to examine each member of A at least once. Keeping in mind the idea of a loop invariant, we would like to find some simple condition Q such that $\vdash$ (Q and not B) $\rightarrow \vdash \Psi$. If such a Q exists, we can make use of the invariant iterative construct theorem (5.22) to conclude

$\vdash Q \longrightarrow \vdash$ wp(while B do s, Ψ),

and therefore

$\vdash \{Q\}$ while B do s $\{\Psi\}$.

The flexibility offered by the modified construction principle suggests that we select for Q a condition stronger than Ψ—for example:

Q: $i \in 1 .. 100$ and $(\exists j \in 1 .. i)(\max = A[j])$ and $(\forall k \in 1 .. i)(\max \geq A[k])$,

which, when conjoined with not B, where

$$B:\ i \neq 100,$$

will imply Ψ. Having made this attempt, we recognize straightforwardly that

$$\vdash (i = 1 \text{ and } \max = A[i]) \longrightarrow \vdash Q,$$

and we posit the following "template" for our program:

$$
\begin{aligned}
&i := 1; \\
&\max := A[i]; \\
&\text{while } i \neq 100 \text{ do} \\
&\qquad \text{begin} \\
&\qquad\qquad . \\
&\qquad\qquad . \\
&\qquad\qquad . \\
&\qquad \text{end.}
\end{aligned}
$$

In order to ensure the termination of the while loop, we must demonstrate the existence of an integer function t that satisfies the theorem (5.22). Intuition suggests choosing

$$t = 100 - i.$$

Clearly,

$$\vdash (Q \text{ and } i \neq 100) \longrightarrow \vdash (i \in 1 .. 99) = \vdash (100 - i > 0)$$
$$= \vdash (t > 0)$$

establishes line two of (5.22). We can ensure that t is a strictly decreasing function [required by the third line of the antecedent in (5.22)] by incrementing the value of i during each iteration of the loop. Suppose we conjecture that i is to be incremented by 2 during each iteration. Then

$$\text{wp}(i := i + 2, Q) = i \in -1 .. 98 \text{ and}$$
$$(\exists j \in 1 .. i + 2)(\max = A[j]) \text{ and} \qquad (5.24)$$
$$(\forall k \in 1 .. i + 2)(\max \geq A[k]).$$

For (5.24) to be acceptable, we must satisfy line one of (5.22); that is, we must have

$$\vdash (Q \text{ and } i \neq 100) \longrightarrow \vdash \text{wp}(i := i + 2, Q).$$

Unfortunately, it is clear that the first term in $\text{wp}(i := i + 2, Q)$—that is, $i \in -1 \ldots,98$—is not implied by Q and $i \neq 100$. If, instead, we try the assignment $i := i + 1$, we obtain

$$\text{wp}(i := i + 1, Q) = i \in 0 .. 99 \text{ and}$$
$$(\exists j \in 1 .. i + 1)(\max = A[j]) \text{ and} \qquad (5.25)$$
$$(\forall k \in 1 .. i + 1)(\max \geq A[k]),$$

and it is clear that

$$\vdash (Q \text{ and } i \neq 100) \longrightarrow \vdash \text{wp}(i := i + 1, Q),$$

as required by (5.22). Unfortunately, $i := i + 1$ is *not* sufficient for the loop body. There must be some other s-unit s to record the current value of max also in the body, say, *before* $i := i + 1$, such that

$$\vdash (Q \text{ and } i \neq 100) \longrightarrow \vdash \text{wp}(s; i := i + 1, Q).$$

The choice of having s *precede* $i := i + 1$ is at this point completely arbitrary. If the choice does not work, we can always come back and try another arrangement.

From (5.19) we have that

$$\text{wp}(s; i := i + 1, Q) = \text{wp}(s, \text{wp}(i := i + 1, Q)). \qquad (5.26)$$

Our goal, then, is to use (5.25) and (5.26) to find some s-unit s such that

$$\vdash ((i \in 1 .. 100) \text{ and } (\exists j \in 1 .. i)(\max = A[j])$$
$$\text{and } (\forall k \in 1 .. i)(\max \geq A[k]) \text{ and } i \neq 100)$$
$$\longrightarrow \qquad\qquad\qquad\qquad\qquad\qquad\qquad\qquad (5.27)$$
$$\vdash \text{wp}(s, (i \in 0 .. 99) \text{ and } (\exists j \in 1 .. i + 1)(\max = A[j])$$
$$\text{and } (\forall k \in 1 .. i + 1)(\max \geq A[k])).$$

One s that satisfies (5.27) is the assignment, $i := i - 1$, but this leads to a contradiction of the monotone-decreasing character of the function t. As no other assignment seems profitable, we venture a guess that s is an alternative construct. Simple inspection of (5.27) shows that

$$\vdash (Q \text{ and } i \neq 100 \text{ and } \text{not } \max < A[i + 1]) \longrightarrow \vdash \text{wp}(i := i + 1, Q)$$

hence, we guess that $\max < A[i + 1]$ is the proper boolean condition for the alternative construct s. In quick order we also discover

$$\vdash (Q \text{ and } i \neq 100 \text{ and } \max < A[i + 1])$$
$$\longrightarrow$$
$$\vdash ((i \in 0 .. 99) \text{ and } (\exists j \in 1 .. i + 1)(A[i + 1] = A[j]) \qquad (5.28)$$
$$\text{and } (\forall k \in 1 .. i + 1)(A[i + 1] \geq A[k])).$$

The implicant of (5.28) is

$$\text{wp}(\max := A[i + 1], \text{wp}(i := i + 1, Q)).$$

An appeal to the alternative construct theorem (5.21) leads to the conclusion that

$$\vdash (Q \text{ and } i \neq 100)$$
$$\longrightarrow \vdash \text{wp}(\text{if } \max < A[i + 1] \text{ then } \max := A[i + 1], \text{wp}(i := i + 1, Q)).$$

With (5.19) we may take the implicant of the above as

$$\text{wp}(\text{if } \max < A[i + 1] \text{ then } \max := A[i + 1]; i := i + 1, Q),$$

which satisfies (5.27).

At this point we apply the invariant iterative construct theorem (5.22) to conclude

$$\vdash Q \longrightarrow \vdash \text{wp}(\underline{\text{while}} \ i \neq 100 \ \underline{\text{do}}$$
$$\underline{\text{begin}}$$
$$\underline{\text{if}} \ \text{max} < A[i + 1] \ \underline{\text{then}} \ \text{max} := A[i + 1]; \qquad (5.29)$$
$$i := i + 1;$$
$$\underline{\text{end}}, Q \ \underline{\text{and}} \ i = 100).$$

Finally, recalling that $\vdash (i = 1 \ \underline{\text{and}} \ \text{max} = A[i]) \longrightarrow \vdash Q$, together with (5.29) and the facts that $\vdash (Q \ \underline{\text{and}} \ i = \overline{100}) \rightarrow \vdash \Psi$, and wp$(i := 1; \text{max} := A[i], Q)$ $= \underline{\text{true}}$, we may conclude that

$$\underline{\text{true}} \longrightarrow \vdash \text{wp}(\underline{\text{program}} \ \text{AMAX3}$$
$$i := 1;$$
$$\text{max} := A[i];$$
$$\underline{\text{while}} \ i \neq 100 \ \underline{\text{do}}$$
$$\underline{\text{begin}}$$
$$\underline{\text{if}} \ \text{max} < A[i + 1] \ \underline{\text{then}} \ \text{max} := A[i + 1];$$
$$i := i + 1;$$
$$\underline{\text{end}}$$
$$\underline{\text{end}} \ \text{AMAX3}, \Psi)$$

and therefore $\vdash \{\underline{\text{true}}\} \ \text{AMAX3} \ \{\Psi\}$.

5.6 REMARKS

The constructive method is generally equivalent to the inductive assertion method and the axiomatic method. In fact, the same conclusions can be deduced from the deductive systems underlying either one of these methods. Furthermore, each of these methods may be applied constructively, as they are all based on predicate transformers that allow an assertion and an s-unit to be mapped to another assertion. Two aspects are responsible for the difference between the constructive method and the inductive assertion and axiomatic methods

1. The backward approach to program construction may be adhered to by the axiomatic method but not by the inductive assertion method.
2. The deduction of unique weakest preconditions is comparable to the deduction of unique strongest postconditions in the inductive assertion method, but such deduction cannot be guaranteed by the axiomatic method.

The backward approach to program construction is advantageous, as generally the information content of a program's postcondition, Ψ, is larger than the information content of its precondition, Φ. Postconditions define the effect of program or s-unit execution as a relation between initial states and final states, whereas preconditions define constraints on initial states only. Furthermore, the information in preconditions is usually more weakly structured than the information in postconditions. For example, many programs considered in this book have a precondition, <u>true</u>, whereas they have highly structured postconditions. Consequently, as shown in Figure 5.2, the backward approach to program construction suggests a reasoning from highly structured, large information contents to loosely structured, small information contents in the assertions specifying the semantics of a program P.

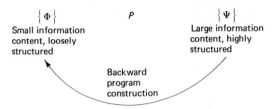

Figure 5.2. Direction of reasoning in the backward approach to program construction

The backward approach to program construction is more appealing in the sense that it is intuitively simpler to apply predicate transformers to reduce explicitly defined requirements on the program semantics (Ψ) to requirements on the input data (Φ) than it is to expand requirements on the program semantics. Again, consider a precondition Φ: <u>true</u>, which allows program execution for any arbitrary set of input data. This condition provides no guidance for constructing a program satisfying a given postcondition, hence the forward approaches usually rely on the prior construction of a program and the definition of intermediate assertions to construct a proof. Contrastingly, the backward approach derives the intermediate assertions while constructing a program, while providing maximum guidance in the process by using all requirements on the program semantics given in the postcondition Ψ. In the case of Φ: <u>true</u>, the program construction is aimed at the reduction of the postcondition to the absolutely weakest precondition, <u>true</u>.

The definition of unique weakest preconditions by the wp transformers in the constructive method and unique strongest postconditions by the svc transformers in the inductive assertion method provides maximum flexibility in the selection of assertion in the program proof and construction processes as illustrated in Figure 5.3. The wp transformers define the largest set of legitimate initial states. Thus, in the construction and proof process, maximum flexibility for the selection of preconditions is obtained, as any subset of the defined largest set is a legitimate set of initial states. This largest set of legitimate initial states might never be derived with the axiomatic method. Consequently, the choice of appropriate preconditions for the continuation or termination of

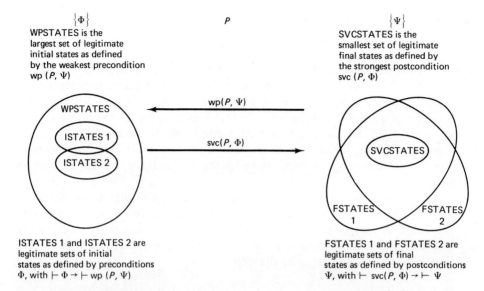

$\{\Phi\}$ P $\{\Psi\}$

WPSTATES is the largest set of legitimate initial states as defined by the weakest precondition wp (P, Ψ)

SVCSTATES is the smallest set of legitimate final states as defined by the strongest postcondition svc (P, Φ)

wp(P, Ψ)

svc(P, Φ)

ISTATES 1 and ISTATES 2 are legitimate sets of initial states as defined by preconditions Φ, with $\vdash \Phi \rightarrow \vdash$ wp (P, Ψ)

FSTATES 1 and FSTATES 2 are legitimate sets of final states as defined by postconditions Ψ, with $\vdash$ svc$(P, \Phi) \rightarrow \vdash \Psi$

Figure 5.3. Predicate transformers and associated sets of legitimate initial and final states

program construction is more limited with the axiomatic method than with the constructive method.

Similarly, the svc transformers define the smallest set of legitimate final states. Thus, in the proof process maximum flexibility is obtained for selecting weaker postconditions that define supersets of this smallest set of legitimate states and are more appropriate for the continuation or termination of the proof. Again, the axiomatic method, which does not guarantee the derivation of the smallest set of legitimate final states, is more limited in its forward application to correctness proofs than the inductive assertion method.

The constructive method offers a practical advantage by virtue of its dictate that we consider program construction and verification as a *single* task. The advantage emanates from the fact that at each step in the construction/ verification process:

1. We employ inference rules to construct the wp(s, R) transformer to test the appropriateness of the selected s-unit s in terms of its effect on the program state. That is, we have immediate feedback as to whether or not a selected s-unit s brings us nearer to the establishment of $\vdash \{\Phi\} P \{\Psi\}$. If we find that, for a given R, an inappropriate s-unit s was selected, we may select another s-unit s' such that wp(s', R) brings us nearer to the ultimate goal, $\vdash \{\Phi\} P \{\Psi\}$, than did wp$(s, R)$.

2. Alternatively, we may employ the rules of consequence (b) to replace a given postcondition R' by another, say R, such that $\vdash R' \rightarrow \vdash R$, with

R being more suitable than R' for the application of the wp transformer associated with the selected s-unit s.

As a result we have *guidance*, via wp(s, R), in the selection of s-units and complete flexibility (during construction) to use the rules of consequence to modify a postcondition R to a form R', which, when coupled with the transformer wp(s, R') $= Q^*$, leads to a Q^* that brings us nearer the establishment of $\vdash \{\Phi\} P \{\Psi\}$ for some program precondition Φ. In other words, the combined step-by-step application of the rules described above gives the constructive method advantages not exhibited by the axiomatic or inductive assertion methods.

We contrast the three methods by giving (again) algorithms for their application (see Section 4.5.4), wherein we use the notation "{ }" to denote the fact that an s-unit or an assertion need not be given a priori to carry out a (construction) verification step, but rather may be selected as part of the step or derived as a consequence of the step.

1. <u>Inductive assertion method</u>:   given $\{Q\} s \{R\}$ for all s-units in program P. Given $\{\Phi\} P \{\Psi\}$, the correctness proof—that is, the establishment of $\vdash \{\Phi\}$ $P \{\Psi\}$—proceeds by establishing $\vdash \{Q\} s \{R\}$ for all s-units. For the proof of each $\{Q\} s \{R\}$, the transformer svc(s, Q) $= R^*$ is first constructed. Then the verification condition $V_s(Q; R) = (\text{svc}(s, Q) \rightarrow R)$ is established so that we may conclude that $\vdash V_s(Q; R) \rightarrow \vdash \{Q\} s \{R\}$.

2. <u>Axiomatic method</u>. (a) <u>Forward approach</u>:   given $\{\Phi\} s \{$ $\}$ for the first executables-unit of program P. Given $\{\Phi\} P \{\Psi\}$, the proof proceeds such that the postconditions R are deduced for all s-units in the program P on the basis of a given precondition Q and the s-unit itself. That is, given $\{Q\} s \{R\}$, deductive transformations $T(s, Q) = R^*$ are applied to establish $\vdash \{Q\} s \{R\}$, for any $R \in \{R | \vdash T(s, Q) \rightarrow \vdash R\}$. Hence in each proof step the postcondition R to be used as precondition in the next proof step can be *selected* from the set $\{R | \vdash T(s, Q) \rightarrow \vdash R\}$, and in the final step we establish $\Psi \in \{R | \vdash T(s_t, Q) \rightarrow \vdash R\}$, where s_t is any s-unit whose execution terminates program execution.

(b) <u>Backward approach</u>:   given $\{$ $\} s \{\Psi\}$ for all s-units terminating execution of program P. Backward application of the axiomatic method requires that in each proof step, $\{$ $\} s \{R\}$ is given in order for each s-unit in the program P. In this case, deductive transformations $T(s, R) = Q^*$ are applied to establish $\vdash \{Q\} s \{R\}$ for any $Q \in \{Q | \vdash Q \rightarrow \vdash T(s, R)\}$. In the final step we establish $\Phi \in \{Q | \vdash Q \rightarrow \vdash T(s_b, R)\}$, where s_b is the s-unit that begins execution of the program P.

3. <u>Constructive method</u>:   given $\{$ $\}$ $\{\Psi\}$ for a program. The program P and the precondition specifying the program state at the beginning of the program execution are deduced in the correctness proof. The proof proceeds by developing s-units s and weakest precondition Q^* with the predicate transformer

$wp(s, R) = Q^*$. That is, given { } $\{R\}$, $\vdash \{Q\} s \{R\}$ can be established for any $Q \in \{Q \mid \vdash Q \rightarrow \vdash wp(s, R)\}$ and any $s \in \{s \mid \vdash T(s, Q) \rightarrow \dashv R\}$. In the last construction/proof step we establish that the deduced precondition $\Phi \in \{Q \mid \vdash Q \rightarrow \vdash wp(s_b, R)\}$ can be satisfied by the data state that is given, before the execution of the first s-unit s_b, in the constructed program P.

Note that the transformation $T(s, Q)$ for the constructive method is the same as for the axiomatic method. This view of legitimate s-units indicates that inference rules such as (5.21) and (5.22) may be employed to deduce preconditions Q, with $\vdash Q \rightarrow \vdash wp(s, R)$, in cases where the weakest precondition Q^* cannot be explicitly formulated via the definition of the predicate transformer $wp(s, R) = Q^*$ for a particular s-unit s. This observation is particularly true for iterative constructs—for example while B do s—as the constructive method considers only total correctness. That is, as the definition of a wp transformer is s-unit dependent, the conditions for the integer selection functions are not explicitly stated in the definition of the wp transformer for an iterative construct. The reason is that the wp transformers for iterative constructs are independent of the semantics of a particular (compound) s-unit that constitutes the loop body. However, given an inference rule, such as (5.22), we may test to find if the (compound) s-unit satisfies the integer selection function conditions necessary to guarantee termination.

To close, we note that none of the approaches is complete in the sense that they do not consider such things as input-output, character manipulations, variable scope control (procedures), pointer variables, error recovery strategies, or parallel programs. As a result, the methods are believed by some [14] to be inadequate for practical real-world applications. We hasten to add, however, that knowledge of verification techniques can mitigate the task of program development and promote the construction of "bug-free" programs. Further, as Chapter 8 will show, they constitute an integral part of program specification techniques that can be employed in real-world applications. Additionally, progress is being made on extending the verification techniques to include rules for some of the omitted items listed above. In particular, rules exist for parallel programs, as will be discussed in the next chapter.

6

CORRECTNESS
OF PARALLEL PROGRAMS

6.1 THE PROBLEM POSED BY PARALLEL PROGRAMS

Verification of parallel programs is considerably more difficult than verification of sequential programs, and no truly satisfactory formalism for the task has appeared. Specifically, verification of parallel programs is complicated by the nondeterministic manner in which parallel programs can affect (*interfere* with) each other through operations on those objects of the state space that are shared. Additionally, there are correctness criteria of interest for parallel programs other than sequential partial or total correctness; for example, parallel programs may be designed to exhibit a cyclic behavior. In this section we outline the extant approaches taken in establishing a formalism for parallel programs.

We begin by giving a syntax for describing parallel programs, and then we discuss the problems that parallel programs pose. For purposes of our discussion, parallel programs (that is, the concurrent execution of processes) will be syntactically indicated by an s-unit of the form

$$\text{cobegin } s_1 \, \| \, s_2 \, \| \, \ldots \, \| \, s_n \text{ coend}.$$

The s-units s_i, $i \in 1 \, . \, . \, n$, may be simple or compound, and execution of cobegin . . . coend results in the execution of the n parallel processes emanating from the s_i, For these processes we may not make assumptions about the way in which the parallel execution is implemented (realized); in particular, nothing can be assumed about the relative speeds of the n processes—that is, about the rates at which execution of the processes progresses. The absence of such information leads directly to nondeterminism, as it is not possible to identify process interruption or process interference* points caused by direct rates of progress of the processes. To illustrate this point consider the semantic definition of the classic example:

$$\{x = 0\} \text{ ADD: } \underline{\text{cobegin}} \; x := x + 1 \,\|\, x := x + 1 \; \underline{\text{coend}} \; \{x = 1 \; \underline{\text{or}} \; x = 2\}.$$

$$(6.1)$$

Given no knowledge about the implementation (the realization) of the two processes resulting from the execution of (6.1), we would be hard pressed to conclude $x = 2$ following execution. The reason is that the process executions may be interleaved so that the *shared object* x is only incremented by one. If we are assured that the implementation employs a single instruction to increment x (that is, an increment-memory instruction), rather than a load register, increment register, store register sequence, then we may conclude $x = 2$ following execution, as the incrementation is done as an *uninterruptable* or *elementary* [27] operation. On the basis of this example, we see that we might proceed by ensuring that s-unit semantics are sufficiently explicit to provide information on possible preemption (or interference) points. Thus, if the weakest precondition semantics for the assignment s-unit are changed from

$$\text{wp}(x := x + a, R) = R[x \longleftarrow x + a]$$

to

$$\text{wp}(x := x + a, R) = \text{wp}(x_0 := x; x_0 := x_0 + a; x := x_0, R), \qquad (6.2)$$

where x_0 is a unique temporary, we are able to conclude that

$$\text{wp}(\text{ADD}, x = 2) = \underline{\text{false}} \qquad (6.3)$$

—that is, there exists no state for which it can be guaranteed that the effect of executing ADD is $x = 2$. However, we may conclude

$$\text{wp}(\text{ADD}, x = 1 \; \underline{\text{or}} \; x = 2) = (x = 0), \qquad (6.4)$$

as the assignment $x := x_0$ may be executed following one or two incrementations of x_0. If, on the other hand, we can be guaranteed that execution of the s-units of (6.1) are serialized (for example, by having been realized by an increment-memory instruction), then by the rule of functional composition (5.19) we have

$$\text{wp}(\underline{\text{cobegin}} \; x := x + 1 \,\|\, x := x + 1 \; \underline{\text{coend}}, R)$$
$$= \text{wp}(x := x + 1; x := x + 1, R)$$
$$= \text{wp}(x := x + 1, \text{wp}(x := x + 1, R))$$
$$= \text{wp}(x := x + 1, R[x \longleftarrow x + 1])$$
$$= R[x \longleftarrow x + 2],$$

---

*Whether preemption or interference is the cause of nondeterminism depends upon whether the realization employs a single processor or multiple processors.

from which we may conclude

$$\text{wp(ADD}, x = 2) = \text{wp}(x := x + 1; x := x + 1, x = 2)$$
$$= (x + 2 = 2) = (x = 0). \tag{6.5}$$

In essence, the approach to parallelism examplified by (6.2) amounts to specifying how s-unit executions are realized—that is, how they are compiled. For the example discussed, the assertion (6.3) results from the possibility of more preemption or interference points than allowed for (6.5). In other words, (6.5) results when we *restrict* the allowable parallelism, in this case by explicitly specifying a synchronization of the parallel programs.

One approach to the verification of parallel programs, then, is the specifying of a synchronization mechanism, such as monitors [28], that guarantees mutually exclusive access to shared objects, and then providing rules for verification in the face of the selected synchronization mechanism. This approach has been applied by a number of writers [29, 30, 31, 32]. It is limited in that, in certain cases, it restricts parallelism beyond that allowable either for the application or for an efficient implementation. In [33], a second approach has been taken that relaxes certain restrictions on parallelism, as they pertain to monitors, so that verification rules for structures more like SIMULA classes [34] are provided.

In this chapter we concentrate on approaches applicable to a general class of parallel programs. We do so by not introducing specific implicit synchronization mechanisms and by not imposing restrictions on the composition of the constitutent s-units s_i. In Section 6.5 we sketch, as an example, how additional results can be obtained if we restrict the s-units s_i to conditional critical region statements [28] of the form

<u>with</u> x_i <u>when</u> B_i <u>do</u> s_i <u>od</u>,

so that the allowable interactions or potential interference patterns are restricted by mutual exclusion.

We begin our discussion by recounting the essence of the axiomatic and constructive methods. Each is based on the definition of a deductive system that models sequential program semantics. With these models we are able to make statements—that is, to derive assertions—about the effect of s-unit execution on program state. As summarized in Section 5.6, the constructive method generates a weakest precondition, $\text{wp}(s, R)$, for a *selected* s-unit s and an associated postcondition R, while the axiomatic method generates a postcondition, R, for a given s-unit s and an associated precondition Q. The important point is that both depend on the sequential nature of program execution to assure determinism and thus verification. It seems reasonable, therefore, to approach the verification of parallel programs by mapping the possible parallelisms into a set of "potential" (possible) sequential programs that may obtain by execution of the <u>cobegin</u> . . . <u>coend</u> s-unit. We then verify the parallel program by verifying, in turn, each sequential program.

The constructive approach to verification of parallel programs to be discussed in Section 6.3 directly considers all possible sequential programs that can result. By doing so, it establishes a rule for obtaining wp(cobegin . . . coend, R). The approach accounts for total correctness and, in a sense, gives a complete characterization of parallel programs. The difficulty in applying the approach increases as the number of possible interactions of the parallel s-unit sequences grows, so that if a large number of interactions must be accounted for, a correspondingly large number of sequential programs must be verified. As a result, the weakest preconditions for a large number of cases must be established and combined.

The axiomatic approach to verification of parallel programs to be discussed in Section 6.2 circumvents the combinatorics of the constructive approach by not directly considering all possible interleavings. Instead, the approach attempts to establish assertions that are true for all (or a class of the) possible resulting sequential programs. This approach proceeds by seeking to identify ways in which the parallel programs do *not* interfere with each other, then establishing assertions on the basis of properties that obtain as a result of the absence of certain interference patterns. These assertions will be valid regardless of the actual manner in which the parallel programs interact under the class of restrictions considered. This reasoning is formalized by the *noninterference principle*, and it, together with the notion of *auxiliary variables*, provides a discipline that may be easier to apply than its constructive counterpart. In a sense, the approaches are orthogonal; the constructive method requires direct verification of each possible resulting sequential program, while the axiomatic method attempts to lump obtainable sequential programs into a class and, based on noninterference properties of that class as a whole, considers as few sequential programs as possible.

Both approaches proceed by decomposing the s-units s_i in a parallel programming construct into *lexically explicit* s-unit sequences, $s_i = s_{i_1}; s_{i_2}; \ldots;$ $s_{i_m(i)}$, so that all possible interaction or interference points are apparent. The form (6.2) represents, for example, a lexically explicit sequence for the assignment $x := x + a$. Additionally, in some cases, we must also know how the sequences s_i are assigned to processors. To clarify this point, consider the program taken from [27]:

$$x := N; y := 0; B := \underline{\text{true}};$$

$$P: \underline{\text{cobegin}}$$

$$L_1: \underline{\text{while }} x > 0 \underline{\text{ do }} y := (y + 1) \underline{\text{ mod }} N \underline{\text{ od}}; B := \underline{\text{false}} \| \qquad (6.6)$$

$$L_2: \underline{\text{while }} B \underline{\text{ do }} x := x - 1 \underline{\text{ od}}$$

$$\underline{\text{coend}},$$

with its obvious intended semantics. If P is implemented on a uniprocessor with no time-slicing [28], P will *never* terminate, as there will be no reason to switch the processor from one sequence, L_i, to the other, L_j, $i, j \in 1 . . 2, i \neq j$.

Even if time-slicing is employed, termination is not guaranteed but depends upon the policy enforced by the processor scheduler. For example, nontermination results if the time-slicing policy is dependent upon process-initiated relinquishment of the processor. If, on the other hand, each program in the parallel set—that is, L_1 and L_2—is assigned its own processor, then termination of the parallel processes is guaranteed regardless of the relative speeds of the individual processors. In subsequent sections, where the semantics of parallel programs depend on the number of processors involved, as they do in (6.6), we will assume that each program in the parallel set is assigned its own processor.

6.2 THE AXIOMATIC METHOD AND PARALLEL PROGRAMS

The axiomatic method as proposed by Hoare allows us to establish partial correctness (see Section 4.5) and total correctness (see Section 5.4) of sequential programs. To apply the method to parallel programs requires first that the deductive system of Section 4.5 be extended so that the reasoning employed to prove partial correctness extends to compound s-units of the form

$$\text{cobegin } s_1 \| s_2 \| \ldots \| s_n \text{ coend.}$$

Second, the deductive system obtained by this extension must be further extended to facilitate proof of total correctness. Note that the latter extension of the deductive system is analogous to the extension of the deductive system of Section 4.5 as given in Section 5.4. In this section we summarize such extensions as given by Owicki [30] and Flon [29], respectively.

6.2.1 The Noninterference Principle and Explicit Synchronization

The fundamental objective of the extension of Hoare's deductive system to accommodate correctness proofs of compound s-units of the form

$$\text{cobegin } s_1 \| s_2 \| \ldots \| s_n \text{ coend}$$

is to formally specify a relationship among the constituent s-units $s_i, i = 1, \ldots, n$, such that the effect on the program state of executing $s_1, \ldots, s_n$ in parallel is the same as executing each s-unit in isolation. Such a relationship can, of course, be established only if the processes resulting from the execution of the s-units s_i do not interfere with each other in their use of shared objects. One possibility for guaranteeing noninterference is to prohibit shared objects. Another possibility is to require that execution of assignment statements and evaluation of expressions in the lexically explicit formulation of each s-unit s_i be considered indivisible operations. This requirement is impractical, as it forces us to make particular assumptions about the implementation of the s-units s_i.

The indivisible-execution requirement may be lifted by the conventions

(1) that the *only* indivisible operation be the memory reference, (2) that each expression e in the s-units s_i refer at most once to each shared object x, and (3) that multiple-assignment s-units are prohibited. As a result, an expression e will never be evaluated using more than a single value for a shared object x.

Noninterference among the processes p_i emanating from the s-units s_i requires that certain assertions used to establish $\vdash \{Q_i\} s_i \{R_i\}$ for each process p_i be *invariantly true* after parallel execution of the other processes p_j, $i \neq j$. That is, if the assertions used to establish $\vdash \{Q_i\} s_i \{R_i\}$ are not falsified by execution of any other process p_j, the establishment of $\vdash \{Q_i\} s_i \{R_i\}$ will still hold after the execution of the s-unit cobegin $s_1 \| s_2 \| \ldots \| s_n$ coend. These ideas are formalized in the *principle of noninterference* as given by Owicki [35].

Noninterference Principle

Let $\{p_j | j \in 1 \ldots n\}$ be the set of processes emanating from the execution of the s-unit cobegin $s_1 \| s_2 \| \ldots \| s_n$ coend, and let each process p_j be represented by the program

$$s_j = s_{j_0}; s_{j_1}; \ldots; s_{j_{m(j)}},$$

where each s_{j_k} is a separate s-unit. By $\vdash \{Q_j\} s_j \{R_j\}$ we denote the following conjunction:

$$\vdash \{Q_{j_0}\} s_{j_0} \{R_{j_0}\}$$
$$\text{and} \vdash \{Q_{j_1}\} s_{j_1} \{R_{j_1}\}$$
$$\vdots$$
$$\text{and} \vdash \{Q_{j_{m(j)}}\} s_{j_{m(j)}} \{R_{j_{m(j)}}\},$$

such that $\vdash Q_j \rightarrow \vdash Q_{j_0}, \vdash R_{j_{m(j)}} \rightarrow \vdash R_j$, and $\vdash R_{j_i} \rightarrow \vdash Q_{j_{i+1}}$, $i = 0, \ldots, m(j) - 1$. Then the set of proofs

$$\{\vdash \{Q_j\} s_j \{R_j\} | j = 1, \ldots, n\}$$

is a proof of

$$\{Q\} \text{ cobegin } s_j \| s_j \| \ldots \| s_n \text{ coend } \{R\}$$

for precondition Q and postcondition R, if

$$(\forall i, j \in 1 \ldots n, i \neq j)(\forall k, k \in 0 \ldots m(j))(\forall h, h \in 0 \ldots m(i))$$

$$(\vdash \{R_{i_h} \text{ and } Q_{j_k}\} s_{j_k} \{R_{i_h}\}). \quad (6.7)$$

That is, the execution of any s-unit s_{j_k} in process p_j between the execution of s-units s_{i_h} and $s_{i_{h+1}}$ in process p_i must not invalidate the postcondition R_{i_h}.

In other words, the processes p_i, $i = 1, \ldots, n$, are interference-free, if the execution of s-units in p_i does not invalidate any of the assertions (or arguments) used in the proof of p_j, $i \neq j$. As a result, the set of sequential proofs and the establishment of (6.7) are sufficient to provide a proof of $\{Q\}$ cobegin $\ldots$ coend $\{R\}$. The latter step is accomplished by the following inference rule:

Rule of Parallelism

$$\vdash \{Q_1\} s_1 \{R_1\} \text{ and } \ldots \text{ and } \vdash \{Q_n\} s_n \{R_n\}$$

$$\text{and} \vdash (\text{noninterference condition (6.7)})$$

(6.8)

$$\vdash \{Q_1 \text{ and } Q_2 \text{ and } \ldots \text{ and } Q_n\} \text{ cobegin } s_1 \| \ldots$$

$$\| s_n \text{ coend } \{R_1 \text{ and } R_2 \text{ and } \ldots \text{ and } R_n\}$$

which explicitly shows how the Q_i's and R_i's are combined to establish Q and R, respectively. Note that if the noninterference property (6.7) is not satisfied, it does not necessarily mean that the consequent of (6.8) cannot be established. For example, consider the compound s-unit

$$s_j = s_{j_0}; s_{j_1} = B := \underline{\text{true}}; A := \underline{\text{true}}$$

with Q_j: true, and for which we would like R_j: A. A sequential proof for s-unit s_j may be

$$\vdash \{\underline{\text{true}}\} B := \underline{\text{true}} \{\text{true}\} \qquad (\text{i.e., } \vdash \{Q_{j_0}\} s_{j_0} \{R_{j_0}\})$$

and   (6.9)

$$\vdash \{\underline{\text{true}}\} A := \underline{\text{true}} \{A\} \qquad (\text{i.e., } \vdash \{Q_{j_1}\} s_{j_1} \{R_{j_1}\})$$

or alternatively

$$\vdash \{\underline{\text{true}}\} B := \underline{\text{true}} \{B\} \qquad (\text{i.e., } \vdash \{Q_{j_0}\} s_{j_0} \{R_{j_0}\})$$

and   (6.10)

$$\vdash \{B\} A := \underline{\text{true}} \{A\} \qquad (\text{i.e., } \vdash \{Q_{j_1}\} s_{j_1} \{R_{j_1}\}).$$

The proof (6.9) violates the noninterference property (6.7) for a postcondition R_{j_1}: $A \rightarrow B$ for some s-units s_i, $i \neq j$, since substitution in $\vdash \{R_{i_h} \text{ and } Q_{j_1}\}$ $s_{j_1} \{R_{i_h}\}$ yields $\vdash \{A \rightarrow B)$ and $\underline{\text{true}}\} A := \underline{\text{true}} \{A \rightarrow B\}$, which is not valid by assignment axiom (4.21). [Note that by (4.21) we obtain for R_{i_h}: $A \rightarrow B$, $\vdash \{\underline{\text{true}} \rightarrow B\} A := \underline{\text{true}} \{A \rightarrow B\} = \vdash \{B\} A := \underline{\text{true}} \{A \rightarrow B\}$.] Contrastingly, the proof (6.10) satisfies (6.7) for R_{i_h}: $A \rightarrow B$, as $\vdash \{(A \rightarrow B) \text{ and } B\}$ $A := \underline{\text{true}} \{A \rightarrow B\}$ is valid according to (4.21). In summary, use of (6.9) surely blocks the application of the rule of parallelism (6.8), although the s-unit cobegin . . . coend may be correct, whereas use of (6.10) does not.

Restricting indivisible operations to the level of memory references has given us the maximum flexibility in the interleavings that can be considered. Two approaches can be taken to raise the granularity to a level appropriate for the intent of a given program. The first approach proceeds by providing *explicit* synchronization mechanisms (as given, for example, by the while construct in the example that follows). The second approach employs *implicit* synchronization (for example, as provided by monitors [28] or resource invariants [33]), which, unlike the first approach, requires the introduction of auxiliary variables to facilitate a proof of correctness.

To demonstrate *explicit synchronization*, we give a proof of a program containing two parallel while constructs.

Example

Consider the program

$$\begin{array}{l} \textbf{cobegin} \\ \quad \textbf{while } x > 0 \textbf{ do } x := x - 2 \textbf{ od} \| \\ \quad \textbf{while } x < 0 \textbf{ do } x := x + 1 \textbf{ od} \\ \textbf{coend,} \end{array} \qquad (6.11)$$

which is to be proven correct with respect to Φ: true and Ψ: $x = 0$ or $x = -1$. Our overall strategy is to (a) give a proof for the first while, (b) give a proof for the second while, (c) demonstrate noninterference for the pair of while statements, and (d) use the rule of parallelism (6.8), to establish the proof of the parallel program.

The precondition Φ: true applies to the initial entry into each while construct. Thus, the loop invariant must be true for each while loop construct.

Demonstration of (a):

1. $\vdash (x > 0) \longrightarrow$ true   by A_{AR} [see (4.19)].
2. $\vdash \{\text{true}\}\, x := x - 2\, \{\text{true}\}$ by (4.21).
3. $\vdash \{\text{true and } x > 0\}\, x := x - 2\, \{\text{true}\}$ by 1 and (4.21).
4. $\vdash \{\text{true}\}\, \text{while } x > 0 \text{ do } x := x - 2 \text{ od } \{\text{true and } x \le 0\}$ by (5.10) and 3.

Demonstration of (b):

5. $\vdash (x < 0) \longrightarrow$ true   by A_{AR}.
6. $\vdash \{\text{true}\}\, x := x + 1\, \{\text{true}\}$ by (4.21).
7. $\vdash \{\text{true and } x < 0\}\, x := x + 1\, \{\text{true}\}$ by 5 and (4.21).
8. $\vdash \{\text{true}\}\, \text{while } x < 0 \text{ do } x := x + 1 \text{ od } \{\text{true and } x \ge 0\}$ by (5.10) and 7.

Demonstration of (c):

Steps 1 through 8 constitute the sequential proofs for the while constructs. Noninterference remains to be proved. Noninterference requires that we show $\{R_{i_h} \text{ and } Q_{j_k}\}$ $s_{j_k} \{R_{i_h}\}$ for *two* cases.

   Case 1. Let R_{i_h}: $x \ge 0$ and s_{j_k}: while $x > 0$ do $x := x - 2$ od. We must show

$$\{x \ge 0 \text{ and true}\} \text{ while } x > 0 \text{ do } x := x - 2 \text{ od } \{x \ge 0\}$$

by showing $\{Q \text{ and } B\}\, s\, \{Q\}$, for Q: $x \ge 0$. We have:

9. $\vdash (x \ge 0 \text{ and } x > 0) \longrightarrow \vdash (x > 0)$ by A_{AR}.
10. $\vdash \{x > 0\}\, x := x - 2\, \{x > -2\}$ by (4.21).
11. $\vdash (x > -2) \nrightarrow (x \ge 0)$ by A_{AR}.

That is, for $x = -1$ the noninterference cannot be shown, as while $x > 0$ do $x := x - 2$ od might violate the postcondition of while $x < 0$ do $x := x + 1$ od. However, by the rule of consequence (b), we know that as

12. $\vdash (x \ge 0) \longrightarrow \vdash (x > -2)$ by A_{AR},

we can replace 8 by

13. $\vdash \{\text{true}\}\, \text{while } x < 0 \text{ do } x := x + 1 \text{ od } \{x > -2\}.$

Doing so eliminates the interference.

Case 2. Let R_{i_h}: $x \leq 0$ and s_{j_k}: while $x <$ do $x := x + 1$ od. We must show

$$\{x \leq 0 \text{ and true}\} \text{ while } x < 0 \text{ do } x := x + 1 \text{ od } \{x \leq 0\}$$

by showing $\{Q \text{ and } B\} s \{Q\}$ for Q: $x \leq 0$. We have:

14. $\vdash (x \leq 0 \text{ and } x < 0) \longrightarrow (x < 0)$ by A_{AR}.
15. $\vdash \{x < 0\} x := x + 1 \{x < 1\}$ by (4.21).
16. $\vdash (x < 1) \longrightarrow (x \leq 0)$ by A_{AR}.

Hence, while $x < 0$ do $x := x + 1$ od does not violate the postcondition of while $x > 0$ do $x := x - 2$ od. Therefore, the rule of parallelism (6.8) can be applied.

Demonstration of (d):

17. (4) and (13) and $\vdash$ (noninterference)

$$\{\text{true}\} \text{ cobegin}$$
$$\quad\quad\quad \text{while } x > 0 \text{ do } x := x - 2 \text{ od} \|$$
$$\quad\quad\quad \text{while } x < 0 \text{ do } x := x + 1 \text{ od}$$
$$\quad\quad \text{coend}$$
$$\{x = 0 \text{ or } x = -1\} \quad\quad\quad\quad\quad\quad\quad\quad \text{by (6.8) and 18.}$$

18. $\vdash (x \leq 0 \text{ and } x > -2) \longrightarrow \vdash (x = 0 \text{ or } x = -1)$

establishing the proof of the parallel program.

For later reference (see Section 6.3) we present a second proof example with explicit synchronization. This second example demonstrates, once more, that the choice of pre- and postconditions in the sequential proofs affects the satisfiability of noninterference (6.7) and hence the applicability of the rule of parallelism (6.8).

Example

Consider the program

$$\text{cobegin}$$
$$\quad\quad \text{if } B \text{ then } x := x + 1 \text{ fi}; B := \text{not } B \|$$
$$\quad\quad \text{if not } B \text{ then } x := x - 1 \text{ fi}$$
$$\quad \text{coend.}$$

Given the precondition Φ: $(B \text{ and } x = 0)$ or $(\text{not } B \text{ and } x = 1)$, we attempt to prove this program and, at the same time, derive the appropriate postcondition Ψ as part of the process. Our strategy is (a) to give a proof of the first if, (b) to give a proof of the second if, (c) to show noninterference for the pair of if statements, and (d) to use the rule of parallelism to establish correctness of the parallel program.

Demonstration of (a).

(Sequential proof for if B then $x := x + 1$ fi; $B := $ not B.)

1. $(((B \text{ and } x = 0) \text{ or } (\text{not } B \text{ and } x = 1)) \text{ and } B)$
   $\longrightarrow \vdash (B \text{ and } x = 0)$ by A_{AR}.
2. $\vdash \{B \text{ and } x = 0\} x := x + 1 \{B \text{ and } x = 1\}$ by (4.21).
3. $\vdash (B \text{ and } x = 1) \longrightarrow \vdash x = 1$ by (4.21).
4. $\vdash \{B \text{ and } x = 0\} x := x + 1 \{x = 1\}$ by 2, 3, and rule of consequence (a).

5. $(((B$ and $x = 0)$ or $($not B and $x = 1))$ and not $B)$
   $\rightarrow \vdash ($not B and $x = 1)$ by A_{AR}.

6. $\vdash ($not B and $x = 1) \rightarrow \vdash x = 1$ by A_{AR}.

7. $\vdash \{(B$ and $x = 0)$ or $($not B and $x = 1)\}$
   if B then $x := x + 1$ fi $\{x = 1\}$ by 4, 6, and rule of conditionals.

8. $\vdash \{x = 1\}$ $B :=$ not B $\{x = 1\}$ by (4.21).

9. $\vdash \{(B$ and $x = 0)$ or $($not B and $x - 1)\}$
   if B then $x := x + 1$ fi; $B :=$ not B $\{x = 1\}$ by 7, 8, and rule of composition.

Demonstration of (b).

(Sequential proof for if not B then $x := x - 1$ fi.)

10. $\vdash \{(B$ and $x = 0)$ or $($not B and $x = 1)\}$
    if not B then $x := x - 1$ fi $\{x = 0\}$ analogous to 1 through 7.

Demonstration of (c).

(Proof of noninterference.) Show

$$\vdash \{R_{i_h} \text{ and } Q_{j_k}\} s_{j_k} \{R_{i_h}\}$$

Case 1. Choose $R_{i_h}: x = 1$ from 9, and $s_{j_k}:$ if not B then $x := x - 1$ fi.

11. $(((B$ and $x = 0)$ or $($not B and $x = 1))$ and $x = 1)$
    $\rightarrow \vdash ($not B and $x = 1)$ by A_{AR}.

12. $\vdash \{$not B and $x = 1\}$ $x := x - 1$ $\{$not B and
    $x = 0\}$ by (4.21).

13. $\vdash ($not B and $x = 0) \not\rightarrow (x = 1)$

That is, the noninterference principle is violated, as

$$\text{if not } B \text{ then } x := x - 1 \text{ fi}$$

might violate the postcondition of

$$\text{if } B \text{ then } x := x + 1 \text{ fi}; B := \text{not } B.$$

Case 2. Choose $R_{j_h}: x = 0$ from 10 and $s_{j_k}:$ if B then $x := x + 1$ fi; $B :=$ not B. Analogous to 11 through 13, the noninterference principle will be violated.

The difficulties with the proof of noninterference may be overcome by choosing weaker postconditions for the two conditional s-units to be executed in parallel. That is, by making weaker statements about the resultant values in the sequential proofs, we increase the allowable interference in the parallel execution of the two s-units. Thus, we make a weaker statement about the parallel program in its entirety by allowing a wider range of result values for the execution of each s-unit. For the case at hand we first modify the postconditions for the sequential proofs:

14. $\vdash (x = 1) \rightarrow \vdash (x = 0$ or $x = 1)$ by A_{AR}.

15. $\vdash (x = 0) \rightarrow \vdash (x = 0$ or $x = 1)$ by A_{AR}.

16. $\vdash \{(B$ and $x = 0)$ or $($not B and $x = 1)\}$ if B
    then $x := x + 1$ fi; $B :=$ not B $\{x = 0$ or $x = 1\}$ by 9, 14.

17. $\vdash \{(B$ and $x = 0)$ or $($not B and $x = 1)\}$
    if not B then $x := x - 1$ fi $\{x = 0$ or $x = 1\}$ by 10, 15.

Then we attempt a new proof of noninterference:

    Case 1. Choose R_{i_h}: $x = 0$ or $x = 1$ from 16 and s_{j_k}: if not B then $x := x - 1$ fi.

18. $\vdash (((B$ and $x = 0)$ or (not B and $x = 1))$ and $(x = 0$ or $x = 1)) \rightarrow \vdash ((B$ and $x = 0)$ or (not B and $x = 1))$ by A_{AR}.

Hence noninterference is established by 17.

    Case 2. Choose R_{i_h}: $x = 0$ or $x = 1$ from 17 and s_{j_k}: if B then $x := x + 1$ fi; $B :=$ not B. Then, analogous to 18, noninterference is established by 16.

Demonstration of (d).

Application of the rule of parallelism gives

19. (16) and (17) and $\vdash$ (noninterference)

$$\vdash \{(B \text{ and } x = 0) \text{ or } (\text{not } B \text{ and } x = 1)\}$$
$$\qquad \text{cobegin}$$
$$\qquad\qquad \text{if } B \text{ then } x := x + 1 \text{ fi}; B := \text{not } B \parallel$$
$$\qquad\qquad \text{if not } B \text{ then } x := x - 1 \text{ fi}$$
$$\qquad \text{coend}$$
$$\{x = 0 \text{ or } x = 1\}$$

establishing the proof of the parallel program.

6.2.2 Implicit Synchronization

Raising the level of granularity from the memory reference level via implicit synchronization mechanisms may result in a cobegin . . . coend s-unit for which the constituent s-units s_j may not contain sufficient information to apply the rule of parallelism (6.8). More specifically, we may be unable to capture sufficient information on possible parallel-program interference patterns to facilitate the proof. The information required may be had by introducing additional or auxiliary variables into the parallel programs in such a way that the statements that use them *do not* affect either the flow of control or the values assigned to the shared objects of the program state space. The need for such variables has been independently recognized by many researchers, including [36, 37]. We hasten to point out that the set of auxiliary variables is *only* necessary to establish properties of the parallel program given by cobegin . . . coend and is not necessary to the correct execution of the program itself. That is, auxiliary variables simplify the proof process by allowing us to establish sequential correctness and noninterference among the set of parallel processes P_j, $j = 1, \ldots, m$.

    Auxiliary variables are defined as follows. Let $A_j = \{a_k\}$ be a set of variables that appear in the process p_j emanating from the s-unit s_j, which are used only in assignment statements of the form $a_k := e$, where $a_k \in A_j$, and e is any expression that does not contain multiple occurrences of any single shared variable. Then A_j is called the set of auxiliary variables for s-unit s_j.

    To demonstrate the use of auxiliary variables, we consider implicit synchronization mechanisms. Let $M(r)$ denote an implicit synchronization mechanism, wherein r is a *resource*—that is, a set of logically connected shared objects. $M(r)$ guarantees sequential access—mutual exclusion—to the resource r. To avoid interference, objects belonging to r cannot be manipulated, except in s-units *protected* by $M(r)$. A typical mechanism $M(r)$ is

$$\text{with } r \text{ when } B \text{ do } s,$$

where with r provides mutual exclusion, hence implicit synchronization. The procedure for proving correctness of parallel programs using implicit synchronization mechanisms is then:

1. Construct the parallel program, cobegin $s_1 \| \ldots \| s_n$ coend.
2. Generate for each s-unit s_j the auxiliary variable set A_j and assertions $I(r)$ that are true whenever a process gains access to r.
3. Prove the correctness of the set of sequential programs $s_j, j = 1, \ldots, n$, from which we can
4. Deduce the correctness of the parallel program using the rule of parallelism (6.8) and the inference rules that define the mechanism $M(r)$ employed.

The assertions $I(r)$ of step 2 are often called *resource invariants* [33]. The implicit sychronization mechanism given above may be defined by the following inference rule:

with rule:

$$\vdash \{Q\} s \{R\} \tag{6.12a}$$

$$\vdash \{B \text{ and } I(r)\} s \{I(r)\} \tag{6.12b}$$

$$\overline{\vdash \{Q\} \text{ with } r \text{ when } B \text{ do } s \{R\}} \tag{6.12c}$$

Step 4 is supported by the inclusion of the *auxiliary variable axiom* [33] in the deductive system. This axiom says that a proof for the s-units s_j with auxiliary variables is also a proof of the parallel program without the auxiliary variables. This axiom derives from the definition of auxiliary variables.

Example:

Consider the parallel program

```
program ADD2
    resource r(x);
    cobegin
        with r when true do x := x + 1 ||
        with r when true do x := x + 1
    coend
end ADD2,
```

which is to be proven correct with respect to $\Phi: x = 0$ and $\Psi: x = 2$.

Our strategy requires specification of the appropriate sets A_1, A_2 of auxiliary variables as well as a resource invariant $I(r)$. Since the parallel program's intention is multiple (two) increments of x, it seems reasonable to declare auxiliary variables that record for each process, whether or not x has been incremented by that process, and that can be used to establish a viable (appropriate) invariant $I(r)$ for the shared resource x. Given these considerations, we define the auxiliary variable sets:

$$A_1 = A_2 = \{y, z\},$$

(which record the individual, parallel s-unit increments to x as shown by their use in the "extended" program bracketed in step 9 of the proof that follows), extend the set of protected resources:

$$\underline{resource}\ r(x, y, z),$$

define the resource invariant:

$$I(r):\ x = y + z,$$

and define an extended precondition Q', with $\vdash Q' \longrightarrow \vdash Q$:

$$Q':\ x = 0\ \underline{and}\ y = 0\ \underline{and}\ z = 0\ \underline{and}\ I(r).$$

Given these constructs, our verification strategy will be to (a) construct a sequential proof for the first $\underline{with}$ statement, (b) construct a sequential proof for the second $\underline{with}$ statement, (c) demonstrate noninterference among the pair of $\underline{with}$ statements, and (d) use (6.12) to demonstrate Ψ.

Demonstration of (a).

The sequential proofs using the $\underline{with}$ rule require demonstration of both (6.12a) and (6.12b).

Demonstration of (6.12a):

1. $\vdash \{y = 0\}\ y := 1\ \{y = 1\}$ by (4.21) and rule of consequence (a).

2. $\vdash \{x = 0 + z\}\ x := x + 1\ \{x = 1 + z\}$ by (4.21).
3. $\vdash \{y = 0\ \underline{and}\ x = y + z\}\ x := x + 1;\ y := 1\ \{y = 1\ \underline{and}\ x = y + z\}$
               by rule of composition and A_{AR} and 2.

Demonstration of (6.12b):

4. $\vdash \{\underline{true}\ \underline{and}\ I(r)\}\ x := x + 1;\ y := 1\ \{I(r)\}$ by 3.

From 1 through 4 we have:

5. $\vdash \{y = 0\ \underline{and}\ x = y + z\}\ \underline{with}\ r\ \underline{when}\ \underline{true}\ \underline{do}\ x := x + 1;$
    $y := 1\ \{y = 1\ \underline{and}\ x = y + z\}$ by using (6.12) with 3 and 4.

Demonstration of (b).

By reasoning analogous to that which gave 5, we have:

6. $\vdash \{z = 0\ \underline{and}\ x = y + z\}\ \underline{with}\ r\ \underline{when}\ \underline{true}\ \underline{do}\ x := x + 1;$
    $z := 1\ \{z = 1\ \underline{and}\ x = y + z\}$ by (6.12).

Demonstration of (c).

We have:

7. $\vdash \{(y = 1\ \underline{and}\ x = y + z)\ \underline{and}\ (z = 0\ \underline{and}$ by 5 and 6, the
    $x = y + z)\}\ \underline{with}\ r\ \underline{when}\ \underline{true}\ \underline{do}\ x := x + 1;\ z := 1$ rule of consequence
    $\{y = 1\ \underline{and}\ x = y + z\}$ (b), and use of (6.7).

Analogously we have:

8. $\vdash \{(z = 1 \text{ and } x = y + z) \text{ and } (y = 0 \text{ and } x = y + z)\}$ with r when true do
   $x := x + 1; y := 1 \{z = 1 \text{ and } x = y + z\}$.

Demonstration of (d).

We have:

9. (5) and (6) and (7) and (8)

   $\vdash \{y = 0 \text{ and } z = 0 \text{ and } x = y + z \text{ and } x = 0\}$
       cobegin
           with r when true do
              begin
              $x := x + 1; y := 1$
           end $\|$ extended program with
           with r when true do   auxiliary variables
              begin
                   $x := x + 1; x := 1$
           end
       coend
   $\{y = 1 \text{ and } z = 1 \text{ and } x = y + z\}$ by (6.8).

Hence we have:

    $\vdash \{x = 0\}$
        resource $r(x)$
        cobegin
           with r when true do $x := x + 1 \|$
           with r when true do $x := x + 1$
        coend
    $\{x = 2\}$ by 9 and the axiom of
                   auxiliary variables.

6.2.3 Total Correctness of Parallel Programs

We must now extend the deductive system to provide for proof of total correctness of iterative s-units s_j contained in cobegin ... coend. Total correctness of cobegin ... coend s-units is given by termination of all its constituent s-units. As a first observation we note that the rule (5.17) may not be sufficient to show termination of a while construct used in a parallel program. For example, consider, from [29], the parallel program

    $x := N; y := 0; B := \text{true};$
    $P:$ cobegin
        $L_1:$ while $x > 0$ do $y := (y + 1) \bmod N$ od; $B := \text{false} \|$
        $L_2:$ while B do $x := x - 1$ od
    coend.

Suppose we wish to prove termination of the loop L_1. Clearly, if each process is assigned its own processor, the selection function governing termination [see (5.17)] is $t = \text{pos}(x)$, where

$$\text{pos}(x) = \underline{\text{if }} x < 0 \underline{\text{ then }} 0 \underline{\text{ else }} x.$$

Let us consider the following abbreviated sequential proofs for L_1 and L_2.

$x := N; y := 0; B := \text{true};$
$\{B\}$
$\underline{\text{cobegin}}$
$\quad L_1: \{B\}$
$\qquad \underline{\text{while }} x > 0 \underline{\text{ do }} \{B\} y := (y + 1) \bmod N \{B\} \underline{\text{ od}};$
$\qquad \overline{\{x \leq 0\}}$
$\qquad B := \text{false}$
$\qquad \{x \leq \overline{0} \text{ and } \underline{\text{not }} B\} \parallel$
$\quad L_2: \{\underline{\text{true}}\}$
$\qquad \underline{\text{while }} B \underline{\text{ do }} \{\underline{\text{true}}\} x := x - 1 \{\underline{\text{true}}\} \underline{\text{ od}};$
$\qquad \overline{\{\underline{\text{not }} B\}}$
$\underline{\text{coend}}$
$\overline{\{x \leq 0 \text{ and } \underline{\text{not }} B\}}.$

The sequential proofs for s-units L_1 and L_2 are interference-free by (6.7). To prove termination of L_1, we have to show that $t = \text{pos}(x)$ eventually reaches the value 0 (see Section 5.4.2). As L_1 does not affect the function t (but L_2 does), we must show that L_2 decrements $t = \text{pos}(x)$ a sufficient number of times, without affecting the assertions about x in the sequential proof of L_1. However, we note that (6.7) is satisfied with respect to the postcondition of the $\underline{\text{while}}$ statement in L_1, as

$$\vdash \{x \leq 1\} x := x - 1 \{x \leq 0\}$$
$$\underline{\vdash (x \leq 0) \longrightarrow \vdash (x \leq 1)}$$
$$\vdash \{x \leq 0\} x := x - 1 \{x \leq 0\} \qquad \text{by rule of consequence (a)}$$
$$\underline{\vdash (x \leq 0 \text{ and } \underline{\text{true}}) \longrightarrow \vdash (x \leq 0)}$$
$$\vdash \{x \leq 0 \text{ and } \underline{\text{true}}\} x := x - 1 \{x \leq 0\} \qquad \text{by rule of consequence (a)}.$$

Hence all that remains to be shown is that the nontermination of L_2 is not affected by L_1. That is, we must prove that L_2 cannot terminate before $t = \text{pos}(x)$ reaches the value 0. However, we note that L_1 and L_2 are interference-free with respect to the $\underline{\text{while}}$ statement in L_2, as

$$\vdash \{\underline{\text{not }} B \text{ and } x \leq 0\} B := \underline{\text{false}} \{\underline{\text{not }} B\}.$$

Hence the proof that $t = \text{pos}(x)$ actually reaches the value 0 proceeds as discussed in Section 5.4.2, and with the termination of L_1 the s-unit $B := \underline{\text{false}}$ is executed, guaranteeing the termination of L_2. To formalize these observations, the following methodology has been given [27].

Owing to the possible interleavings of parallel processes, *loop invariants* as defined in (5.17) are not sufficient to establish total correctness of parallel programs. Instead, loop invariants used for the latter purpose must hold after every step of the compound, interative construct, not just at entry and exit.

A loop invariant of this type is called a *weak loop invariant*. In the <u>while</u>-statement

$$\underline{\text{while}}\ \underline{\text{true}}\ \underline{\text{do}}$$
$$\{Q\ \underline{\text{and}}\ B\}$$
$$B := \underline{\text{false}};$$
$$\{Q\}$$
$$B := \underline{\text{true}}$$
$$\{Q\ \underline{\text{and}}\ B\}$$
$$\underline{\text{od}}$$

the predicate Q is the weak loop invariant, whereas Q <u>and</u> B is the loop invariant. Additionally we define a *steady-state loop invariant* to be any predicate that is guaranteed to be satisfied after a finite number of executions of the loop body and that remains true thereafter. Finally, a *steady-state weak loop invariant* is, by analogy to the distinction between a normal and a weak invariant, any steady-state loop invariant that is also a weak invariant.

For parallel programs, the following two loop invariants are defined. A *weak parallel loop invariant* is a weak loop invariant for which a proof of noninterference can be exhibited. A *steady-state weak parallel loop invariant* is a steady-state weak invariant for which a proof of noninterference can be exhibited. To prove termination then, the rule (5.17) is modified to read as follows:

1. Define an integer function t of the program state and prove $t \geq 0$ is invariant.
2. Find a steady-state weak parallel loop invariant Q for the loop in question and prove

$$\vdash Q\ \underline{\text{and}}\ B \longrightarrow \vdash t > 0.$$

3. For those s-units (in other processes and within the loop in question) that may affect the value of t, show that, in any state in which Q holds, none of these can increase t unboundedly.
4. Show that in any state in which Q <u>and</u> B holds, some s-units will cause a decrease in t.
5. Show that as long as Q <u>and</u> B holds, s-units that decrease t must continue to be executed.

These conditions must imply termination of the loop in question, since a steady decrease in t and $\vdash Q$ <u>and</u> $B \longrightarrow \vdash t > 0$ imply termination, when $t = 0$.

6.3 THE CONSTRUCTIVE METHOD AND PARALLEL PROGRAMS

As discussed in Section 6.1, the extant constructive approach to parallel programs does not attempt to find properties (assertions) common to a class of possible interleavings, but instead directly considers all allowable interleavings. To wit, the definition offered by Flon [27] for two parallel processes p_1 and p_2 resulting from s-units s_1 and s_2 is

wp($\underline{\text{cobegin}}\ s_{1_1}; s_{1_2}; \ldots; s_{1_n} \| s_{2_1}; s_{2_2}; \ldots; s_{2_n}\ \underline{\text{coend}}, R$)
$$= \text{wp}(\{\langle s_{1_1}; s_{1_2}; \ldots; s_{1_n}\rangle, \langle s_{2_1}; s_{2_2}; \ldots; s_{2_n}\rangle\}, R),$$

where

1. wp($\{\ \}, R$) = R,
2. wp($\{\langle\ \rangle, \langle s\rangle\}, R$) = wp($\{\langle s\rangle, \langle\ \rangle\}, R$) = wp($\{\langle s\rangle\}, R$),
3. wp($\{\langle s\rangle\}, R$) = wp(s, R),
4. wp($\{\langle s_{1_1}; s_{1_2}; \ldots\rangle, \langle s_{2_1}; s_{2_2}; \ldots\rangle\}, R$)
   = wp(choose 1 from $\{\langle s_{1_1}; s_{1_2}; \ldots\rangle, \langle s_{2_1}; s_{2_2}; \ldots\rangle\}, R$) $\underline{\text{and}}$
   wp(choose 2 from $\{\langle s_{1_1}; s_{1_2}; \ldots\rangle, \langle s_{2_1}; s_{2_2}; \ldots\rangle\}, R$),
5. wp(choose j from $\{\langle s_{1_1}; s_{1_2}; \ldots\rangle, \langle s_{2_1}; s_{2_2}; \ldots\rangle\}, R$)
   = $\underline{\text{if}}\ j = 1\ \underline{\text{then}}$ wp $(s_{1_1}; \{\langle s_{1_2}; \ldots\rangle, \langle s_{2_1}; s_{2_2}; \ldots\rangle\}, R)$
   $\underline{\text{else if}}\ j = 2\ \underline{\text{then}}$ wp $(s_{2_1}; \{\langle s_{1_1}; s_{1_2}; \ldots\rangle, \langle s_{2_2}; \ldots\rangle\}, R)$,
6. wp($s; \{P\}, R$) = wp(s, wp($\{P\}, R$)).

The weakest preconditions of assignment and $\underline{\text{when}} \ldots \underline{\text{do}}$ are defined as

(p1) wp($x := e, R$) = $R[x \leftarrow e]$,

(p2) wp($\underline{\text{when}}\ B\ \underline{\text{do}}\ s\ \underline{\text{od}}, R$) = B $\underline{\text{and}}$ wp(s, R).

In using the above definition, no simplification can be made until the expansions directed by rules 4 and 5 are finished.

Example:

wp ($\underline{\text{cobegin}}$
$\qquad L_1$: $\underline{\text{when}}\ I = 0\ \underline{\text{do}}\ I := 1\ \underline{\text{od}}; t_1; I := 0 \|$
$\qquad L_2$: $\underline{\text{when}}\ I = 0\ \underline{\text{do}}\ I := 1\ \underline{\text{od}}; t_2; I := 0$
$\qquad \underline{\text{coend}}, R$)
= wp ($\{\langle\underline{\text{when}}\ I = 0\ \underline{\text{do}}\ I := 1\ \underline{\text{od}}; t_1; I := 0\rangle$,
$\qquad\qquad\qquad\qquad\qquad \langle\underline{\text{when}}\ I = 0\ \underline{\text{do}}\ I := 1\ \underline{\text{od}}; t_2; I := 0\rangle\}, R$)
= wp ($\underline{\text{when}}\ I = 0\ \underline{\text{do}}\ I := 1\ \underline{\text{od}}; \{\langle t_1; I := 0\rangle$,
$\qquad\qquad\qquad\qquad \langle\underline{\text{when}}\ I = 0\ \underline{\text{do}}\ I := 1\ \underline{\text{od}}; t_2; I := 0\rangle\}, R$) $\underline{\text{and}}$
$\quad$ wp ($\underline{\text{when}}\ I = 0\ \underline{\text{do}}\ I := 1\ \underline{\text{od}}; \{\langle\underline{\text{when}}\ I = 0\ \underline{\text{do}}\ I := 1\ \underline{\text{od}}; t_1; I := 0\rangle$,
$\qquad\qquad\qquad\qquad\qquad\qquad\qquad\qquad\qquad\qquad \langle t_2; I := 0\rangle\}, R$)

= $\ldots$

= $I = 0$ $\underline{\text{and}}$ wp $(t_1, \text{wp}\ (t_2, R))$ $\underline{\text{and}}$ wp $(t_2, \text{wp}\ (t_1, R))$

If the s-unit

$$\underline{\text{if}}\ B\ \underline{\text{then}}\ t_1\ \underline{\text{else}}\ t_2\ \underline{\text{fi}}$$

is added, we must consider that even if B evaluates to true at some point, its value may change by the time t_1 is actually executed. To account for this potentiality we require that the lexically explicit form of the conditional be such that B contains no divisible references to shared objects, and t_1 and t_2 are themselves indivisible. For example, the statement

$$\underline{\text{if}}\ c_1\ \underline{\text{and}}\ c_2\ \underline{\text{then}}\ x := x + 1\ \underline{\text{else}}\ y := y + 1\ \underline{\text{fi}}$$

must be converted to

$$T_1 := c_1;$$
$$T_1 := T_1 \text{ and } c_2;$$
$$\underline{\text{if }} T_1 \underline{\text{ then }} \overline{T_2 := x;\ T_2 := T_2 + 1;\ x := T_2}$$
$$\underline{\text{else }} \overline{T_3 := y;\ T_3 := T_3 + 1;\ y := T_3}$$
$$\underline{\text{fi}}.$$

With this observation we then modify the preceding definition of rule 5 to:

5′. wp (choose j from $\{\langle s_{1_1}; s_{1_2}; \ldots \rangle, \langle s_{2_1}; s_{2_2}; \ldots \rangle\}, R)$

    $= \underline{\text{if }} j = 1 \underline{\text{ then}}$

        $\underline{\text{if }} s_{1_1} \text{ is "}\underline{\text{if }} B \underline{\text{ then }} t_1 \underline{\text{ else }} t_2 \underline{\text{ fi}}\text{"}$

            $\underline{\text{then }} (B \underline{\text{ and }} \text{wp}(\{\langle t_1; s_{1_2}; \ldots \rangle, \langle s_{2_1}; s_{2_2}; \ldots \rangle\}\ R) \underline{\text{ or}}$

                $(\text{not } B \underline{\text{ and }} \text{wp}(\{\langle t_2; s_{1_2}; \ldots \rangle, \langle s_{2_1}; s_{2_2}; \ldots \rangle\}, \overline{R}))$

           $\underline{\text{else }} \text{wp}(s_{1_1}; \{\langle s_{1_2}; \ldots \rangle, \langle s_{2_1}; s_{2_2}; \ldots \rangle\}, R)$

    $\underline{\text{else if }} j = 2 \underline{\text{ then}}$

        ⋮

(analogous).

To include the $\underline{\text{while}}$ s-unit

$$\underline{\text{while }} B \underline{\text{ do }} t \underline{\text{ od}},$$

where t and B are in lexically explicit form, we must consider that although the boolean B may evaluate to $\underline{\text{true}}$ and the loop may be entered, B may no longer hold by the time t is executed. To account for the potentiality, we further change rule 5 to

5″. wp(choose j from $\{\langle s_{1_1}; s_{1_2}; \ldots \rangle, \langle s_{2_1}; s_{2_2}; \ldots \rangle\}, R)$

    $= \underline{\text{if }} j = 1 \underline{\text{ then}}$

        $\underline{\text{if }} s_{1_1} \text{ is "}\underline{\text{while }} B \underline{\text{ do }} t \underline{\text{ od}}\text{"} \underline{\text{ then}}$

            $(B \underline{\text{ and }} \text{wp}(\{\langle t; \underline{\text{while }} B \underline{\text{ do }} t \underline{\text{ od}}; s_{1_2}; \ldots \rangle, \langle s_{2_1};$

                                    $s_{2_2}; \ldots \rangle\}, R)) \underline{\text{ or}}$

            $(\text{not } B \underline{\text{ and }} \text{wp}(\{\langle s_{1_2}; \ldots \rangle, \langle s_{2_1}; s_{2_2}; \ldots \rangle\}, R))$

        $\underline{\text{else if }} s_{1_1} \text{ is "}\underline{\text{if }} B \underline{\text{ then }} t_1 \underline{\text{ else }} t_2 \underline{\text{ fi}}\text{"} \underline{\text{ then}}$

            ⋮

Example:

We consider the example

    $\underline{\text{cobegin}}$
    $\underline{\text{if }} B \underline{\text{ then }} x := x + 1 \underline{\text{ fi}};\ B := \underline{\text{ not }} B \parallel$
    $\underline{\text{if }} \underline{\text{not }} B \underline{\text{ then }} x := x - 1 \underline{\text{ fi}}$
    $\underline{\text{coend}},$

for which we have shown, using the axiomatic method (see Section 6.2.1),

$$\{(B \underline{\text{ and }} x = 0) \underline{\text{ or }} (\text{not } B \underline{\text{ and }} x = 1)\}$$
$$\underline{\text{cobegin}} \ldots \underline{\text{coend}}$$
$$\{x = 0 \underline{\text{ or }} x = 1\}.$$

The constructive proof that follows uses neither the noninterference principle (6.7) nor the rule of parallelism (6.8). Rather, it explicitly considers all possible interleavings of the execution of the constituent s-units, thus accounting for all effects that might result from these interleavings.

Proof:

1. wp(cobegin **if** B **then** $x := x + 1$ **fi**; $B :=$ **not** B ‖ **if not** B **then** $x := x - 1$ **fi coend**, $x = 0$ **or** $x = 1$)

= wp({⟨**if** B **then** $x := x + 1$ **fi**; $B :=$ **not** B⟩, ⟨**if not** B **then** $x := x - 1$ **fi**⟩}, $x = 0$ **or** $x = 1$).

Applying rule 5′, we obtain

2a. B **and** wp({⟨$x := x + 1$; $B :=$ **not** B⟩, ⟨**if not** B **then** $x := x - 1$ **fi**⟩}, $x = 0$ **or** $x = 1$)

   or

2b.   **not** B **and** wp({⟨$B :=$ **not** B⟩, ⟨**if not** B **then** $x := x - 1$ **fi**⟩}, $x = 0$ **or** $x = 1$)

   and

2c.   **not** B **and** wp({⟨**if** B **then** $x := x + 1$ **fi**; $B :=$ **not** B⟩, ⟨$x := x - 1$⟩}, $x = 0$ **or** $x = 1$)

   or

2d. B **and** wp({⟨**if** B **then** $x := x + 1$ **fi**; $B :=$ **not** B⟩, $x = 0$ **or** $x = 1$).

Applying rule 5′ to 2a, we obtain

3a. B **and** wp($x := x + 1$; {⟨$B :=$ **not** B⟩, ⟨**if not** B **then** $x := x - 1$ **fi**⟩}, $x = 0$ **or** $x = 1$)

   and

   not B **and** wp({⟨$x := x + 1$; $B :=$ **not** B⟩, ⟨$x := x - 1$⟩}, $x = 0$ **or** $x = 1$)

    or

   B **and** wp({⟨$x := x + 1$; $B :=$ **not** B⟩}, $x = 0$ **or** $x = 1$).

Applying the simplification rules 1 through 6 to 3a, we obtain

4a. B and wp$(x := x + 1,$ wp$(\{\langle B := \text{not } B\rangle, \langle\text{if not } B \text{ then } x := x - 1 \text{ fi}\rangle\}, x = 0 \text{ or } x = 1)$

and

not B and wp$(x := x + 1,$ wp$(\{\langle B := \text{not } B\rangle, \langle x := x - 1\rangle\}, x = 0 \text{ or } x = 1)$

and

wp$(x := x - 1,$ wp$(\{\langle x := x + 1; B := \text{not } B\rangle\}, x = 0 \text{ or } x = 1)$

or

B and wp$(x := x + 1,$ wp$(\{\langle B := \text{not } B\rangle\}, x = 0 \text{ or } x = 1)).$

Applying the simplification rules 1 through 6 to 4a, we obtain

5a. B and wp$(x := x + 1,$ wp$(B := \text{not } B,$ wp$(\{\langle\text{if not } B \text{ then } x := x - 1 \text{ fi}\rangle\}, x = 0 \text{ or } x = 1)$

and

not B and wp$(\{\langle B := \text{not } B\rangle, \langle x := x - 1\rangle\}, x = 0 \text{ or } x = 1))$

or

B and wp$(\{\langle B := \text{not } B\rangle\}, x = 0 \text{ or } x = 1))$

and

not B and wp$(x := x + 1,$ wp$(B := \text{not } B,$ wp$(\{\langle x := x - 1\rangle\}, x = 0 \text{ or } x = 1))$

and

wp$(x := x - 1,$ wp$(\{\langle B := \text{not } B\rangle\}, x = 0 \text{ or } x = 1)))$

and

wp$(x := x - 1,$ wp$(x := x + 1,$ wp$(B := \text{not } B, x = 0 \text{ or } x = 1)))$

or

B and wp$(x := x + 1, x = 0 \text{ or } x = 1).$

Applying the simplification rules 1 through 6 to 5a and (3.15), we obtain

6a. B and $\text{wp}(x := x + 1, \text{wp}(B := \underline{\text{not}}\ B, (\underline{\text{not}}\ B\ \underline{\text{and}}\ x = 1\ \underline{\text{or}}\ x = 2)\ \underline{\text{or}}\ (B\ \underline{\text{and}}\ x = 0\ \underline{\text{or}}\ x = 1))$

$\qquad\qquad \underline{\text{and}}$

$\qquad\qquad \underline{\text{not}}\ B\ \underline{\text{and}}\ \text{wp}(B := \underline{\text{not}}\ B, \text{wp}(x := x - 1, x = 0\ \underline{\text{or}}\ x = 1))$

$\qquad\qquad\qquad \underline{\text{and}}$

$\qquad\qquad\qquad \text{wp}(x := x - 1, \text{wp}(B := \underline{\text{not}}\ B, x = 0\ \underline{\text{or}}\ x = 1))$

$\qquad \underline{\text{or}}$

$\qquad\qquad B\ \underline{\text{and}}\ x = 0\ \underline{\text{or}}\ x = 1)$

$\underline{\text{and}}$

$\qquad \underline{\text{not}}\ B\ \underline{\text{and}}\ \text{wp}(x := x + 1, \text{wp}(B := \underline{\text{not}}\ B, x = 1\ \underline{\text{or}}\ x = 2)$

$\qquad\qquad \underline{\text{and}}$

$\qquad\qquad\qquad \text{wp}(x := x - 1, x = 0\ \underline{\text{or}}\ x = 1))$

$\qquad \underline{\text{and}}$

$\qquad\qquad \text{wp}(x := x - 1, \text{wp}(x := x + 1, x = 0\ \underline{\text{or}}\ x = 1))$

$\underline{\text{or}}$

$\qquad B\ \underline{\text{and}}\ x = -1\ \underline{\text{or}}\ x = 0.$

Further simplification of 6a leads to

7a. $B\ \underline{\text{and}}\ \text{wp}(x := x + 1, (B\ \underline{\text{and}}\ x = 1\ \underline{\text{or}}\ x = 2)\ \underline{\text{or}}\ (\underline{\text{not}}\ B\ \underline{\text{and}}\ x = 0\ \underline{\text{or}}\ x = 1))$

$\qquad\qquad \underline{\text{and}}$

$\qquad\qquad \underline{\text{not}}\ B\ \underline{\text{and}}\ \text{wp}(B := \underline{\text{not}}\ B, x = 1\ \underline{\text{or}}\ x = 2)$

$\qquad\qquad\qquad \underline{\text{and}}$

wp(x := x − 1, x = 0 $\underline{or}$ x = 1)

$\underline{or}$

B $\underline{and}$ x = 0 $\underline{or}$ x = 1)

$\underline{and}$

$\underline{not}$ B $\underline{and}$ wp(x := x + 1, x = 1 $\underline{or}$ x = 2)
$\underline{and}$

wp(x := x − 1, x = −1 $\underline{or}$ x = 0)

$\underline{or}$

B $\underline{and}$ x = −1 $\underline{or}$ x = 0.

Further simplification of 7a leads to

8a. B $\underline{and}$ wp(x := x + 1, (B $\underline{and}$ x = 1 $\underline{or}$ x = 2) $\underline{or}$ ($\underline{not}$ B $\underline{and}$ x = 0 $\underline{or}$ x = 1)
$\underline{and}$

$\underline{not}$ B $\underline{and}$ x = 1 $\underline{or}$ x = 2
$\underline{and}$ x = 1 $\underline{or}$ x = 2

$\underline{or}$

B $\underline{and}$ x = 0 $\underline{or}$ x = 1)

$\underline{and}$

$\underline{not}$ B $\underline{and}$ x = 0 $\underline{or}$ x = 1
$\underline{and}$ x = 0 $\underline{or}$ x = 1

$\underline{or}$

B $\underline{and}$ x = −1 $\underline{or}$ x = 0.

Further simplification of 8a leads to

9a. B and $\text{wp}(x:=x+1, (B \text{ and } x=1 \text{ or } x=2) \text{ or } (\text{not } B \text{ and } x=0 \text{ or } x=1))$

   and

      not B and $x=0$ or $x=1$

   or

      B and $x=-1$ or $x=0$.

Further simplification of 9a leads to

10a. B and $(B \text{ and } x=0 \text{ or } x=1)$ or $(\text{not } B \text{ and } x=-1 \text{ or } x=0)$ and $(\text{not } B \text{ and } x=0 \text{ or } x=1)$ or $(B \text{ and } x=-1 \text{ or } x=0)$,

11a. B and $x=0$.

Applying rule 5' to 2b, we obtain

3b. not B and $\text{wp}(B:=\text{not } B, \text{wp}(\{\langle\text{if not } B \text{ then } x:=x-1 \text{ fi}\rangle\}, x=0 \text{ or } x=1)$

   and

      not B and $\text{wp}(\langle B:=\text{not } B\rangle, \langle x:=x-1\rangle\rangle, x=0 \text{ or } x=1)$

   or

      B and $\text{wp}(\langle\langle B:=\text{not } B\rangle\rangle, x=0 \text{ or } x=1)$.

Applying the simplification rules 1 through 6 and (3.15) to 3b, we obtain

4b. not B and $\text{wp}(B:=\text{not } B, (\text{not } B \text{ and } x=1 \text{ or } x=2) \text{ or } (B \text{ and } x=0 \text{ or } x=1))$

   and

      not B and $\text{wp}(B:=\text{not } B, \text{wp}(\langle\langle x:=x-1\rangle\rangle, x=0 \text{ or } x=1))$

      and

      $\text{wp}(x:=x-1, \text{wp}(\langle\langle B:=\text{not } B\rangle\rangle, x=0 \text{ or } x=1))$

or
$$B \text{ and } \mathrm{wp}(B := \text{not } B, x = 0 \text{ or } x = 1).$$

Further simplification of 4b leads to

5b. $\text{not } B \text{ and } (B \text{ and } x = 1 \text{ or } x = 2) \text{ or } (\text{not } B \text{ and } x = 0 \text{ or } x = 1)$
and
$\text{not } B \text{ and } \mathrm{wp}(B := \text{not } B, x = 1 \text{ or } x = 2)$
and
$\mathrm{wp}(x := x - 1, x = 0 \text{ or } x = 1)$
or
$B \text{ and } x = 0 \text{ or } x = 1.$

Further simplification of 5b leads to

6b. $\text{not } B \text{ and } (B \text{ and } x = 1 \text{ or } x = 2) \text{ or } (\text{not } B \text{ and } x = 0 \text{ or } x = 1)$
and
$\text{not } B \text{ and } x = 1 \text{ or } x = 2$
and
$x = 1 \text{ or } x = 2$
or
$B \text{ and } x = 0 \text{ or } x = 1.$

Analogous to the reasoning that led from 9a to 10a, we obtain from 6b

7b. $\text{not } B \text{ and } x = 1.$

Applying rule 5′ to 2c, we obtain

3c. not B and B and wp({⟨$x := x + 1$; $B := $ not B⟩, ⟨$x := x - 1$⟩}, $x = 0$ or $x = 1$)

or

not B and wp({⟨$B := $ not B⟩, ⟨$x := x - 1$⟩}, $x = 0$ or $x = 1$)

and

wp($x := x - 1$, wp({⟨if B then $x := x + 1$ fi; $B := $ not B⟩}, $x = 0$ or $x = 1$)).

Applying the simplification rules 1 through 6 to 3c, we obtain

4c. not B and B and wp($x := x + 1$, wp({⟨$B := $ not B⟩, ⟨$x := x - 1$⟩}, $x = 0$ or $x = 1$))

and

wp($x := x - 1$, wp({⟨$x := x + 1$; $B := $ not B⟩}, $x = 0$ or $x = 1$))

or

not B and wp($B := $ not B, wp({⟨$x := x - 1$⟩}, $x = 0$ or $x = 1$))

and

wp($x := x - 1$, wp({⟨$B := $ not B⟩}, $x = 0$ or $x = 1$))

and

wp($x := x - 1$, wp(if B then $x := x + 1$ fi, wp($B := $ not B, $x = 0$ or $x = 1$))).

Further simplification of 4c leads to

5c. not B and B and wp($x := x + 1$, wp($B := $ not B, wp({⟨$x := x - 1$⟩}, $x = 0$ or $x = 1$))

and

wp($x := x - 1$, wp({⟨$B := $ not B⟩}, $x = 0$ or $x = 1$)))

and

$$\text{wp}(x := x - 1, \text{wp}(x := x + 1, \text{wp}(B := \underline{\text{not}} \ B, x = 0 \ \underline{\text{or}} \ x = 1)))$$

<u>or</u>

<u>not</u> B <u>and</u> $\text{wp}(B := \underline{\text{not}} \ B, \text{wp}(x := x - 1, x = 0 \ \underline{\text{or}} \ x = 1))$

<u>and</u>

$$\text{wp}(x := x - 1, \text{wp}(B := \underline{\text{not}} \ B, x = 0 \ \underline{\text{or}} \ x = 1))$$

<u>and</u>

$$\text{wp}(x := x - 1, \text{wp}(\underline{\text{if}} \ B \ \underline{\text{then}} \ x := x + 1 \ \underline{\text{fi}}, x = 0 \ \underline{\text{or}} \ x = 1)).$$

Further simplification of 5c leads to

6c. <u>not</u> B <u>and</u> B <u>and</u> $\text{wp}(x := x + 1, \text{wp}(B := \underline{\text{not}} \ B, x = 1 \ \underline{\text{or}} \ x = 2)$

<u>and</u>

$$\text{wp}(x := x - 1, x = 0 \ \underline{\text{or}} \ x = 1))$$

<u>and</u>

$$\text{wp}(x := x - 1, \text{wp}(x := x + 1, x = 0 \ \underline{\text{or}} \ x = 1))$$

<u>or</u>

<u>not</u> B <u>and</u> $\text{wp}(B := \underline{\text{not}} \ B, x = 1 \ \underline{\text{or}} \ x = 2)$

<u>and</u>

$$\text{wp}(x := x \to 1, x = 0 \ \underline{\text{or}} \ x = 1)$$

<u>and</u>

$$\text{wp}(x := x - 1, (B \ \underline{\text{and}} \ x = -1 \ \underline{\text{or}} \ x = 0) \ \underline{\text{or}} \ (\underline{\text{not}} \ B \ \underline{\text{and}} \ x = 0 \ \underline{\text{or}} \ x = 1).$$

Further simplification of 6c leads to

7c. not B and B and wp($x := x + 1$, $x = 1$ or $x = 2$)

$$\text{and}$$

$$x = 1 \text{ or } x = 2)$$

$$\text{and}$$

$$\text{wp}(x := x - 1, x = -1 \text{ and } x = 0)$$

or

not B and $x = 1$ or $x = 2$
and $x = 1$ or $x = 2$

and

(B and $x = 0$ or $x = 1$) or (not B and $x = 1$ or $x = 2$).

Further simplification of 7c leads to

8c. not B and B and $x = 0$ or $x = 1$
and $x = 0$ or $x = 1$

or

not B and $x = 1$ or $x = 2$

and

(B and $x = 0$ or $x = 1$) or (not B and $x = 1$ or $x = 2$).

Further simplification of 8c leads to

9c. not B and $x = 1$ or $x = 2$.

Further simplification of 2d leads to

3d. B and wp(if B then $x := x + 1$, wp($\langle\langle B := \text{not } B\rangle\rangle$, $x = 0$ or $x = 1$)).

Further simplification of 3d leads to

4d. B and wp(if B then $x := x + 1$, $x = 0$ or $x = 1$).

Further simplification of 4d leads to

5d. B and (B and $x = -1$ or $x = 0$) or (not B and $x = 0$ or $x = 1$)
6d. B and $x = -1$ or $x = 0$.

Combining 11a, 7b, 9c, and 6d according to 2, we obtain

12. ((B and $x = 0$) or (not B and $x = 1$)) and ((not B and $x = 1$ or $x = 2$) or (B and $x = -1$ or $x = 0$)).

Rewriting 12 yields

13.   (B and $x = 0$) and (not B and $x = 1$ or $x = 2$)

    or

    (B and $x = 0$) and (B and $x = -1$ or $x = 0$)

    or

    (not B and $x = 1$) and (not B and $x = 1$ or $x = 2$)

    or

    (not B and $x = 1$) and (B and $x = -1$ or $x = 0$).

Simplification of 13 leads to

14. B and $x = 0$ and B and $(x = -1$ or $x = 0)$

    or

    not B and $x = 1$ and not B and $(x = 1$ or $x = 2)$.

Finally, we obtain

15. $(B$ and $x = 0)$ or $($not B and $x = 1)$;

that is, we have proved

16. $\{(B$ and $x = 0)$ or $($not B and $x = 1)\}$

    cobegin

      if B then $x := x + 1$ fi; $B := $ not $B||$

      if not B then $x := x + 1$ fi

      coend

    $\{x = 0$ or $x = 1\}$.

6.4 COMMUNICATING SEQUENTIAL PROCESSES

The preceding discussion has assumed that the parallel processes have all been able to access (read, write) the shared objects. Generally, this common access-ability results from the set of parallel processes operating out of or having access to a common shared memory that retains the objects (values). For certain classes of systems—for example, truly distributed systems and local networks—such direct sharing of objects is not possible. Processes in these latter categories share objects (object values) by direct communication, wherein processes communicate the value of objects among themselves. The communication is effected by sending and receiving messages. There are myriad policies and techniques whereby message passing may be formalized. For most techniques it is difficult to adequately formalize the semantics of the communication techniques for purposes of verification. One of the major hurdles is the lack of knowledge on the states of the communicating processes during the interval between the sending and receiving of the message. In one proposal, communicating sequential process (CSP) [135], the synchronization between the partners is quite explicit, and as a result the semantics of message passing can be captured.

In CSP, message passing between processes named A and B is effected by a combination of the execution of

$$A\,?x \qquad \text{(we call? huh)}$$

in B, and

$$B\,!e \qquad \text{(we call! shriek)}$$

in A. The result of the pairwise execution of huh and shriek with complementary named processes is the transfer of the value of the object denoted by expression e (in A) to B, where it becomes the value of the object named x. The passing of the value e to x occurs only when A executes $B\,!e$ and B executes $A\,?x$. Should either A or B execute its construct without B or A executing its counterpart, A or B becomes "blocked" until the complementary construct is executed. (A slightly different circumstance obtains when either command appears in a guard of one of Dijkstra's guarded commands [23, 136]—a circumstance of no consequence to us here.)

The explicit process synchronization necessary to effect the passing of e to x facilitates the formalization of the semantics of shriek and huh in the sequential execution of the processes in which they appear. The observation has been pursued in [136, 137], where sequential proofs of the constituent processes proceed by associating assertions with both shriek or huh that can be used in the sequential correctness proofs of the processes in which they appear. Specifically we would construct assertions P_1 and Q_1 in B and assertions P_2 and Q_2 in A to be used in the sequential proofs of

$$\vdash \{P_1\}\, A\,?x\, \{Q_1\}$$

in B and

$$\vdash \{P_2\}\, B\,!e\, \{Q_2\}$$

in A, respectively. These assertions must reflect not only the result of the local sequential proofs of processes A and B, but the effect of the passing of e to x as well. The latter is very much in the spirit of an assignment, hence the assignment axiom (4.21) is applicable. Direct application of (4.21) would serve to characterize the effect of the communication from B's point of view but not A's. To aid in deducing facts about the communication in A, direct use of (4.21) is replaced in [136, 137] by

$$\vdash (P_1 \text{ and } P_2) \longrightarrow \vdash (Q_1[x \longleftarrow e] \text{ and } Q_2[x \longleftarrow e]). \tag{6.13}$$

[Note that not $(P_1 \text{ and } P_2)$ prevents the processes A and B from synchronizing and hence prevents communication from occurring.] In [136] establishment of (6.13) is referred to as a satisfaction proof—satisfaction in the sense that the assertions used in the sequential proofs reflect the effect of (or are valid as a result of) the synchronized passing of e to x. Use of (6.13) and the sequential proofs of A and B is facilitiated by use of *auxiliary variables*, which to be viable in the context of A and B must also be able to appear as elements of the object e, for transfer to elements of the object x. Use of auxiliary variables also necessitates a proof of noninterference, which must include verification of (6.7) for every assertion in A and B as well as verification that for every assertion P

$$\vdash (P \text{ and } P_1 \text{ and } P_2) \longrightarrow \vdash P[x \longleftarrow e],$$

where P_1 and P_2 are as in (6.13). Examples, details, and variations in approach may be found in [136, 137].

6.5 REMARKS

In this chapter we have considered approaches to proving the correctness of parallel programs. While these approaches, as yet, do not offer a completely satisfying formalism for the task, they do represent approaches based on the mainstream axiomatic and constructive verification methods. For parallel programs, the constructive approach tends to explicitly consider all possible interleavings as we can see by examination of the definition of wp(cobegin . . . coend) as given in Section 6.3. The axiomatic approach, on the other hand, attempts to find properties common to a class of possible interleavings and then to prove the correctness of all interleavings included in the class. Such a proof establishes the correctness of the class as a whole by using the common properties. The common properties employed are found and verified by use of the noninterference principle, and in particular the noninterference property (6.7). Classification of this approach may be further refined by considering whether or not the synchronizations of the set of parallel programs are explicitly specified. With explicit synchronizations, the variables and s-units used generally contain sufficient information to allow proof of correctness. Typical s-units that exhibit explicit synchronization are the constructs, while B do s od, as discussed in Section 6.2.1, and await B then s, as given in [35]. When high-level more "implicit" synchronization mechanisms are used (for example, with r when B do s), the parallel program may not contain sufficient information to complete a proof of correctness. To complete correctness proofs for these cases we introduce auxiliary data objects to supply the required missing information. These objects allow us to define resource invariants $I(r)$, which explicitly state what each process can assume about the objects it shares with other processes. If it can be guaranteed that the resource invariants are preserved by all processes accessing shared objects, then the reasoning involved in proving a parallel program correct can be reduced to the strictly sequential case.

The material we have introduced speaks to partial and total correctness only. We note, however, that we are also able to prove properties of non-terminating cyclic parallel programs [42]. Proof rules to show the absence of blocking and deadlock are also given for cyclic parallel programs in which the s-units s_i in cobegin $s_1 \| \ldots \| s_n$ coend are restricted to the *single* construct,

$$\text{with } r \text{ when } B \text{ do } s \text{ od.}$$

Specifically, in [33] a mechanism is presented that allows us to use the information given in a partial correctness proof (using auxiliary variables and resource invariants) to prove (in the sense of partial correctness) the absence of blocking and deadlock. An extension of these mechanisms through the definition of (nonblocking, nondeadlock, and nonstarvation) invariants is given in [27] and extended in [41, 137]. These invariants provide means for proving (in the sense of total correctness) the above-named properties, plus others. Additional material may be found in [140, 138] and a somewhat more complex but robust axiomatic approach in [139].

Axiomatic proofs *may* be easier to constuct than constructive proofs, even though application of the wp(cobegin . . . coend, R) rule is mechanistic. The difficulty in applying the rule stems from the need to *decompose* the postcondition R. This need is exemplified in the proof given in Section 6.3. Generally, the situation is as follows. In (6.8) the postcondition R is composed of the postconditions R_i, $i = 1, \ldots, n$, resulting from the sequential proofs of the s-units s_i in cobegin $s_1 \| \ldots \| s_n$ coend. With the constructive method, R is decomposed into $R(s_{i_h}, s_{j_k})$, which result from all possible interleavings of s-units s_{i_h} with s-units s_{j_k}, $i, j \in 1 .. n, i \neq j, k \in 0 .. m(j), h \in 0 .. m(i)$, [see (6.7)], such that

$$\bigwedge \qquad\qquad R(s_{i_h}, s_{j_k}) = R$$
$$(\forall i, j \in 1 .. n, i \neq j)$$
$$(\forall k \in 0 .. m(j))$$
$$(\forall h \in 0 .. m(i))$$

This decomposition is not always obvious, even in the face of rules 3, 5, and 6 in the definition of wp(cobegin $s_1 \| \ldots \| s_n$ coend), which specify a mechanism for it.

7

APPLICATIONS
OF THE VERIFICATION
APPROACHES

The late 1960s and the 1970s saw significant activity in the area of program verification, but interest in showing that programs "do as they are intended" predates these efforts considerably. Informally, programmers have always been aware of the verification process. In a paper by Goldstine and von Neumann, published in 1947, we see the first seeds of the ideas that were later to form the basis for formal program verification [87]. In that paper the authors describe "assertion boxes" which they attach to program flowchart representations to describe the state of the program at various control points during its execution. Interestingly, these assertion boxes are introduced simultaneously with substitution (assignment) boxes; the notion of the "equal" importance of state description and state modification has not been lost on the researchers who have followed these pioneers.

Since the publication of Floyd's paper in 1967, the literature has offered literally hundreds of articles relating to the verification of computer programs, with untold numbers of "proven" programs being produced along the way. While it is not within the scope of this chapter to give a complete survey of that body of literature, we will present an overview of the accomplishments and setbacks encountered in the application (primarily paper-and-pencil) of verification methods.

Our discussion centers on two points. First, we look at the body of published proofs to give the reader an idea of the kinds of programs that have been proven, as well as some of the limitations on the effectiveness of verification techniques. Second, we survey the extension and refinements of some of the popular proof techniques.

7.1 PUBLISHED PROOFS

Published "proofs" of programs seldom have as their principal motivation a demonstration of the correctness of the particular program at hand. Rather, they are intended to give evidence of the feasibility of proof methods. The programs used to demonstrate the viability of verification techniques are generally drawn from small "classical" algorithms of computer science. The general philosophy is to use problems that are "well-understood," to avoid complicating the exposition unnecessarily with problem-dependent issues when the concern is with the process of verification.

Published proofs tend to emphasize certain aspects of the verification process while avoiding others. For instance, the "programming languages" used are usually not production languages, but simpler representations such as flowcharts or pidgin ALGOL, in which detail is deemphasized. Details of hardware implementation often are omitted also. Finally, many of the proofs are presented informally or only partially.

These comments are not intended as criticisms of published proofs, but rather as a means of describing the intellectual environment in which they were offered. Later, when we review some of the "failures" of proof efforts, we shall return to this point so as to ensure that the proofs are judged in the same spirit in which they were created.

7.1.1 Mathematical Functions

Mathematical functions make good candidates for examples of program proofs, because they are easily specified in terms of input-output relationships. Perhaps the most often used example for program verification centers around one of the oldest known algorithms: that for finding the greatest common divisor of two positive integers [23, 93, 117]. Other mathematical algorithms whose correctness has been established include prime determination [44, 77, 103, 126], exponentiation and factorial computation [126], integer and real division [115, 129], Gaussian elimination and the approximate solution of ordinary differential equations [116], the maximum of a series of powers of matrices [106], and the calculation of hashing functions [92].

In proofs of mathematical functions, most authors have chosen not to confine themselves to the kind of finite arithmetic available on digital computers; indeed, as Hoare pointed out [18], the problems of machine arithmetic greatly complicate the process of establishing the correctness of a program. Typically, functions are proven under the assumption that any integer (and occasionally that any real) value is representable. An important exception to this idealized approach is presented in [88], where the problem of interval arithmetic is treated explicitly. In [88] the authors present a proof of correct implementation of part of an ALGOL multiplication algorithm using a finite arithmetic range.

Habermann, in his article outlining the correctness proof of a quadratic-hash algorithm [92], notes that the proof of an algorithm often requires an intimate knowledge of the application area, and that "there is more to proving the correctness of a program than applying the inductive assertion method." Often, program proofs depend on subtle mathematical theorems that are far from apparent in the context of the algorithm itself. "The statements of a program do not always provide sufficient information for proving its correctness. The correctness of the algorithm implemented by the program must often be proved with the pure mathematical techniques or exhaustive enumeration."

7.1.2 Sorting, Searching, and Complex Data Structures

Arrays and the operations associated with them have received a great deal of attention. Many of the "standard" array search routines have been "verified," including linear search [119], binary search [77], and logarithmic search [75]. Array and table look-up routines are common examples in many verification tutorials.

Most mathematical functions and search routines share the property that they treat their major internal data structures as inviolate rather than variable. In algorithms that permute data, the opposite is true. Examples of verified permutation algorithms range from simple interchange [93] to list reversal [115] to in-place permutation [80] to full array sorts such as radix sort [107], quicksort [84] and treesort [74, 109].

One noteworthy proof was that offered by Hoare of the correctness of the FIND algorithm [95]. (FIND(k) arranges the array elements $A[1] \ldots A[N]$ so that $A[k]$ contains the kth largest value of the original array, with $A[k] \geq A[i], 1 \leq i < k$, and $A[k] \leq A[j], k + 1 < j \leq N$.) Hoare pays particular attention to the problem of structuring proofs to make them manageable; he uses a stepwise refinement approach to simplify both program and proof design.

A historically interesting sorting proof was developed by London [109] concerning the correctness of the TREESORT 3 algorithm [83]. London's article represented a kind of landmark in that it offered a formal proof as an alternative to the usual "certification" techniques applied to algorithms published in the *Communications of the Association for Computing Machinery* (*CACM*). The proof used the inductive assertion method, showing total correctness in an informal but analytic manner.

The article is interesting not only for the proof it contains, but also for the controversy that it sparked. In a letter to CACM appearing a few months later, K. A. Redish criticized this "new kind of certification" when he attributed to London "a common confusion between an *algorithm*, its *representation*, and its implementation on a processor—a *code* [124]." In that same issue, London responded: "To the extent that the proof accounts for the features of a particular processor on a particular machine, the well-known distinctions between an algorithm, its representation, and its code can be ignored. . . . It seems unlikely that either standard [testing] or proof certification ever can, or should, cover all properties for all machines."

More complex data structures have also been investigated [101]. Several authors have verified the Fisher-Galler algorithm [85], which uses tree structures to identify equivalence classes from the element pairs defining the relation [111, 117]. More recently, several proofs of the Schorr-Waite graph-marking algorithm [125] have appeared [76, 91, 128]. This problem presents an interesting challenge to the verifier, as it involves list structures and pointer variables—difficult items to handle via formal verification mechanisms. The prime sieve algorithm, which produces a collection of primes as its output and depends on the data type set, has also been verified [97]. Stacks and queues have also been treated [127].

7.1.3 Large Programs

One of the prevailing criticisms of program verification is that it is not applicable to production software. Critics cite the use of "toy" examples as evidence that verification methods are really only feasible on a small scale. As we have noted, the use of such "toy" problems is well motivated and does not mean that the authors were incapable of applying the methods to larger problems, only that they chose small problems as a vehicle for the demonstration of methods.

In a very early article, Naur used the concept of "general snapshots" (state descriptions) to motivate the construction of an algorithm to reformat text [120]. Although the program itself is not large, it certainly falls within the spirit of "realistic software." (A historical note: the method Naur used was very similar in intent to the system ultimately formalized by Floyd [10], and for that reason the inductive assertion method is sometimes known as the Floyd-Naur method.)

Larger-scale system software has also been the object of several verification efforts. Several parsers have been verified [100, 123], as have segments of compilers [99, 111, 118]. Verification tools have also been the focus of proof attempts [123]. (This last point is especially important if we are to put faith in machine-assisted verification. This will be treated in greater detail in Chapter 9.)

7.1.4 Parallel Programs

As can be seen in Chapter 6, the problem of verifying parallel programs is not an easy one. The proofs required tend to be extremely long, and for this reason errors are likely to be generated in the verification process. It is not surprising, then, that relatively few examples of proofs of parallel programs have appeared in the literature. Moreover, those that have appeared are intended to be suggestive of complete proofs rather than complete in themselves.

The correctness of multiprocess programs depends not only on the functionality of the individual processes but also on interactions, or the absence of interactions, among those processes [78]. For noncommunicating concurrent processes, for example, the proof process requires demonstrations of mutual exclusion of access to shared data. Examples of such proofs have been given in [102, 105, and 130].

Among communicating processes, there is a need to describe the "joint" effect of process execution; the text of each individual process may not contain sufficient information to permit verification with respect to the function of the multiprocess program. Examples of proofs concerning communicating processes may be found in [35, 102] and [108, 122]. In a more "realistic" vein, Ashcroft has proven a number of properties of a simple airline reservation system that involves issues of concurrency [73].

7.1.5 An Example

Having surveryed the range of manual verification efforts, we now turn our attention to the examination of a "typical" proof as reported in the literature. We draw our example from a modern text on software engineering [132].

The program in question describes an additive algorithm for realizing the product of two numbers. Procedure MULTIPLY is defined with two input parameters, A and B, representing the values to be multiplied, and an output parameter, R, intended to hold their product upon termination of the procedure. The procedure text and input-output specifications are given below:

MULTIPLY (A, B, R)
   begin
      $R := 0; X := B;$
      while $X \neq 0$ do
      begin
         $R := R + A;$
         $X := X - 1;$
      end
   end MULTIPLY
   Specifications: $\{B \geq 0\}$ MULTIPLY (A, B, R) $\{R = A * B\}$

The cited text uses the axiomatic method of proof (see Section 4.5), and the proof itself is preceded by a presentation of the rules of inference and basic axioms necessary to effect verification of programs written in the ALGOL-like language presented in Section 4.5.2.

Owing to the brevity of the algorithm, the proof given is fairly complete. The authors first establish

$$\vdash \{B \geq 0\} \, R := 0; \, X := B \, \{X = B \text{ and } R = 0 \text{ and } B \geq 0\}^+$$

and then, using the invariant

$$I: \; R = A * (B - X),$$

they show

$$\vdash \{R = A * (B - X)\}$$
$$\text{while } X \neq 0 \text{ do}$$

$$\begin{aligned}
&\text{begin}\\
&\quad R := R + A;\\
&\quad X := X - 1\\
&\text{end}\\
&\{R = A * B\}^{+}.
\end{aligned}$$

The proof that

$$\vdash (X = B \text{ and } R = 0 \text{ and } B \geq 0) \longrightarrow (R = A * (B - X))$$

is left as an exercise to the reader. The authors also offer an informal proof that the loop indeed terminates, thus establishing the total correctness of MULTIPLY with respect to the given input-output specifications.

The proof given by the authors is simple and clear; however, part of that clarity comes from a necessarily abstract view of the processor that is to execute the program. Several points, common to many manual proofs, are worthy of note. First, with respect to the data objects manipulated by MULTIPLY, the authors choose not to distinguish between real and integer types, nor do they identify the parameter-passing mechanisms used to communicate among procedures. If all parameters are passed by value, for instance, then the procedure fails to satisfy its specifications from the viewpoint of the invoking procedure.

Assuming that the data objects are integers and that parameters are to be passed by name or reference, there remain certain problems limiting the utility of the proof in a production environment. First, the authors make the common assumption that arithmetic operations operate on an infinite domain; clearly this program is *not* correct with respect to the specifications if any of the values A, B, or R do not fall within the range of values representable in the processor. Second, even discounting the domain of the arithmetic operations, there remain problems with the definition of arithmetic operations. While the authors include commutativity, associativity, and distributivity among their basic arithmetic axioms, for example, programming languages that permit side effects on function calls can make no such claims to order-independent evaluation.

7.1.6 An Assessment

As we have seen, the verification process requires a considerable amount of bookkeeping and attention to detail. Although most of the theorems that must be proven in establishing a program's correctness are very simple, their number can be large, and the sheer volume of text required to effect the proof, often an order of magnitude greater than the body of the program itself, is an invitation to error.

Most of the proofs cited in this chapter were undertaken without the benefit of automated verification aids. It is no surprise, then, that despite usually careful refereeing of articles, some errors have been able to slip through. What *is* surprising, however, is that many of the errors result not from simple bookkeeping mistakes, but rather from fundamental errors in the design of programs.

In a provocative article published in 1976, Gerhart and Yelowitz explored the problem of errors in manually "proven" programs [86]. They analyzed a number of proofs in detail to see if they could discover errors, and they present about a dozen examples of "proven" programs that in fact contained errors, either in the specifications given for the program, in the program construction, or in the proofs themselves.

Concerning errors in "proven" programs, the authors observed three common causes: informality in the use of the inductive assertion method, informality in the treatment of program termination, and inattention to "standard" methods of verification, such as review and testing. This latter point is especially important, as the authors found that many of the errors were "easily discovered by the standard methods of hand simulation and testing," belying some of the early hopes for the potential of formal verification, some researchers having held that, "given the proof of correctness . . . [one] can dispense with testing altogether" [121].

The Gerhart and Yelowitz article, and a companion piece by Goodenough and Gerhart [89], tempt us to paraphrase Dijkstra's admonition about the limits of testing [79]: while it may be true that "testing can be used to show the presence of bugs, but never to show their absence," experience has shown that, at least with respect to manual efforts, "formal" verification can be used to show the absence of bugs, but not their presence. The prudent observer, we hope, would view these two maxims not as evidence of the futility of both approaches, but rather as practical guidelines to their limitations. We hold to the philosophy, propounded by Goodenough and Gerhart [89], that formal verification and testing are not mutually exclusive, but rather "*complementary* methods for decreasing the likelihood of program failure."

Two final points remain to be discussed. The first concerns the placement of "blame" for the errors found in "proven" programs. Though in each case there are a number of causes for an error, we must ask whether the reason was the lack of automated aids, or rather something more basic. Unfortunately, no definitive answer can be given. Undoubtedly, as we shall see in Chapter 9, automated systems are a great aid to keeping track of the details of a proof, and perhaps such aids could have prevented some of the errors which Gerhart and Yelowitz found. Nonetheless, many of the errors resulted not from clerical mistakes, but rather from incomplete and incorrect specifications. Thus, while we might reasonably attribute the source of proof errors to "human frailty," it is clear that automation of the proof process cannot be expected to completely alleviate the problem.

The other question we must ask is whether published "proofs" have been of use despite their mistakes; to this we can respond with a hearty affirmative. In light of our recognition of the motivation for presenting the proofs, we view these efforts as positive steps toward a methodology for producing correct, reliable software. Mistakes do not invalidate the methods, but rather inspire us to make the methods less error-prone. In addition, verification techniques offer us not only proof methods, but also systematic program design methods, which have already produced benefits in the construction of production software.

7.2 EXTENSIONS

Verification "technology" has come a long way since the appearance of the first papers of Floyd, Naur, and Hoare. In this section we discuss a few of the extensions and applications growing out of verification research.

7.2.1 Definitions of Programming Language Semantics

One outgrowth of the research in program verification has been a renewed interest in formally defining the semantics of programming language constructs, and indeed of providing semantic definitions of entire programming languages, especially "production" languages.

The first major effort in this area was an attempt to define the semantics of the Pascal programming language [98]. In a relatively short article, Hoare and Wirth provide a set of axioms and proof rules for specifying the semantic content of programming constructs, with the exceptions of real arithmetic and goto statements. Taken together with the formal *syntactic* definition for Pascal [131], the two documents form the basis for an implementation specification for Pascal language processors.

Interestingly, the axiomatic definition of Pascal is as useful for what it doesn't say as for what it does. For instance, there are no constraints placed on the value of the index variable of for loops at loop termination. Hoare and Wirth write that "the definition must . . . give enough freedom to achieve efficiency by leaving certain less important aspects undefined" [98].

Using the Pascal definition as a prototype, a set of proof rules for an axiomatic definition of the programming language Euclid has recently been presented [112], which defines the entire language except for features involving machine dependencies and storage allocation. Other, similar definitions—for example, for the Ada language—can be expected in the future.

7.2.2 Research into the Definition of General Language Constructs

Axiomatic language definition requires semantic definition of the constructs that comprise the language, and many authors have focused their attention on particular classes of constructs rather than on individual languages.

In this section we discuss research on specifying the meaning of various language elements, some of which are contained within the language definitions mentioned previously.

Since Hoare's brief definition of an ALGOL-like language in his "axiomatic basis" paper [18], researchers have made intensive efforts to axiomatize certain "troublesome" features in programming languages. Chief among these is the goto construct, which has come under serious criticism since the advent of "structured programming." A number of authors have attempted to provide very general rules for goto statements [36, 104], with mixed success; the rules derived are general enough to handle arbitrary branching, but lack the "punch" needed to characterize meaning in particular "useful" uses of the goto. More recently, Arbib and Alagic [72] have offered proof rules for certain "bridled" uses of the goto, such as multiple loop exits, in which contextual information can be used to "sharpen" goto semantics in a manner that would not be possible with arbitrary uses of the construct.

There has also been considerable interest in means for specifying the semantics of procedure invocation and definition constructs [36, 81, 90, 91, 96]. One point on which researchers agree is the difficulty of specifying proof rules for procedures that permit side effects; if "nonfunctional" state changes are permitted, modeling of semantics becomes very difficult, and the general strategy has been to prohibit side effects with procedure usage. Other control flow issues that have been treated include the coroutine mechanism [75] and event-actuated invocations [114].

Section 7.1.2 mentions several examples of program proofs involving data structures of varying complexity, and those references will not be repeated here. We shall simply mention name management as one area where data structures have caused special problems [82, 113]. The problem arises particularly with respect to pointer variables, which carry the potential for generating multiple access paths to data items, thus complicating the proof process.

7.3 CONCLUSIONS

This chapter has presented an overview of the now vast literature available on program verification. We have not attempted, nor could we have hoped, to survey all available material, and we apologize to those authors whose work was not mentioned. Readers with a deeper interest in the field can use our bibliography as a starting point.

Our attention has focused primarily on verification efforts that did not have the advantage of machine assistance. As we shall see in Chapter 9, automated aids can help with the "bookkeeping" tasks inherent in program verification. Certainly, without such aids, proofs can become tedious and error-prone. Finally, we must recognize that automated verification systems have become possible only because of the efforts of those for whom such tools were not available. Even if their efforts were not always correct and complete, they marked the beginning of a discipline that may have a profound impact on the quality of software in the years to come.

8

APPROACHES TO SPECIFICATION

8.1 USES OF SPECIFICATION

The formal specification techniques described in this chapter are generally employed within a model of computation that is common to all of them but that is described (or assumed) in the literature using a variety of terminology. Briefly, the specification process centers around the definition of a set of "functions" in a notation that varies with the technique being used. These functions define outputs produced from given inputs, and (again, depending upon the technique being used) may or may not have side effects.

Such sets of functions may be used to give a behavioral definition of an interesting object. Thus a pushdown stack may be defined purely or abstractly by the results of the "push," "pop," "top," and "empty" operations. Such a "representation-free" definition is called a *type abstraction*, and the object being represented is referred to as an *abstract data type*, an object of known properties that may be used by programs. Alternatively, a set of functions may describe a large functional unit, such as an operating system. In this latter case the functions may be thought to define an *abstract machine* or an *interface*, to be used by programs in a manner analogous to elements or entry points in an operating system interface.

Functions of the type described can be used to break the verification task into two parts, separating the problem of verifying the program using the functions from that of verifying the programs that implement the defined functions. (Verification as discussed in the previous chapters refers, of course, to the problem of verifying the programs that implement the defining functions of an abstract data type or abstract machine.) The program that "uses" the functions (called the "using program") is able to rely on the behavior and correctness of the programs implementing the defined functions (sometimes called the "concrete programs" or "internal programs") to the degree that the behavior of the functions defined in their specifications, and the concrete programs have been verified. The functions thereby become part of the semantics of the using program, just as an operating system function (such as "get-record") informally becomes part of a program that references it (for example, by "call get-record"). The verifier of the using program therefore does not have to be concerned with details of the implementing programs, and the verifier of the implementing programs does not have to be concerned with the specific context in which they may be used.

Once a set of invariants has been proven for the implementing programs (by first proving them for the specifications of the functions and then verifying the implementations), the invariants can be used to draw conclusions about the using programs. In particular, they may be used as lemmas in the proofs of verification conditions generated by the inductive assertion method. Typical invariants provide, for example, the knowledge that a data object will never exceed a defined range or that a particular relationship between values (for example, *a* always greater than *b*) will hold for all possible sequences of function invocations.

An important technique for separating the two concerns of verification is known as *type induction* or *generator induction* [44]. This technique is used most often to prove invariant properties for an abstract data type or abstract machine. The technique breaks such a proof down into two steps analogous to those of mathematical induction. The property is first shown to hold for the initial state of the object or abstract machine. Next, for each function a proof is presented that shows that all invocations of the function made with the property holding will preserve the property. If the property holds initially, and holds before and after the invocation of each function, then the property is invariant.

The relationship between using and implementing programs is summarized by Figure 8.1. This structure can be extended in both directions. The implementing programs can themselves be viewed as using programs that use a second, lower-level set of functions from a second, lower-level abstract machine or abstract data type. Thus (in the data-type viewpoint) complex objects can be built up out of simpler ones, or (in the abstract-machine viewpoint) a powerful abstract machine can be described as a hierarchy of progressively more detailed abstract machines.

When we add specifications to the diagram, we obtain the complete relationship between using and implementing programs shown in Figure 8.2. This diagram is a decomposition of the box entitled "Program Specification" in Figure 1.2.

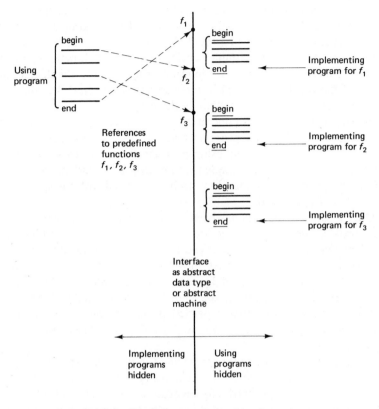

Figure 8.1. Relationship between using and implementing programs

In addition to the overall structure shown in Figure 8.2, each specification-program relationship may be broken down into levels. This breakdown is a consequence of the differing needs of the validator and the verifier (see Section 1.3). The validator requires a specification that is abstract enough to be self-evidently correct. The verifier requires a specification that can be used to produce assertions for proof methods such as those described in previous chapters. Thus the validator requires a specification in terms of high-level objects and powerful operations; the verifier requires specifications in terms of objects and operations that are part of the implementation of the program to be verified.

The conflicting requirements of validator and verifier are reconciled by introducing two specifications and a mapping between them. The validator uses the *abstract specification*; the verifier uses the *concrete specification*. The manner of mapping between the two levels of abstraction varies among techniques and will be described in subsequent sections. The input and output assertions, Φ and Ψ, used in the proof examples of previous chapters can be viewed as concrete specifications for the programs being proven.

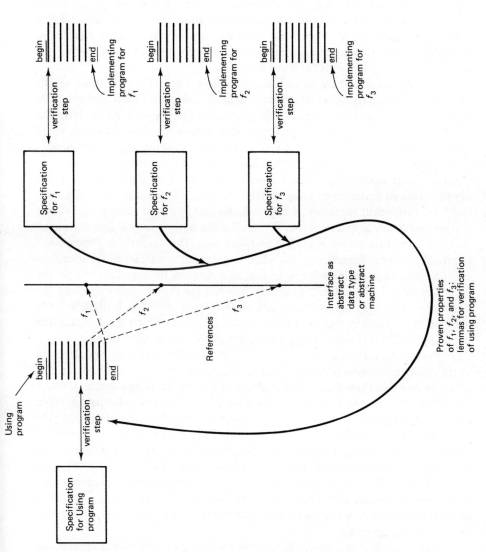

Figure 8.2 Using and implementing programs with specifications

8.2 SPECIFICATION APPROACHES

There presently exist three basic families of specification approaches: the algebraic, the state-machine, and the abstract model (occasionally also called the predicate transform method). As mentioned above, these approaches define behavior in units called "functions," and do so in a result-oriented or "non-procedural" way that suppresses most detail of implementation, including the step-by-step procedures that achieve the result.

The approaches share other features as well. Each of them defines results in terms of "underlying abstractions," usually associated with some known mathematical entity about which it is possible to reason with rigor. With the algebraic and state-machine approaches, the underlying abstraction is part of the approach; with the abstract model technique, it is chosen by the specifier.

Some variants of each approach have facilities for stating "exceptions"— input or usage patterns which the specifier declares to be unacceptable. There are two ways of making exception statements. One way employs the "precondition" or "restriction" notation, which tells the author of the using program that a given condition is unacceptable and makes the author responsible for seeing that the condition never occurs. The other way, the "error" or "exception" approach, includes detection of the offending condition as part of the specification and defines a special value to be passed out across the interface, should the exception occur. The abstract program then has the responsibility to check for that value and take appropriate action. The responsibility is thereby split between the implementing program for the function (which must detect the offending condition) and the using program (which must react to it).

Finally, all three approaches share an attribute that has been characterized as the "hidden function problem." This problem is inherent in the breakdown of behavior into functions that are defined separate from the using programs. When so defined, the functions cannot conveniently capture any information from previous invocations. The solution to the problem, which is viewed with varying degrees of satisfaction by workers in the field, is to have "hidden" or "auxiliary" functions that are not accessible to the using program and that define results that depend upon prior invocations. These functions are called "hidden" because they cannot be directly referenced by a using program. In general, hidden functions provide results that other functions require, but that the specifier has decided are not part of the visible behavior of the abstract data type or abstract machine being specified.

The sections that follow will describe each of the specification approaches by means of an annotated example. The example to be used is that of an integer pushdown stack with a bounded size of three. Visible behavior of the stack is defined by four functions: push, which adds an integer to the stack; pop, which discards the top of the stack; top, which returns the last integer pushed and leaves the stack unchanged; and empty, which tells whether or not the stack contains any elements.

The examples will be presented in an informal syntax, which has been designed for readability and freedom from clutter. For simplicity, each example is written as the specification of a single stack; it is a simple matter to syntactically extend the example to the class idea of SIMULA [45] or the form concept of Alphard [46], so that templates of objects are specified as one syntactic element and instances of the object are defined and named as needed.

8.3 ALGEBRAIC SPECIFICATIONS

The initial theoretical work on algebraic specifications was done by Guttag [47]. Two specification languages in this family that are supported by "tools"* are the AFFIRM language [48] and the OBJ language [49]. AFFIRM is used for verification (as discussed in previous chapters), and the tools provide syntax and consistency checks; OBJ is used to validate specifications by experimentation. With experimentation, functions are specified and then referenced in using or abstract programs. The OBJ system computes the specified result using a rewrite technique developed by Goguen. The author of a specification can thereby "debug" his work in a manner analogous to that used by programmers. Our example uses a simplified form of the OBJ syntax, chosen because OBJ treats errors and exceptions. (The authors of the AFFIRM system hold that errors are a property of an implementation and not a specification concern.) The error-handling mechanism of OBJ is of the "exception" model described above; later work of Guttag [50] incorporates the precondition model.

The underlying abstraction for algebraic specifications is the set of integers. Algebraic specification languages also assume "built-in" functions, typically if-then-else and the boolean operators, which can be defined trivially using the technique.

Functions are defined in the algebraic technique by stating their relation to each other. They are functions in the mathematical sense that they may not have side effects but may only map a value in their domain to a value in their range. The technique is called "algebraic" because the values and functions of a specification can be viewed as forming an abstract algebra (see Section 8.3.3).

8.3.1 Algebraic Specification of Bounded Stack

We present the specification in this section; in the following section we present explanatory notes.

1. obj   stack;
2. sorts   stack/integer, boolean;
3. ok-ops
4.   push: stack, integer → stack;
5.   pop: stack → stack;

---

*Tools imply computer programs that aid in the use of a specification language that supports a given approach. We will examine such tools in Chapter 9.

6.   top: stack $\longrightarrow$ <u>integer</u>;
7.   empty: stack $\longrightarrow$ <u>boolean</u>;
8.   newstack: $\longrightarrow$ stack;
9.   depth: stack $\longrightarrow$ <u>integer</u>; <u>hidden</u>;
10. <u>error-ops</u>
11.   underflow $\longrightarrow$ stack;
12.   no_more $\longrightarrow$ <u>integer</u>;
13.   overflow $\longrightarrow$ stack;
14. <u>ok-eqn's</u>
15.   pop (push (s, item)) = s;
16.   top (push (s, item)) = item;
17.   empty (newstack) = <u>true</u>;
18.   empty (push (s, item)) = <u>false</u>;
19.   depth (newstack) = 0;
20.   depth (push (s, item)) = 1 + depth (s);
21. <u>error-eqn's</u>
22.   pop (newstack) = underflow;
23.   top (newstack) = no_more;
24.   push (s, item) = overflow <u>if</u> depth (s) > 2;
25. <u>jbo</u>

8.3.2 Notes on the Stack Specification

Throughout this chapter notes refer to numbered lines in the specification. In this and other examples the specifier has decided that the "boundedness" of the stack is to be made visible only by an error value that is returned upon overflow, and the exact depth of the stack at any instant is not to be provided to using programs.

1. The basic units of specification in OBJ are "objects," which correspond to abstract data types.
2. The <u>sorts</u> statement in OBJ names the new type being defined in OBJ (preceding the "/") and the old types used in the definition (following the "/").
3. The <u>ok-ops</u> section defines the argument types and results for normal operation of each of the functions defined.
4. This statement defines "push" as a function that accepts a stack and an integer and returns an integer. Lines 5 through 8 provide similar information for other functions.
9. Hidden or auxiliary functions (not accessible to an abstract program) are explicitly denoted as such in OBJ.

10. An error result in OBJ is a specifier-defined value of the type normally returned by a function that could be misused (see note to line 22). This section of the specification defines those error values.

11. This line states that under some circumstances some function that normally returns a stack will instead return an error value of type "stack" equal to "underflow." The appropriate encoding of this value (for example all 1's) is left to the implementor. Lines 12 and 13 provide similar information for other functions. As with the decision to "hide" the stack depth, it was a conscious choice of the specifier to have this error value be of type "stack"; if a new type (say, "exception") were used, line 11 would read

$$\text{underflow: stack} \longrightarrow \text{exception}$$

and the type "exception" would be added on line 2 as an old (predefined) type.

14. This section of the specification defines the normal semantics of the functions of the object under consideration. The definitions are in the form of equations (also known as rewrite rules or algebraic axioms).

15. The nesting of functions implies sequence; this equation informally reads: "a 'push' of an 'item' on a stack '*s*' followed by a 'pop' yields the original stack." Lines 16 through 20 provide other defining equations.

21. This section of the specification defines the circumstances under which functions will return designated error values (see note to line 10) instead of the normal values defined in the ok-eqn's section (see note to line 14).

22. This line states that a "pop" following a "newstack" will return the special error value "underflow," which is of type "stack" (as defined by line 11). Line 23 provides similar information for function "top."

23. The OBJ statement "$f(x) = g$ if b" means: "If b is true, then $f(x)$ returns the value g; otherwise, $f(x)$ returns the value previously defined for it." In this case, if depth exceeds 2, push $(s, item)$ is to return "overflow."

The semantics of the algebraic technique are shown by the following abstract or using program. The reader should recall the earlier discussion (see Section 8.1) on the relationship between using and implementing programs. We *elaborate*, or symbolically execute, the using program, computing results from the specifications of functions it uses. The elaboration is presented to illustrate the manner in which the specification approach defines results, and not as an argument that the specification is "correct" or "reasonable." The reader should also note the difference between the semantics of the programming constructs of the abstract programming language (here restricted to variables, results, and the assignment statement), and the extensions provided by the specified functions. The OBJ system permits these extensions to have a wide variety of syntactic forms, so that the specification technique can be used to define the semantics of various programming languages.

ABSTRACT PROGRAM

1. <u>begin</u>
2.   <u>integer</u> result, stack s;
3.   push $(s, 5)$;
4.   push $(s, 3)$;
5.   pop (s);
6.   result: $=$ top (s);
7. <u>end</u>

ELABORATION FOR THE ALGEBRAIC SPECIFICATION

Line no.	*Notes*
3.	push $(s, 5)$ = push (newstack, 5) = <u>if</u> depth (push (newstack, 5)) > 2 <u>then</u> overflow <u>else</u> push (newstack, 5) [by line 24 of the specification]; depth push $(s, 5)$ = push (newstack, 5) ["newstack" because this is the first push encountered in the using program] = $1 +$ depth (newstack) = $1 + 0 = 1$ [by line 20 of the specification]; . . . push (newstack, 5) = push (newstack, 5). This identity occurs because there is no equation in the specification with "push" on the left-hand side.
4.	push $(s, 3)$ = push (push (newstack, 5), 3) = <u>if</u> depth (push (push (newstack, 5), 3) > 2 <u>then</u> overflow <u>else</u> push (push (newstack, 5), 3) [by line 24 of the specification]; depth (push (push (newstack, 5), 3) = $1 +$ depth (push (newstack, 5) = $1 + 1 +$ depth (newstack) = $1 + 1 + 0 = 2$ [by repeated application of line 24 of the specification]; . . push $(s, 3)$ [*in this context*] = push (push (newstack, 5), 3).
5.	pop (s) = pop (push (push (newstack, 5), 3) = push (newstack, 5) [by line 15 of the specification].
6.	result := top (s) = top (push (newstack, 5)) = 5 [by line 16 of the specification].

8.3.3 Comments on the Algebraic Specification Approach

The algebraic specification technique derives its name from its relationship to a form of abstract algebra called a heterogeneous or many-sorted algebra [51]. An abstract algebra consists of a nonempty set (called the *phylum* or *carrier*) and a set of named functions, each of which takes a finite number of arguments from the carrier and maps them onto an element of the carrier. A heterogeneous algebra is one that has a set of named carriers or phyla. Thus our stack specification can be considered as a heterogeneous algebra in which the set of carriers is

{integer, boolean, stack},

and each function can be considered as mapping from the carriers onto the carriers—"pop," for example, being a function that maps an element from the carrier set "stack" onto an element of the carrier set "integer."

The *rewrite rules* are an important aspect of abstract algebras. Rewrite rules are used to reduce expressions systematically in the given algebra. Each rewrite rule defines a transformation or "rewrite" that may be applied to an expression in the algebra. The rules are of the form

$$\underline{\text{left}} \longrightarrow \underline{\text{right}},$$

which defines a rewrite of any expression containing $\underline{\text{left}}$: the replacement of the subexpression $\underline{\text{left}}$ by the subexpression $\underline{\text{right}}$. The principle can be made clear by an example. Consider the following set of rewrite rules for a group [52]:

1. $+(x, 0) \longrightarrow x$
2. $+(0, x) \longrightarrow x$
3. $+(x, -(x)) \longrightarrow 0$
4. $+(-(x), x) \longrightarrow 0$
5. $+(+(x, y), z) \longrightarrow (x, +(y, z))$
6. $-(0) \longrightarrow 0$
7. $-(-(x)) \longrightarrow x$
8. $-(+(x, y)) \longrightarrow +(-(y), -(x))$
9. $+(x, +(-(x), y)) \longrightarrow y$
10. $+(-(x), +(x, y)) \longrightarrow y$

Note that the number of variables in $\underline{\text{right}}$ is always a subset of those in $\underline{\text{left}}$; this permits the reduction. Now these rules can be applied to an arbitrary expression for a group, say:

$$+(+(d, +(c, -(c))), -(+(0, -(a)))),$$

would reduce first to

$$+(+(d, +(c, -(c))), -(-(a)))$$

by recognizing a $\underline{\text{left}}$ of $+(0, -(a))$ and applying rule 2 to obtain $-(a)$. The next reduction would be to

$$+(+(d, 0), -(-(a)))$$

by noting a $\underline{\text{left}}$ of $+(c, -(c))$ and applying rule 3 in order to replace this with a $\underline{\text{right}}$ of 0. Similarly, rule 1 would yield a next reduction to

$$+(d, -(-(a)))$$

and finally

$$+(d, a)$$

by rule 7.

The similarity of this rewrite process to the elaboration of our abstract program is obvious and illustrates that the ok-eqn's and error-eqn's can be viewed, for purposes of formal analysis, as a set of rewrite rules. In particular, two basic questions can be asked of any set of rewrite rules (and, therefore, any algebraic specification):

1. Will the reduction terminate? If yes, the so-called *finite termination property* holds.
2. Will the result be independent of the order in which the rules are applied? Rewrite rules that produce results independent of their order of application exhibit *unique termination* or the *Church-Rosser property* [52].

A set of rules that is both finitely and uniquely terminating is said to be *convergent*. The problem of determining whether an arbitrary set of rewrite rules is convergent is algorithmically undecidable. There do exist sufficient conditions for convergence that appear to cover "reasonable" specifications. Several algorithms exist for determining finite and unique termination of restricted sets of rewrite rules. The AFFIRM system contains mechanisms to determine unique termination (finite termination is presently assumed); an overview of the problem is given in [48].

The incorporation of error results (called "partial operations" in [53]) can prevent even simple algebraic specifications from terminating uniquely. The stack example previously given contains the potential for ambiguous results. This can be shown most easily by considering the using program:

```
begin
    integer result, stack s;
    pop (s);
    push (s, 5);
    result := top (s);
end
```

The existence of the error equation

pop (newstack) = underflow;

in the specification introduces a new value which must be defined for the other functions by means of "implicit axioms" [54]. A reasonable set of axioms for the case at hand would be:

push (underflow, item) = underflow;
top (underflow) = no_more;
pop (underflow) = underflow;

It is these "implicit axioms" that generate the ambiguous results; since the "normal" (nonerror) axioms are defined for *all* values (including error values), the pathological abstract program given above can be elaborated in two ways:

1. top (push (pop (newstack), 5))
   = top (push (underflow, 5))
   = 5 [(by line 16 of the specification)]
2. top (push (pop (newstack), 5))
   = top (push (underflow, 5))
   = top (underflow) [(by the first "implicit axiom" above)]
   = no_more [(by the second "implicit axiom" above)]

Several strategies for producing consistent results have been presented [53]; they fall into two classes. One class prevents inconsistent results by restricting the order in which axioms are applied. Strategies in the second class use a technique in which each axiom incorporates a predicate that tests to see if an error can be produced. Boolean hidden functions are introduced to determine whether an error results from a particular argument value. By adopting this strategy for our stack example, we begin with the set of equations:

$$\text{pop (newstack)} = \text{underflow};$$

$$\text{top (newstack)} = \text{no\_more};$$

$$\text{push } (s, \text{item}) = \text{overflow} \underline{\text{if}} \text{ depth } (s) > 2;$$

to define errors (as in lines 22 through 24 of the specification) and add the following hidden functions to test for them:

$$\text{is\_underflow (underflow)} = \underline{\text{true}};$$

$$\text{is\_underflow (new\_stack)} = \underline{\text{false}};$$

$$\text{is\_underflow (push } (s, \text{item})) = \underline{\text{if}} \text{ is\_underflow } (s)$$
$$\underline{\text{then}} \text{ true}$$
$$\underline{\text{else}} \text{ false};$$

$$\text{is\_overflow (overflow)} = \underline{\text{true}};$$

$$\text{is\_overflow (push } (s, \text{item})) = \underline{\text{if}} \text{ is\_overflow } (s)$$
$$\underline{\text{then}} \text{ true}$$
$$\underline{\text{else}} \text{ false};$$

Each equation can then have a predicate attached that tests for the possibility of error. Thus "pop" (line 15 of the specification) would become

$$\text{pop (push } (s, \text{item})) = \underline{\text{if}} \text{ is\_underflow } (s)$$
$$\underline{\text{then}} \text{ underflow}$$
$$\underline{\text{else}} \underline{\text{if}} \text{ is\_overflow } (s)$$
$$\underline{\text{then}} \text{ overflow}$$
$$\underline{\text{else}} s;$$

Note that this technique involves the controlled propagation of error values. Besides complicating the specification, the technique requires an implementor to propagate and "track" these values in the implementing programs.

Another way of dealing with error values was discovered in the note to line 11 of the specification. This approach involved using an old (predefined) type called "exception" and having the values "underflow," "no-more," and "overflow" be of that type. Since the stack itself is of type "stack" and its constituent values are of type "integer," there is then no possibility of error values propagating across successive function references by the using program. In the case of our pathological using program, elaboration would cause a result of type "exception" and value "underflow" to be returned as a consequence of the attempt to "pop" a "newstack." Returning a value of type "exception" is an example of the "error" or "exception" approach to unacceptable use of functions by using programs. Note that this approach requires that the using program be able to accept exception values from functions that normally do not return values, and that the using program language must define the behavior of a using program when exception values are returned but no action is stated in the using program—that is, the exceptions are not explicitly "handled."

Another problem with algebraic specifications is the number of hidden or auxiliary functions required to specify (in the abstract data type case) even simple objects. It has been shown [55] that an object as elementary as a stack that can be searched (traversed like an array) cannot be specified in a specification of finite size unless hidden functions (such as "depth" in the previous example) are introduced. For complex objects, the number of hidden functions can be greater than the number of those visible (to the using program). This means that the specification contains more information about artifacts of the specification language than information that is directly descriptive of the desired behavior.

From the validator's point of view, algebraic specifications are difficult to reason about (except in purely formal terms, such as the termination properties discussed above) because they are difficult to read. This difficulty derives from the way functions are defined "indirectly" or in terms of each other. This point can be appreciated by considering the following two specifications, one for a multiset* or "bag," the other for a set.

1. obj multiset;
2. sorts multiset/integer, boolean;
3. ok-ops
4. empty: → multiset;
5. member: multiset, integer → boolean;
6. insert: multiset, integer → multiset;
7. delete: multiset, integer → multiset;
8. ok-eqn's
9. member (empty, item_in_question) = false;

*That is, a set that may contain multiple elements of the same value.

10. member (insert (m, item), item_in_question) =
11.   if item = item_in_question
12.   then true
13.   else member (m, item_in_question);
14. delete (empty, item_to_go) = empty;
15. delete (insert (m, item), item_to_go) =
16.   if item = item_to_go
17.   then m
18.   else insert (delete (m, item_to_go), item);
19. jbo

1. obj set;
2. sorts set/integer, boolean;
3. ok-ops
4. empty: ⟶ set;
5. member: set, integer ⟶ boolean;
6. insert: set, integer ⟶ set;
7. delete: set, integer ⟶ set;
8. ok-eqn's
9. member (empty, item_in_question) = false.
10. member (insert (s, item), item_in_question) =
11.   if item = item_in_question
12.   then true
13.   else member (s, item_in_question);
14. delete (empty, item_to_go) = empty;
15. delete (insert (s, item), item_to_go) =
16.   if item = item_to_go
17.   then delete (s, item_to_go)
18.   else insert (delete (s, item_to_go), item);
19. jbo

It has been argued [50] that the crucial difference between a set and a multiset is given by the single difference in line 17 of the respective specifications. The argument can be followed by considering the using program fragment:

S1: insert (x, 3);
S2: insert (x, 5);
S3: insert (x, 3);
S4: delete (x, 3)
S5: test := member (x, 3)

for both the set and the multiset. In the case of the set, the results of each step of the elaboration are

S1: insert (empty, 3) [no equation for insert; see the note to line 3 of using
            program for "stack"]
S2: insert (insert (empty, 3), 5)
S3: insert (insert (insert (empty, 3), 5), 3)
S4: delete (insert (insert (insert (empty, 3), 5), 3), 3) = [by lines 16 and 17]
    delete (insert (insert (empty, 3), 5), 3) = [by lines 16 and 18]
    insert (delete (insert (empty, 3), 3), 5) = [by lines 16 and 17]
    insert (delete (empty, 3), 5) = [by line 14]
    insert (empty, 5)
S5: test := member (insert (empty, 5), 3) = [by line 10]
          member (empty, 3) = [by line 9] <u>false</u>.

For the multiset, the elaboration would be identical up to statement:

S4: delete (insert (insert (insert (empty, 3), 5), 3), 3) = [by lines 16 and 17]
    insert (insert (empty, 3), 5)
S5: test := member (insert (insert (empty, 3), 5), 3) = [by line 10]
          member (insert (empty, 3), 3) = [by line 10]
          <u>true</u>.

The elaborations make clear that the uniqueness of values in a set is maintained by the behavior of the delete function. This is obvious from the respective specifications. Less obvious is the manner in which the property is maintained.

In both specifications the delete function tests, in line 16, to see if the value to be deleted is equal to the last value inserted. If the values do not match, both specifications, in line 18, apply the delete function to the next-to-last value inserted. (The reader may review the stack example to understand the manner in which the sequence of applications of functions is defined by nesting in function definitions.)

Difference occurs as a result of different consequences when the values match. In the case of the multiset, the function returns the value of the multiset before the insertion. In the case of the set, the function returns a delete applied to the value of the set before the insertion. Thus the delete for a multiset is applied until the first equality, and it deletes only one of possibly many insertions of that value; a delete for a set is reapplied after equality, and therefore it deletes all insertions of the value. We leave it to the reader's judgment of whether this characterization of the difference between sets and multisets, and its expression in the language, is natural or not.

From the point of view of the implementor, algebraic specifications may be difficult to read. Programmers appear to be, by temperament and training, much more comfortable with logical statements and the first-order predicate calculus than with the transformational rewrite statements used in the algebraic technique. Implementors also risk being misled by the hidden functions, a problem shared by all the techniques described in this chapter. For example, there is a strong suggestion in the stack specification that "depth" should be implemented by a separate subroutine called before performing the operations of a "push." This is clearly less efficient and more complex than a simple depth variable that is adjusted as a side effect of "push" and "pop." While the better implementation may be clear for simple objects such as stacks, it is often unclear for complex objects. Also, the restriction that functions may not have side effects can cause the specification breakdown into functional units to occur in an "unnatural way." Thus in the stack example "pop" and "top" are shown as distinct functions, whereas one useful form of stack has "pop" as a side effect of "top."

8.3.4 Link Between Specification and Verification

A verifier who is given an algebraic specification has two options: to verify the programs against the specification as it stands, using Guttag's method [56], or to transform the specification into a form that can be used with the inductive assertion method.

Guttag's method involves showing that each equation of the specification is satisfied by the implementing programs. Since the programs will, in general, implement specified functions in terms of concrete objects (for example, arrays instead of stacks), two preliminary tasks must be performed before the actual proof of the implementations can be done:

1. The concrete objects must be formally specified using the algebraic method.
2. A relationship must be defined between the abstract objects (such as stacks) and the concrete objects (such as arrays). This relationship is formally expressed using a *representation* or *mapping* function. (This step is common to the verification of programs specified using any of the approaches discussed.)

The representation function maps the concrete objects onto the abstract ones:

$$\text{abstract} = \text{map (concrete),}$$

and the verification of some program p (concrete), whose specifying function is f (abstract, arg), would involve first locating each reference to f in the specification—for example,

$$g(f \text{ (abstract, arg)}) = \text{arg}$$

—and then demonstrating in this case that

$$g(p \text{ (map (concrete), arg)}) = \text{arg.}$$

In order to simplify the proof procedure, Guttag insists that a restricted implementation language be used that greatly resembles the specification language, and he argues that any reasonable programming language can be translated into this form. The verification problem is thereby reduced to one of showing the consistency between two sets of algebraic specifications. This can be illustrated (via an example taken from Guttag [56]) by considering an implementation of our stack in terms of arrays, as shown next.

ALGEBRAIC SPECIFICATION OF ARRAYS

1. obj array
2. sorts array/integer;
3. ok-ops
4.   new: → array
5.   assign: integer, array, integer → array;
6.   read: array, integer → integer;
7. ok-eqn's
8.   read (assign (val, array, index1), index2) = if index1 = index2
9.   then val
10.   else read (array, index2);
11.   read (new, index) = 0;
12. bjo

We can then define a mapping function "map":

$$map (array, \text{integer}) \longrightarrow stack (\text{integer}),$$

which simply states that we intend to represent our stack by an integer array and an index. We can then consider two implementing programs:

```
PUSH (array, index, arg)
    begin
        array (index + 1) := arg;
        index := index + 1;
    end
```
and
```
TOP (array, index)
    begin
        TOP := array (index);
    end
```

These programs must then be translated into the restricted implementation language, which is restricted in that each program must be expressed as a single equation. At the same time the "map" function is applied so that the program is a single equation involving abstract objects.

The translation problem is straightforward for TOP, since it is a one-line program:

$$\text{TOP (map (array, index))} = \text{read (array, index)}.$$

This equation states that TOP applied to an object represented by an array and an index returns or assumes the value of the element of the array designated by the index.

PUSH is more complicated, since it is given by two lines in the procedural notation. The first line sets the value of an element of the stack; the second line changes the value of the index. Both these changes can be captured in one equation:

PUSH (map (array, index), arg)

$$= \text{map (assign (arg, array, index} + 1), \text{index} + 1).$$

This states that a PUSH is applied to an object (represented by an array and an index) and an argument. The object changes value in that the argument is added to the array and the index is increased by one. Note that both lines of the original program can be expressed this way only because each line defines an operation on parts of the representation of the abstract object "stack." Having made the above transformations and substitutions, we are able to verify these two programs for the axiom:

$$\text{top (push } (s, \text{ item})) = s,$$

where s = stack
item = arg
push is implemented by PUSH
top is implemented by TOP.

We begin with the conjecture

$$\text{TOP (PUSH (stack, arg))} = \text{arg}$$

to be proven. The left side of the conjecture becomes, by the mapping of stacks onto array/index pairs,

$$\text{TOP (PUSH (map (array, index), arg))},$$

which then becomes, by the definition of the PUSH program in terms of array functions,

$$\text{TOP (map (assign (arg, array, index} + 1), \text{index} + 1).$$

Since the subexpression

$$\text{assign (arg, array, index} + 1)$$

is, by the array specification, of type array, we can apply the definition of the TOP program to obtain

$$\text{read (assign (arg, array, index} + 1), \text{index} + 1),$$

which can be reduced, using lines 8 through 10 of the array specification, to arg, thereby proving the conjecture.

In the above verification, the reductions were straightforward identity replacements. More complex functions may require the definition of an *equality interpretation*. An equality interpretation expresses the equality of abstract objects in terms of mapped concrete objects. Thus in our example it may become necessary to make the equality relation

$$\text{stack1} = \text{stack2}$$

for stacks and derive a corresponding equality relation for

$$\text{map (array1, index1)} = \text{map (array2, index2)}.$$

Equality of abstract objects is defined in terms of the functions that use those objects as arguments. In particular, two objects are equal if all possible sequences of function invocations yield identical results when begun with each of the objects. Proof of equality is therefore had by application of generator induction.

An equality relation must make the same statement for the mapping of concrete objects; that is, if map (array1, index1) = map (array2, index2), then any sequence of function invocations for the stack functions will yield the same result, whether begun with

$$\text{map (array1, index1)}$$

or

$$\text{map (array2, index2)}.$$

In addition, an equality relation must have the properties of an equality operator, namely:

Reflexivity: $x = x$

Symmetry: $x = y \longrightarrow y = x$

Transivity: $x = y$ and $y = z \longrightarrow x = z$

Substitution: $x = y \longrightarrow p = p[y \longleftarrow x]$, where p is any expression.

To illustrate the use of the equality operator, we introduce a program for POP in the restricted notation:

$$\text{POP (map (array, index))} = \underline{\text{if}} \quad \text{index} = 0$$
$$\underline{\text{then}} \quad \text{map (array, 0)}$$
$$\underline{\text{else}} \quad \text{map (array, index} - 1);$$

Note that this program assumes that

$$\text{map (array, 0)} = \text{no\_more}$$

We next attempt a proof for the equation in the stack specification

$$\text{pop (push (} s, \text{item))} = s,$$

which yields the conjecture

$$\text{POP (PUSH (map (array, index), arg))} = \text{map (array, index)}.$$

By the definition of the PUSH program we obtain for the left-hand side

POP (map (assign (arg, array, index + 1), index + 1)).

Applying the definition of the POP program and simplifying the subexpression (index + 1) − 1 to index, we obtain

if   index + 1 = 0
then map (assign (arg, array, index + 1), 0)
else map (assign (arg, array, index + 1), index).

Considering the nonerror case (the else clause), we obtain the following reduced form for our conjecture:

map (assign (arg, array, index + 1), index) = map (array, index).

In order to prove this we introduce the equality relation:

map (array1, index1) = map (array2, index2)
iff
index1 = index2
and
$(\forall k \in 1 .. index1)(read (array1, k) = read (array2, k))$.

This equality relation states that, if we represent stacks as arrays, then the two representations are equal (in the stack sense) if all their values from base to the current value of the pointer are equal; that is, the "garbage" values left in the array by "popped pushes" are not taken into account in determining equality in the stack sense. After proving that this is a valid equality relation (the proof appears in [56]), we can apply it to the reduced conjecture to yield

(index = index) and $(\forall k \in 1 .. index)(read (assign (arg, array, index + 1), k)$

$= read (array, k))$,

which can be reduced by integer equality and the definition of the read axiom for arrays to

$(\forall k \in 1 .. index)$
(if   index + 1 = k
then arg
else read (array, k)
=   read (array, k)),

which reduces, for $1 \leq k \leq index$, to

true ⟶ read (array, k) = read (array, k)

or true, and

false ⟶ arg = read (array, k),

which is

false ⟶ false

or true otherwise, thereby showing that the programs for POP and PUSH relate to each other in the same way that their defining functions pop and push do in their specifications.

The laboriousness of the above verification method, and in particular its requirement that every specification reference to a given function be reverified when the implementing program is changed (for example, "push" is referenced five times in the stack specification), has motivated researchers to seek other ways to verify the implementing programs of algebraically specified functions. Flon and Misra [57] have developed a method based, as suggested earlier, on the transformation of the specification into a form more adaptable to the inductive assertion method. This transformation is based on the observation that a rewrite rule of the form

$$\text{pop (push } (s, \text{item})) = s$$

can be altered to the

$$\{\underline{\text{pre}}\} \text{ function}\{\underline{\text{post}}\}$$

form required by the inductive assertion method:

$\{\text{old\_stack} = \text{push (oldest\_stack, item)}\}$

$$\text{pop (old\_stack) } \{\text{new\_stack} = \text{oldest\_stack}\}.$$

Once transformed, this specification can be used with the verification technique associated with the abstract model approach, discussed in Section 8.5. A more complete example of a transformation from algebraic to abstract model form will be given in Section 8.6.

Despite the practical difficulties posed by the algebraic technique, it remains a rich field for research, primarily because of its attractive mathematical grounding in abstract algebra. As the formal specification field matures, it appears that a major role for the algebraic technique will be the formal definition of objects, such as stacks and queues, that more implementation-oriented approaches will use as primitives.

8.4 STATE-MACHINE SPECIFICATIONS

The state-machine technique was first developed on an ad hoc basis [58] and was subsequently formalized [59, 60]. Specification languages based on this technique include SPECIAL [61], which was developed and is supported by tools at SRI International, and INA JO[62], which is part of a verification system at the System Development Corporation. The two languages are very similar, and the example given later in this section can be viewed as being represented in a simplified form of either.

The underlying abstractions of state-machine specifications are integers and boolean objects. The existing languages also use real numbers and character strings. In addition, they make available to the specifier elementary extension mechanisms such as vectors, sequences, and structures.

A state-machine specification resembles other specifications in that it defines a set of functions that specify transformations on inputs. The set of functions may be viewed (depending on the particular specification) as defining the nature of an abstract data type or describing the behavior of an abstract machine. A state-machine specification is given in terms of states and transitions. Its functions are divided into two classes:

V-functions allow an element of the state to be observed but do not define any aspect of transitions.

O-functions define transitions by means of *effects*. The effect of an O-function is to change the state; this is done by denoting a V-function and altering the value it will return.

The relationship between O-functions and V-functions is very similar to that between variables and operations in a programming language. Informally, a V-function is analogous to an unbounded array with symbolic indices, one index corresponding to each argument position. Another way to think of V-functions is as mappings between names and values. The V-function name designates a multiset of values, and the argument values for a specific invocation select a value from the multiset. Thus a V-function may look exactly like an array:

<u>vfun</u> table (i, j, k),

with a specific value in the table being denoted by actual argument values, such as

table (5, 13, 26).

Since arguments may take symbolic value—for example,

color = {red, white, blue},

direction = {north, south, east, west},

—a V-function could be defined in these terms:

<u>vfun</u>   color_pointer_set (color, direction).

In this case a specific value would be denoted by symbolic "actual" argument values—for example,

color_pointer_set (blue, east).

In this, the general case, the symbolic actual values can be thought of as being appended to the V-function name to uniquely denote an element of the state space, such as

color_pointer_set.blue.east.

V-functions can therefore readily describe any structure that resembles an array, list, tree, or constructs obtainable by the structuring facilities of languages such as PL/I or COBOL. Further aspects of V-functions and O-functions are presented in the following example.

8.4.1 State-Machine Specification of Bounded Stack

1. <u>module</u> stack;
2. <u>declarations</u> <u>integer</u> index, item; <u>boolean</u> flag;
3. <u>functions</u>
4.   <u>vfun</u> h_depth $\longrightarrow$ index;
5.   <u>hidden</u>;
6.   <u>initially</u> index $= 0$;
7.   <u>vfun</u> h_set_of_items (index) $\longrightarrow$ item;
8.   <u>hidden</u>;
9.   <u>initially</u> item $=$?;
10.   <u>ofun</u> push (item);
11.   <u>exceptions</u> h_depth > 2;
12.   <u>effects</u> 'h_set_of_items (h_depth) $=$ item;
13.   'h_depth $=$ h_depth $+ 1$;
14.   <u>ofun</u> pop;
15.   <u>exceptions</u> h_depth < 0;
16.   <u>effects</u> 'h_depth $=$ h_depth -1;
17.   <u>vfun</u> top ( ) $\longrightarrow$ item;
18.   <u>exceptions</u> h_depth < 0;
19.   <u>derivation</u> item $=$ h_set_of_items (h_depth -1);
20.   <u>vfun</u> empty ( ) $\longrightarrow$ flag;
21.   <u>derivation</u> flag $=$ (h_depth $= 0$);
22. <u>end module</u>;

8.4.2 Notes on the Stack Specification

Line no.   *Notes*

1.   A <u>module</u> in SPECIAL is an arbitrary collection of functions and does not necessarily correspond to an abstract data type.
2.   Types in SPECIAL are defined mappings between allowable values (<u>integer</u>, <u>real</u>, <u>boolean</u>, <u>character</u>) and names. There exists a mechanism for defining new types by explicit enumeration (for example, traffic_light_color $=$ red, yellow, green) and elementary type extension mechanisms such as <u>set-of</u>, <u>sequence-of</u>, and <u>structure</u>.
4.   The identifier "index" is local to this <u>vfun</u> and is used (a) to signify the type of the value returned and (b) to reference the returned value in the body of the function. Since this <u>vfun</u> has no arguments, it defines a one-element multiset.

5.   "h-depth" is a <u>hidden</u> <u>vfun</u> and therefore cannot be referenced in a using program that employs stacks. (It is standard usage in SPECIAL to prefix <u>hidden</u> function names with "h_".)

6.   This statement sets the initial value of "h_depth" to 0. Note that the name "index" serves only to denote the returned value.

7.   Since <u>vfun</u>, h_set_of_items, has an input argument, it defines a set of values whose maximum size is the maximum range of possible arguments. Note that this size is not given in the function definition; see the note to line 11 for a further discussion.

9.   "?" means "undefined."

10. The actual value of the argument "item" will be provided by the using program.

11. Exceptions are tested in order (there is only one here). The first exception that is <u>true</u> returns a value "exception-n" to the abstract program and terminates the instantiation of the function. This exception expresses the bounded size of the stack. It could be placed here or in the definition of "h_set_of_items" (lines 7 through 9). The choice to place it here is based on a goal of clarity and a feeling on the part of the specifier that the restriction is more appropriately associated with the visible "push" function than with some hidden part of the abstract machine. Note that checking for <u>exceptions</u> is the responsibility of the implementor, and avoiding or responding to them is the responsibility of the using programmer; see the example using program given below.

12. The <u>effects</u> of an <u>ofun</u> are defined to take place "instantly"; the reader of the specification is not to infer anything whatever from the order in which the <u>effects</u> are stated. In order to express changes in value, some notation must be adopted to differentiate between the "old" (preinvocation) and the "new" (postinvocation) values of referenced <u>vfuns</u>; the leading prime is used in SPECIAL to denote the new value. Note that since the old value of "h_depth" is used to select an element of the set of values denoted by "h_set_of_items," "h_depth" becomes in effect the pointer to the next free element instead of the pointer to the last used. This subtle distinction is an artifact of the specification and is not binding on the implementor; there is no mechanism except a comment to denote nonbinding distinctions. The inability to readily separate essential from nonessential aspects of formal specification is a major weakness of this genre as a guide to implementors.

13.   This <u>effect</u> could be directly implemented by the assignment statement

$$h\_depth := h\_depth + 1;$$

14.   This <u>ofun</u> affects the internal state of the stack machine without passing any information to or from the abstract program.

15.   See the note to line 11.

17.   Visible <u>vfuns</u> are "derived"; the values they show to a using program are derived from the values of hidden <u>vfuns</u>. The identifier "item" is used, as is "index" in line 4, as a local identifier to denote the type of the returned result and to enable the derivation to be defined.

19.   Note that the <u>vfuns</u> "h_set_of_items" and "h_depth" are invoked (as a consequence of their reference here) whenever "top" is invoked by a using program.

As in the previous section, the semantics of the state-machine specification technique will be shown by elaboration of a using program:

1. <u>begin</u>
2. <u>integer</u> result, stack s;
3. push $(s, 5)$;
4. push $(s, 3)$;
5. pop (s);
6. result $:=$ top (s);
7. <u>end</u>

ELABORATION FOR STATE-MACHINE SPECIFICATION

Line no.   *Notes*

3.   push $(s, 5)$ $\rightarrow$ h_set_of_items $(0) = 5$ [by line 12 of the specification] <u>and</u> h_depth $= 1$ [by line 13 of the specification]

4.   push $(s, 3)$ $\rightarrow$ h_set_of_items $(1) = 3$ [by line 12 of the specification] <u>and</u> h_depth $= 2$

5.   pop (s) $\rightarrow$ h_depth $= 1$. Note that the set h_set_of_items now contains a "garbage" value; a fastidious specifier might have added a line 16a to the specification reading

$$'h\_set\_of\_items\,(h\_depth) = ?$$

and thereby have made a statement about

the underlying abstraction that had no effect upon the visible attributes of the stack. Note also that this issue does not arise in algebraic specifications, since the value returned by any function instantiation is evaluated from the prior instantiations and not "extracted" from an underlying abstraction.

6.   result := top (*s*) $\longrightarrow$ result := h_set_of_items (0) = 5

8.4.3 Comments on the State-Machine Specification Approach

The state-machine technique arose from more pragmatic roots than did the algebraic approach, and perhaps for this reason the state-machine technique has not received as much attention in the literature. It has, however, been the technique most used in actual practice. It has been the specification technique used for some ten experimental prototype and feasibility models of secure operating systems [158]. It has also been used to specify an experimental fault-tolerant computer [141, 142].

The practical use of the state-machine model is largely a result of its suitability for validation of security. Current practice in the development of secure systems includes a requirement for a "proof of security." The most prevalent technical approach to obtaining such a proof involves a combination of validation and verification. First a specification is produced and by formal means is shown to be a specification of a secure system; then an implementation is produced and verified to correspond to the specification. The conclusion is then drawn that the implementation is secure. (This approach is in accord with Figure 2.2.) The state of the art permits complete validation (under a set of assumptions), and several validated specifications exist [158]; as the ability to verify is still limited, typically only "illustrative" or sample proofs are produced. The disciplines imposed by writing a formal specification, however, lead to very modular and straightforward programs in which confidence of correctness exists exceeding that resulting from walk-throughs [63].

8.4.3.1 Proof of Properties: Security

As an example of formal validation of specifications, we will show how security is demonstrated for a state-machine specification. For this example we will use a simplified form of the military security policy and the validation methods developed at SRI International [64].

To understand the security policy we first consider a time-shared system used by two classes of personnel, which we will call *cleared* and *uncleared*. Likewise all information in the system is identified as being cleared or uncleared. The military security policy can then be characterized as stating that information may flow only from uncleared to cleared. If we define a type* security_level = {cleared, uncleared}, and operations

$$\underline{\text{gtr}}, \underline{\text{lss}}, \underline{\text{eq}}, \underline{\text{geq}}, \underline{\text{leq}}$$

such that

cleared $\underline{\text{gtr}}$ uncleared $= \underline{\text{true}}$

cleared $\underline{\text{lss}}$ uncleared $= \underline{\text{false}}$

clear $\underline{\text{eq}}$ cleared $= \underline{\text{true}}$

cleared $\underline{\text{eq}}$ uncleared $= \underline{\text{false}}$

and so forth, we can restate the above policy as follows:

A user may obtain knowledge of a piece of information $\underline{\text{iff}}$:

the security_level associated with the user

$\underline{\text{geq}}$

the security_level associated with the information.

This restatement of the informal definition is the first in converting the definition to permit formal proof that a given formal specification exhibits the security property. Subsequent steps in the conversion require

1. A definition of "user" in terms of specification language syntax and semantics.
2. A definition of "information" in the same sense.
3. A means of associating a value of security_level with each user and element of information.
4. A method of proving that the flows are legal—that is, from lesser (uncleared) to greater (cleared) values of security_level.

We will consider each point in turn. A user in a computer system is viewed as a program in execution—that is, a process. In the state-machine model this is an arbitrary using program. An arbitrary using program is one that can invoke a specified function in any context whatever—that is, after any sequence of invocations of other functions in the abstract machine and with any possible combination of argument values.

An element of information is any denotable element of the state space—that is, any directly or indirectly observable V-function value as well as any exception value. Exceptions are categorized as information because they are observable by using programs (and, therefore, by users).

A value of security_level is associated with each user by having the abstract program include an argument of type security_level in every function invocation. This argument is defined to carry the unforgeable security_level of

*The actual classes in the military model form a lattice; our restriction to two ordered levels simplifies exposition without omitting any key points.

the user on whose behalf the using program is executed. A value of security_level is associated with every item of information by requiring that every primitive V-function carry an argument of type security_level in its argument list. Thus a V-function

<u>vfun</u> eyes (color)   where   color = {blue, brown, green, grey}

would carry, in its "basic" form, four possible values:

> eyes (blue),
> eyes (brown),
> eyes (green),
> eyes (grey).

With the additional argument it would be defined as

<u>vfun</u> eyes (color, info_level)

and carry eight possible distinct values:

> eyes (blue, cleared),
>
> eyes (blue, uncleared),
>
> .
> .
> .
>
> eyes (grey, uncleared).

Another way of viewing this requirement is that every denotable value in the state space must have its security_level appended to its name (remembering that eyes (blue, cleared) is the same as eyes.blue.cleared). This step is called "partitioning the state space."

The final step, proving that the flows defined in a given specification are only from uncleared to cleared, is somewhat more elaborate. It begins with the observation that a state-machine specification technique permits only three constructs in which information flow is defined:

1. Into the state space, by having a using program provide a value as an argument to a visible O-function.
2. Out of the state space, by having a using program invoke a visible V-function, or by having an exception returned by a visible function.
3. Within the state space, by having a using program invoke an O-function whose <u>effect</u> moves a value from one denotable element of the state space to another. This can occur either between named V-functions, as in

   'one_V-function (arg, security_level)
   > = other_V-function (arg2, security_level-2),

   or within a single V-function, as in
   'one_V-function (arg, security_level)
   > = one_V-function (arg2, security_level-2).

For each kind of information flow in the specification, a "security property" can be formulated that defines the mandatory relations between values of security_level for that flow to be secure according to the model. For the cases mentioned immediately above, the properties are

P1. Any "new value" of a V-function referenced in the effects of an O-function must be at a security_level geq the security_level of the invoking abstract program.

P2. Any "old value" of a V-function mentioned in the derivation of a visible V-function or the exceptions of any visible function must be at a security_ level leq the security_level of the invoking abstract program.

P3. Any "old value" of a V-function referenced in the effects of an O-function must be at a security_level leq that of any "new value" referenced in the same effects clause.

These properties are more restrictive than the informal definition in that they cover potential as well as actual flows; a "cleared" value could be entered in a state-space element at a security_level "uncleared" and never read by any but "cleared" programs. The properties do not recognize this circumstance because they apply to functions specified to be secure for all possible using programs. In other words, the security proof method places the entire burden of restricting information flow upon constraints on the function definition and avoids constraints on the abstract programs. In practice this leads to many cases where useful and clearly benign flows (such as the returning of a "not ready" signal from a device at a higher security_level) are forbidden and an "escape" from the model (called "trusted processes") must be invoked.

Once the properties have been defined, it is a syntactic operation to scan a specification and locate the statements where a given property may apply. A formula generator has been developed at SRI International that does this and generates formulas whose truth implies that the property holds. The general form of such formulas is:

for all values of all arguments to the functions, the truth of the circumstances that permit this statement implies that the statement obeys the relevant property.

The universal quantification on the argument values reflects the insistence that the function be secure in any invocation context. The truth of the circumstances that permit the statement is the conjunction of the negative of each preceding exception, plus the appropriate value of any conditional expression whose scope includes the statement.

We illustrate the proof process by showing a "stack machine" that contains information at different security_levels, but permits an item to be examined only at a security_level geq to that at which it was "pushed." This is done by partitioning the state space of the machine into a stack and index per level.

We will present a machine that is not secure and show how the proof method treats both secure and insecure flows.

1. module secure_stack_machine;
2. types security_level = [cleared, uncleared];
3. declarations integer index, item; boolean flag; security_level   user_level,
4.   stack_level;
5. functions
6. vfun h_depth (stack_level) $\longrightarrow$ index;
7.   hidden;
8.   initially index = 0;
9. vfun h_set_of_items (stack_level, index) $\longrightarrow$ item;
10.   hidden;
11.   initially item = 0;
12. ofun push (user_level, stack_level, item);
13.   exceptions not (user_level leq stack_level);
14.   h_depth (stack_level) > 2;
15.   effects 'h_set_of_items (stack_level, h_depth (stack_level))
16.   = item;
17. ofun pop (user_level, stack_level);
18.   exceptions not (user_level leq stack_level);
19.   h_depth (stack_level) < 0;
20.   effects 'h_depth (stack_level) = h_depth (stack_level) −1;
21. vfun top (user_level, stack_level) $\longrightarrow$ item;
22.   exceptions not (user_level geq stack_level);
23.   h_depth (stack_level) < 0;
24.   derivation item
25.   = h_set_of_items (stack_level, h_depth (stack_level))
26. vfun empty (user_level, stack_level) $\longrightarrow$ flag;
27.   exceptions not (user_level geq stack_level);
28.   derivation flag = (h_depth (stack_level) = 0);
29. end module;

Line no.	Notes
2.	This illustrates the state-machine concept of a type as a restriction on allowable values.
6.	Note how the addition of the stack_level argument permits the denotation of multiple indices under one generic name.
9.	Likewise, multiple sets of values for the individual stacks.
12.	In order to define as flexible a stack machine as possible, each

visible function accepts both the security_level of the user and the security_level of the stack upon which the operation can be performed. It is thus a "multilevel" machine in the sense that operations may be performed at security_levels other than that of the user, subject to the constraints of the security properties.

13.   A "push" is a "write" access, which the properties constrain to occur only upward in level. We assume that the specification language has some facility for introducing the leq operator on the type security_level. Note that this exception is valid for any type security_level for which a partial ordering function can be defined.

18.   A "pop," since it changes the value of the state space, is a "write" access.

22.   A "top" is clearly an instance of a "read" access.

26.   An "empty," since it permits knowledge (albeit indirect) of the state space, is likewise a "read."

The secure-stack-machine is defined in terms of states and transitions in a partitioned state space. One subspace contains all values associated with security level "cleared"; the other contains all values associated with "uncleared." Operations may be performed on either subspace. The exception clause of each function seeks to prevent flow violations by comparing user_level and stack_level before any flows occur. The reader is invited to examine the specification informally for security flaws before the formal analysis is presented.

We will now show the kinds of formulas that are typically generated by the SRI tools. Consider line 19 of the specification, the second exception for the "pop" function. Property P2 [no flow out unless security_level (user) geq security_level (information)] applies here. The formula generated would be

    ($\forall$ user_level, stack_level)   (all using programs)
       (user_level leq stack_level   (negative of first exception)
       implies user_level geq stack_level) (property),

which is clearly false for user_level lss stack_level. The insecure flow detected here is the result of returning an exception from a function whose effect is to "write," and an exception that is a "read." Thus an attempt to perform a legitimate upward flow contains, via the exception mechanism, the potential for an upward "read," which is illegal. This is an example of how the properties are overly restrictive for practical systems; the one bit of information contained in the presence or absence of an exception represents a trivial "leak" but requires either the invocation of the "trusted process" escape or the rewriting of the specification to only allow "push" and "pop" on stacks where user_level eq stack_level.

Consider, alternatively, line 24, the derivation of the "top" function.

This likewise is an instance of property P2. The formula to be proven would be

> (∀ user_level, stack_level) (all abstract programs)
> (user_level <u>geq</u> stack_level
> <u>and</u> (conditions permitting
> h_depth (stack_level) ≥ 0   application)
> <u>implies</u>
> user_level <u>geq</u> stack_level) (property),

which is trivially <u>true</u>.

8.4.3.2 The State-Machine Approach in Practice

State-machine specifications have proved readable in practice and therefore reviewable for purposes of determining functional correctness and for guiding implementors. The existing languages (SPECIAL and INA JO) have a rich syntax that permits the expression of very similar semantics in a range of alternative forms. This richness in turn means that the specifier's style is very lightly constrained by the language. The quality of a given specification therefore depends greatly upon the skill of the specifier—much more than does the quality of a program upon the skill of the programmer, especially with languages like Ada, where the language syntax explicitly forbids stylistic pathologies.

The appropriateness of the state-machine technique for specification of a given system also depends on the relationship between the nature of the system being specified and the underlying abstraction of the technique itself. As can be seen by a study of the hidden V-function "h_set_of_items" (lines 7 through 9 in the stack specification), this underlying abstraction is conveniently visualized as a set of named elements, where the name of the set is the name of the V-function and the name of an element is the concatenation of the values of the arguments. Thus the first element entered into the state space of the stack machine would be "the element named zero within the set h_set_of_items." Since a V-function may have multiple arguments, and the arguments may take nonnumeric values, more complex organizations based upon subsetting may be readily represented. Thus a "shared stack" could be specified by adding the "user name" as an argument:

1. <u>module</u> shared_stack;
2. <u>declarations</u> <u>integer</u> index, item; <u>boolean</u> flag; <u>vector</u> <u>of</u>
3.   characters user_name;
4. <u>functions</u>
5.   <u>vfun</u> h_depth (user_name) → index;
6.   <u>hidden</u>;
7.   <u>initially</u> index = 0;
8.   <u>vfun</u> h_set_of_items (user_name, index (user_name)) → item;

9.   hidden;
10.   initially item = ?;
11.   ofun push (user_name, item);
12.   exceptions h_depth (user_name) > 2;
13.   effects 'h_set_of_items (user_name, h_depth (user_name))
14.   = item;
15.   'h_depth (user_name) = h_depth (user_name) + 1;
16.   ofun pop (user_name);
17.   exceptions h_depth (user_name) < 0;
18.   effects 'h_depth (user_name) = h_depth (user_name) − 1;
19.   vfun top (user_name) → item;
20.   exceptions h_depth (user_name) < 0;
21.   derivation item = h_set_of_items (user_name, h_depth − 1);
22.   vfun empty (user_name) → flag;
23.   derivation flag = (h_depth (user_name) = 0);
24. end module

In this example, the using program is obligated to provide a "user_name." If there are, say, three users named alpha, beta, and gamma, then h_set_of_items will contain named values such as "element alpha-1 of h_set_of_items." As an example of syntactic variation with equivalent semantics, note that a specifier could have exploited the small fixed size of the stack to write the following pathological version of "shared_stack," restricted for simplicity here to the "push" function.

1. module bad_shared_stack;
2. declarations integer index, item; boolean flag; vector of
3.   characters user_name;
4. functions
5.   vfun h_depth (user_name) → index;
6.   hidden;
7.   initially index = 0;
8.   vfun h_zero_stack_slice (user_name) → item;
9.   hidden;
10.   initially item = 0;
11.   vfun h_one_stack_slice (user_name) → item;
12.   hidden;
13.   initially item = 0;

14.   vfun h_two_stack_slice (user_name) → item;
15.   hidden;
16.   initially item = 0;
17.   ofun push (user_name, item);
18.   exceptions h_depth (user_name) > 2;
19.   effects
20.   if h_depth (user_name) = 0
                    then 'h_zero_stack_slice (user_name) = item
22.   else
23.   if h_depth (user_name) = 1
24.   then 'h_one_stack_slice (user_name) = item
25.   else 'h_two_stack_slice (user_name) = item;
26.   'h–depth (user_name) = h_depth (user_name) + 1;
27. end module

While such pathologies are amusingly obvious in structures as simple as shared stacks, they can be subtle in more complex specifications. In general, "clean" state-machine specifications can be written for functions whose behavior is easily expressed in terms of "set-oriented" name/value relations such as are encountered in lists, trees, and arrays. The state-machine approach is less satisfactory for more complex and arbitrary structures and for expressing effects that involve the evaluation of algebraic formulas.

Another inadequacy of state-machine specifications that has been discovered in the course of practical use is the exception semantics. The subject of exception definition and handling is one of the least developed in programming languages, and it is even less understood for practical specification languages. The sequential evaluation of the exceptions violates the "functional" or "non-procedural" spirit of formal specifications. The distinct "exception number" that is returned to the using program requires that the language for that program recognize a type "exception." This is no problem when using programs are written in a language designed for that purpose. There are, however, circumstances in which it is desirable to use an existing language for using programs (when this is done, the state-machine specification can be viewed as a statement of all or part of the formal semantics of the language), and the exception semantics often mate poorly with such languages.

8.4.4 Link Between Specification and Verification

There are presently two approaches to the verification of implementations of state-machine specifications. Both approaches begin with a mapping of concrete objects (for example, primitive data types in the implementation language) to the V-functions. In the verification system associated with INA JO, the O-functions are used to provide input and output assertions for a verification condition generator for the implementation language, which at present is a subset of Jovial. Proofs by inductive assertion are then produced directly in terms of the implementation language.

The verification system associated with SPECIAL takes a slightly different approach. A "low-level specification" is written in SPECIAL. This low-level specification captures the semantics of the implementation environment, which is usually some combination of hardware instructions, compiler code generation strategy, and operating system functionality. Implementation language programs are translated into a common internal language whose semantics are defined by the low-level specification. The result is an internal language program that uses low-level specification functions and "implements" or procedurally defines the O-functions of the abstract specification. The higher-level specification then provides input and output assertions for "subprograms" in the internal language. Verification conditions are then produced and an inductive assertion proof is generated in internal language terms. Note that this is similar, but not identical, to mappings from concrete to abstract objects. Concrete objects are those of the implementation language; the common internal language will, in general, use "low-level" objects that are even more primitive.

Example:

The process can be shown in outline by considering the following example. Consider first a low-level specification for a one-register integer machine on which we wish to implement our stack.

1. module simple_integer_machine;
2. declarations integer word, address;
3. functions
4.   vfun h_memory (address) → word;
5.   hidden;
6.   initially word = ?;
7.   vfun register → word;
8.   initially word = ?;
9.   ofun load (address);
10.   effects 'register = h_memory (address);
11.   ofun store (address);
12.   effects 'h_memory (address) = register;
13.   ofun add (address);
14.   effects 'register = register + h_memory (address)
15.   vfun display (address) → word;
16.   derivation word = h_memory (address);
17. end module;

Next we define an internal language IL with BNF:

$$\langle\text{integer}\rangle::=0\,|\,1\,|\,2\,|\,3\,|\,4\,|\,5\,|\,6\,|\,7\,|\,8\,|\,9$$
$$\langle\text{source}\rangle::=\langle\text{integer}\rangle\,|\,\langle\text{V-function}\rangle$$
$$\langle\text{destination}\rangle::=\langle\text{V-function}\rangle$$
$$\langle\text{statement}\rangle::=\langle\text{call}\rangle\,|\,\langle\text{assignment}\rangle\,|\,\langle\text{conditional}\rangle\,|\,\langle\text{compound}\rangle$$
$$\langle\text{compound}\rangle::=\underline{\text{begin}}\ \langle\text{statement}\rangle\ldots\langle\text{statement}\rangle\ \underline{\text{end}}$$
$$\langle\text{call}\rangle::=\underline{\text{call}}\ \langle\text{O-function}\rangle;$$
$$\langle\text{assignment}\rangle::=\langle\text{destination}\rangle:=\langle\text{source}\rangle;$$
$$\langle\text{conditional}\rangle::=\underline{\text{if}}\ \langle\text{conditional expression}\rangle\ \underline{\text{then}}\ \langle\text{statement}\rangle$$
$$\underline{\text{else}}\ \langle\text{statement}\rangle;$$
$$\langle\text{conditional expression}\rangle::=\langle\text{destination}\rangle\langle\text{compare}\rangle\langle\text{source}\rangle$$
$$\langle\text{compare}\rangle::=>\,|\,<\,|\,\leq\,|\,\geq\,|\,=\,|\,\neq.$$

Note how the semantics of a "complete" machine, which would have branch instructions and so on, are divided between the "basic" semantics of IL and the "extensions" provided by the specification of "simple_integer_machine."

The next step is to provide an implementation for some function such as "push" in the top-level specification in some higher-order language (HOL) with self-evident syntax and semantics:

```
proc push (frame);
    begin
        integer frame, pointer;
        integer array real_stack [1: 3];
        global pointer, real_stack;
        real_stack [pointer] := frame;
            pointer := pointer + 1;
    end push.
```

This program could be translated for verification purposes into the following IL fragment:*

```
if display (5) ≤ 3              /* bounds check, stack depth in loc 5 */
    then
    begin
        call load (0);             /* fetch input argument */
        call store (display (5));  /* store input arg */
        call load (5);
        call add (4);              /* constant 1 */
        call store (5);            /* update pointer */
    end
    else
    /* some error-handling code here */.
```

Thus the nonprocedural specification of "push" given in lines 10 through 13 of the specification or "stack" has been implemented in a higher-order language, which has been translated into an IL program whose semantics are largely defined by the specifi-

---

*"Proper" initialization is assumed. The input argument is in h-memory (0).

cation of "simple_integer_machine." There are two things to note about this process. One is that the bounds check in the IL program is immediately derived from the semantics of an array in the higher-order language and relates only indirectly to the exception on line 11 of the "stack" specification. The second is that there are three sets of mappings in this structure. The first is from the concrete objects of the higher-order language to the V-functions of the stack machine. They are

the variable "pointer" $\longrightarrow$ "h_depth"

the integer array "real_stack" $\longrightarrow$ "h_set_of_items"

The second set of mappings is from the V-functions of "simple_integer_machines" to the concrete objects. They are

h_memory (5) $\longrightarrow$ the variable "pointer"

h_memory (4) $\longrightarrow$ the constant "1"

h_memory (1) through h_memory (3) $\longrightarrow$ the array "real_stack"

With these two mappings we can map "through" the implementing program for "push" and relate the state space of "simple_integer_machine" to the state space of "stack":

h_memory (5) $\longrightarrow$ h_depth

h_memory (1) $\longrightarrow$ h_set_of_items (0)

h_memory (2) $\longrightarrow$ h_set_of_items (1)

h_memory (3) $\longrightarrow$ h_set_of_items (2)

With this mapping it is possible to express the preconditions and effects of "push" in terms of the objects of the IL program (the V-functions of "simple_integer_machine"). The conjecture to be proven in order to verify the higher-order language implementation of "push" then becomes

{h_memory (5) $<$ 3} IL program fragment

{h_memory (h_memory (5)) = h_memory (0) and h_memory (5)

$$= \text{h\_memory (5)} + 1\}.$$

As is often the case with simple functions, once the mappings have been made the proof follows by inspection.

In summary the verification method's steps are:

1. Write a specification of the desired function in SPECIAL (the "top-level specification" or "TLS").
2. Write a specification of the implementation environment (the semantics of the implementation language) in SPECIAL (the "low-level specification" or "LLS").
3. Write an implementation of the TLS function in the implementation language.
4. Translate the implementation into internal language (IL).

5. Map the LLS V-functions "through" the implementation language objects to the TLS V-functions.

6. Using the mappings, express the TLS exceptions (if any) as preconditions in terms of IL objects (that is, LLS V-functions).

7. Using the mappings, express the TLS effects as postconditions in terms of IL objects.

8. Using the resultant pre- and postconditions, prove the IL equivalent of the implementation.

To repeat a point made earlier, the state-machine technique has very pragmatic roots. It occupies a position akin to that of FORTRAN in the programming language family: it is the first technique that was supported by tools and that was subjected to the rigors of practical use. As with FORTRAN, it was devised before many of the principles of the language family were fully understood. The language designers devised features before a significant body of literature existed in any similar language and as a consequence designed very rich and "large" languages. Work on the second generation of state-machine specification languages has begun.

8.5 ABSTRACT MODEL SPECIFICATIONS

The abstract model technique, which is also sometimes called the predicate transform method, differs in both syntax and semantics from the techniques previously discussed. For syntax it uses the basic precondition/postcondition format developed by Hoare (see Section 4.5). It defines its functions in terms of an underlying abstraction that is selected by the specifier. The specifier can use any abstraction (sets, multisets, lists, arrays, and so on) about which it is possible to reason formally. An abstract model specification, therefore, has no intrinsic meaning derived from a specific abstract model specification language; instead, its meaning depends upon the underlying abstraction selected. As the examples will show, the usefulness of a given abstract model specification depends greatly upon the appropriateness of the selected underlying abstraction to the functions being specified.

The approach was developed by Hoare as part of a unified technique for the specification and verification of abstract data types. As a result, it is the most "verification-oriented" of the techniques discussed in this chapter. It is very compatible with (but not defined as part of) the programming languages Alphard [46] and Euclid [65].

In our first example we present a "clean" specification of a bounded integer stack by choosing the sequence (used by Hoare in some of his examples) as the underlying abstraction, with sequence defined in advance by an algebraic specification. The algebraic approach is used because it specifies simple objects well and expresses their behavior in a mathematically rigorous way.

8.5.1 Algebraic Specification of Sequence

1. obj iseq;
2. sorts iseq/integer, iarray;
3. ok-ops
4.   append: iseq, integer $\longrightarrow$ iseq;
5.   leader: iseq $\longrightarrow$ iseq;
6.   trailer: iseq $\longrightarrow$ iseq;
7.   first: iseq $\longrightarrow$ integer;
8.   last: iseq $\longrightarrow$ integer;
9.   nullseq: $\longrightarrow$ iseq;
10.   length: iseq $\longrightarrow$ integer;
11.   seq: iarray $\longrightarrow$ iseq;
12. error-ops
13.   no_leader $\longrightarrow$ iseq;
14.   no_trailer $\longrightarrow$ iseq;
15.   no_first $\longrightarrow$ integer;
16.   no_last $\longrightarrow$ integer;
17.   no_iarray $\longrightarrow$ iseq;
18. ok-eqn's
19.   leader (append (s, element)) = s;
20.   trailer (append (s, element) =
21.   if s = append (append (nullseq, element_1), element_2)
22.   then append (nullseq, element_2)
23.   else append (trailer (s), element);
24.   first (append (s, element) =
25.   if s = nullseq
26.   then element
27.   else first (leader (s));
28.   last (append (s, element)) = element;
29.   length (nullseq) = 0;
30.   length (append (s, element)) = length (s) + 1;
31.   seq (iarray, m, n) =
32.   if $m = n$
33.   then append (nullseq, read (iarray, m))
34.   else append (seq (iarray, m, $n - 1$), read (iarray, n));

35. error-eqn's
36.   leader (nullseq) = no_leader;
37.   trailer (nullseq) = no_trailer;
38.   first (nullseq) = no_first;
39.   last (nullseq) = no_last;
40.   seq (new, m, n) = no_array;
41.   seq (iarray, m, n) = no_array $\underline{if}$ $m > n$;
42. bjo

8.5.2 Notes on Algebraic Specification of Sequence

Line no.   Notes

2.   This object contains a transform from iarrays to iseqs; see Section 8.5.6 for an algebraic specification of the object iarray.

4.   The function append adds an integer to the sequence.

5.   The function leader returns a sequence minus the last integer.

6.   The function trailer returns a sequence minus the first integer.

7.   The function first returns the first integer in the sequence.

8.   The function last returns the last integer in the sequence.

9.   The function nullseq is the empty sequence.

10.   The function length gives the current length of the sequence.

11.   The function seq forms a sequence from contiguous members of an iarray. This function is not part of any intuitive view of sequences but is required for verification.

33.   Since seq maps from iarray to iseq, its semantics reference those those of iarray given in Section 8.5.5. The function constructs a new iseq from contiguous elements of an iarray by "reading" the elements from the iarray and appending them to the iseq in order.

40.   The semantics of this error refer to the semantics of "new" for iarray.

41.   Absence of this error_eqn would define infinite recursion for seq if $m > n$.

8.5.3 Abstract Model Specification of Stack as Sequence

1. type stack;
2. stack is modeled as iseq;
3. invariant $0 \leq$ length (stack) ≤ 2;
4. initially stack = nullseq;
5. functions
6.   push (item: integer)

7.   pre $0 \leq$ length (stack) ≤ 2;

8.   post 'stack = append (stack, item);

9.   pop

10.   pre stack $\neq$ nullseq;

11.   post 'stack = leader (stack);

12.   top returns (item: integer)

13.   pre stack $\neq$ nullseq;

14.   post item = last (stack);

15.   empty returns (flag;   boolean)

16.   post flag = (stack = nullseq);

17. end

8.5.4 Notes on Stack Modeled as Sequence

Line no.   Notes

1.   We use the keyword type because this technique strongly supports the abstract data type.

2.   This clause (aux in Euclid and aux var in Alphard*) denotes the underlying abstraction upon which the new type will be modeled. The underlying abstraction must be defined elsewhere with mathematical rigor.

3.   This line is used in the verification methodology (see Section 8.5.9).

4.   The reader must refer to the semantics of "iseq" to understand what "nullseq" means.

6.   The type being defined (stack) is implied.

8.   We adopt the SPECIAL notation that "'s" means the "value of s after instantiation of the function" rather than the Alphard usage of "before."

11.   The meaning of "leader," like "nullseq" (lines 4, 10, 13, 16), "length" (lines 3, 7,), and "last" (line 14) must be obtained from the formal definition of an "iseq." Note also how similar the definition of an "iseq" is to the algebraic specification of a stack when only the functions append, leader, last, and length are considered.

To further demonstrate the technique we will show the elaboration of the same using program presented in the previous sections:

1. begin

*Replaced by the "let" clause in later versions of the language.

2.   <u>integer</u> result, stack s;
3.   push $(s, 5)$;
4.   push $(s, 3)$;
5.   pop (s);
6.   result := top (s);
7. <u>end</u>

Note that the elaboration follows the form of the elaboration of the algebraic specification for the stack because the underlying abstraction was specified algebraically; if the underlying abstraction had been specified informally or by the state-machine technique, then the elaboration would change accordingly. This observation illustrates our point about the semantics of an abstract model specification depending on the semantics of the underlying abstraction.

ELABORATION FOR THE ABSTRACT MODEL SPECIFICATION
(STACK AS SEQUENCE)

Line no.	Notes

3.   push $(s, 5)$ = append (nullseq, 5) [by line 4 of the stack specification and abstract program context, which shows that this is the first reference, and line 8 of the stack specification].

4.   push $(s, 3$ = append $(s, 3)$ [by line 8 of the stack specification]
= append (append (nullseq, 5), 3) in terms of iseq.

5.   pop (s) = leader (s) [by line 11 of the stack specification]
= leader (append (append (nullseq, 5), 3) in terms of iseq
= append (nullseq, 5) [by line 19 of the iseq specification].

6.   result := top (s) = last (s) [by line 14 of the stack specification]
= last (append (nullseq, 5)) in terms of iseq
= 5 [by line 28 of the iseq specification].

Note that the basic similarity of iseq to stack makes this elaboration very similar to that of the algebraic specification of stacks. In particular, the question of "garbage" values does not arise.

In order to illustrate the relationship between an abstract model specification and the underlying abstraction, we specify a bounded integer stack in terms of arrays. As in the immediately preceding example, the underlying abstraction will be specified algebraically. Note how, in the "stack as array," the depth attribute is visible throughout the pre- and postconditions of the abstract model specification, whereas in the "stack as sequence" it is clearly expressed through an appropriate attribute ("length") of the underlying abstraction. Other implications of the choice of abstraction are given in the elaboration of our standard using program.

8.5.5 Algebraic Specification of Array

1. <u>obj</u> iarray
2. <u>sorts</u> iarray / <u>integer</u>;
3. <u>ok-ops</u>
4.   new: $\longrightarrow$ iarray;
5.   assign: <u>integer</u>, iarray, <u>integer</u> $\longrightarrow$ iarray;
6.   read: iarray, <u>integer</u> $\longrightarrow$ <u>integer</u>;
7. <u>error-ops</u>
8.   empty $\longrightarrow$ <u>integer</u>;
9. <u>ok-eqn's</u>
10.   read (assign (val, array, index 1), index 2)
                  $=$ <u>if</u> index 1 $=$ index 2
11.   <u>then</u> val
12.   <u>else</u> read (array, index 2);
13. <u>error-eqn's</u>
14.   read (new, index) $=$ empty;
15. <u>bjo</u>

8.5.6 Abstract Model Specification of Stack as Array

1. <u>type</u> stack;
2. stack is <u>modeled</u> as iarray and (depth: <u>integer</u>);
3. <u>invariant</u> $0 \leq$ depth ≤ 2;
4. <u>initially</u> stack $=$ new <u>and</u> depth $= 0$;
5. <u>functions</u>
6.   push (item: <u>integer</u>)
7.   <u>pre</u> $0 \leq$ depth ≤ 2;
8.   <u>post</u> 'stack $=$ assign (item, stack, depth) <u>and</u> 'depth $-$ depth $+ 1$;
9.   pop
10.   <u>pre</u> stack $\neq$ new;
11.   <u>post</u> 'depth $=$ depth $- 1$;
12.   top <u>returns</u> (item: <u>integer</u>)
13.   <u>pre</u> stack $\neq$ new;
14.   <u>post</u> item $=$ read (stack, depth $- 1$);
15.   empty returns (flag: <u>boolean</u>)
16.   <u>post</u> flag $=$ (stack $=$ new);
17. <u>end</u>

8.5.7 Notes on Stack Modeled as Array

Line no.	Notes
2.	Here the stack is in terms of an iarray and an auxiliary integer variable.
8.	Note that, in contrast to the previous example, the depth variable must be explicitly changed, because the underlying abstraction does not have as a visible attribute the number of items in it.
16.	This could also be <u>post</u> flag = (depth = 0); to do this "empty" would have to have an input argument of type <u>integer</u> rather than the implied one of stack.

ELABORATION FOR THE ABSTRACT MODEL SPECIFICATION
(STACK AS ARRAY)

Line no.	Notes
3.	push $(s, 5)$ = assign (5, new, 0) [by line 4 of the stack specification and abstract program context, which shows that this is the first reference, and line 8 of the stack specification and depth = 1].
4.	push $(s, 3)$ = assign $(3, s, 1)$ [by line 4 of the stack specification and current value of "depth"] = assign (3, assign (5, new, 0), 1) in terms of iarrays.
5.	pop $(s) \Rightarrow$ depth = 0 [by line 11 of the stack specification]. Note that the underlying abstraction now has a "garbage" value: read (assign (3, assign (5, new, 0), 1), 1) = 3 [by line 10 and 11 of the iarray specification]. As in the state-machine case, the "garbage" value is not reachable by any sequence of push, pop, and therefore is irrelevant to the visible characteristics of the stack.
6.	result := top (s) = read $(s, \text{depth} - 1)$ [by line 14 of stack specification] = read $(s, 0)$ based on current value of depth = read (assign (3, assign (5, new, 0), 1), 0)) = read (assign $(s, \text{new}, 0), 0)$ [by lines 10 and 12 of the iarray specification: index 1 $\neq$ index 2] = 5 [by lines 10 and 11 of iarray specification: index 1 = index 2].

Note that the "read" function took as its argument the entire instantiation sequence of "assigns," since the underlying abstraction did not have an equivalent to "leader."

8.5.8 Comments on Abstract Model Specification Approach

The appropriateness of the abstract model approach to a given problem depends upon two factors. The first factor is whether the functions to be specified can be readily expressed in the precondition/postcondition format. The potential problem area is concerned with exceptions or unacceptable input states. The abstract model technique takes the "proscribing" viewpoint that the specifier's responsibility ends with the definition of necessary conditions for the successful operation of the function. The second factor is whether the chosen underlying abstraction permits a "clean" specification of the desired functions.

The first factor is inherent in the approach; the second is under the control of the specifier. From the validator's point of view, the applicability of the abstract model technique is almost completely a function of the underlying abstraction used in a specific specification. Very few proofs of properties have been published for abstract model specifications. One [27] gives proof of the fairness of a process multiplexer whose underlying abstraction is a very detailed process state vector.

An implementor who is reading an abstract model specification will receive a very definite idea of a favored data representation from the underlying abstraction that was chosen by the specifier. There is considerable disagreement on the desirability of such guidance. In general, the adherents of the abstract model technique believe that the specification should be as concrete as possible, in order to simplify the verification task. Those who favor the algebraic technique believe that a specification should be as abstract as possible, expressing only the essential aspects of the item being specified and thereby coming closer to the mathematical concept of abstraction under which seemingly disparate entities may be described in a way that demonstrates their true similarity.

8.5.9 Link Between Specification and Verification

As noted earlier, the abstract model technique was developed from the outset to support formal verification. Its particular, attendant verification methodology [67] is based on demonstration of correspondence between two sets of specifications: the abstract, which defines function behavior in terms of an underlying abstraction, and the concrete, which defines behavior in terms of the objects of the implementation language. This verification method for abstract data types proceeds as shown in Figure 8.3, where the verification chain contains the following steps.

1. The abstract data type (that is, object and access functions) is defined behaviorally by a set of functions. Each function is specified in terms of pre- and postconditions using the abstract model specification technique. This is called the *abstract specification*.

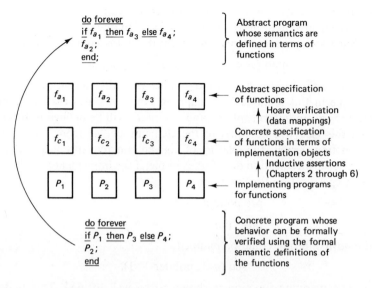

$$do\ \underline{forever}$$
$$\underline{if}\ f_{a_1}\ \underline{then}\ f_{a_3}\ \underline{else}\ f_{a_4};$$
$$f_{a_2};$$
$$\underline{end};$$

Abstract program
whose semantics are
defined in terms of
functions

f_{a_1} f_{a_2} f_{a_3} f_{a_4} ← Abstract specification of functions

↑ Hoare verification (data mappings)

f_{c_1} f_{c_2} f_{c_3} f_{c_4} ← Concrete specification of functions in terms of implementation objects

↑ Inductive assertions (Chapters 2 through 6)

P_1 P_2 P_3 P_4 ← Implementing programs for functions

$$do\ \underline{forever}$$
$$\underline{if}\ P_1\ \underline{then}\ P_3\ \underline{else}\ P_4;$$
$$P_2;$$
$$\underline{end}$$

Concrete program whose
behavior can be formally
verified using the formal
semantic definitions of
the functions

Figure 8.3 Verification method for abstract data types

2. A *concrete representation* of the data type is selected or devised by the implementor. This representation is "concrete" because it is in implementation-language form. Thus the concrete representation of a stack may be an array.

3. A *concrete specification* is written. This, like the abstract specification, is in the pre- and postcondition format. It differs from the abstract specification in that the semantics of each pre- and postcondition are defined in terms of concrete representation rather than the underlying abstraction. As a result of this step, function behavior becomes defined in implementation language terms.

4. The implementing programs for each function are written.

5. The implementing programs for each function are proved to correspond to their respective concrete specifications. This is a straightforward application of the inductive assertion method. Each precondition becomes an input assertion and each postcondition becomes an output assertion. These assertions (unlike those of the abstract specification) are semantically consistent with the implementing programs. Once this step is complete, we must show that the abstract and concrete specifications are semantically identical. We do so by the steps that follow, by showing that the concrete specification "maps up" to the abstract specification.

6. The process begins by the defining of a *mapping function* that maps the concrete specification onto the underlying abstraction of the abstract specification. The mapping function relates the semantics of the concrete specification to the semantics of the abstract specification by means of references

to a common underlying abstraction. This process can be shown by considering a stack implemented in terms of an array "*a*" and an integer "pointer" (presented in [46]). Such an implementation could yield the following mapping function:

$$\underline{\text{map}}\ (a,\ \text{pointer}) = \text{seq}\ (a,\ 1,\ \text{pointer}),$$

where "seq" is the seq function for the underlying abstraction iseq used in the first example in this section. This mapping function states that the semantics of operations given in terms of "*a*" and "pointer" will be defined in terms of an iseq, and this iseq will be equal to the elements of "*a*" from 1 to "pointer." Such a function permits the relating of a given concrete specification clause to a given abstract specification one. For example, if the implementor had proposed a concrete specification for "pop" of

$$\underline{\text{pre}}\ \text{pointer} > 0$$

$$\underline{\text{post}}\ '\text{pointer} = \text{pointer} - 1,$$

then the postcondition could be mapped:

$$\text{seq}\ (a,\ 1,\ \text{pointer} - 1).$$

7. The mapping function is shown to be well formed. This is done by first defining an *abstract invariant*, some condition that universally holds and is defined in terms of the underlying abstraction. Next a *concrete invariant* is devised, some condition that universally holds for the concrete specification. We then show that the mapping function is well formed by demonstrating that it maps the concrete invariant onto the abstract invariant. In the example used above (stack specified in terms of sequence and implemented by an array and a pointer), the abstract invariant is

$$\text{length (stack)} \leq 2,$$

and the concrete invariant would be

$$\text{pointer} \leq 2.$$

The demonstration of well-formedness then becomes the proof of the following conjecture:

$$\text{pointer} \leq 2\ \text{implies length}\ (\underline{\text{map}}\ (a,\ \text{pointer})) \leq 2,$$

which can be done by noting that

$$\text{length}\ (\underline{\text{map}}\ (a,\ \text{pointer})) = \text{length}\ (\text{seq}\ (a,\ 1,\ \text{pointer}))$$

$$= \text{pointer}.$$

8. By means of the mapping function, the concrete specification is shown to have the same semantics as the abstract one. To continue the example, this means that the concrete postcondition of "pop,"

$$'\text{pointer} = \text{pointer} - 1,$$

must be shown to be semantically identical to

$$'\text{stack} = \text{leader (stack)},$$

which proceeds according to the following argument:

$$\text{stack} = \underline{\text{map}}\ (a, \text{pointer})$$
$$= \text{seq}\ (a, 1, \text{pointer})$$
$$'\text{stack} = \underline{\text{map}}\ ('a, '\text{pointer})$$
$$= \underline{\text{map}}\ (a, \text{pointer} - 1)$$
$$= \text{seq}\ ('a, 1, \text{pointer})$$
$$\text{leader}\ (\text{stack}) = \text{leader}\ (\underline{\text{map}}\ (a, \text{pointer}))$$
$$= \text{leader}\ (\text{seq}\ (a, 1, \text{pointer}))$$
$$= \text{seq}\ (a, 1, \text{pointer} - 1),$$

and since a is not referenced in the concrete postcondition

$$'a = a,$$

then

$$\text{seq}\ ('a, 1, \text{pointer} - 1) = \text{seq}\ (a, 1, \text{pointer} - 1),$$

and therefore

$$'\text{pointer} = \text{pointer} - 1 \longrightarrow '\text{stack} = \text{leader}\ (\text{stack}),$$

which is precisely the conjecture to be proven.

The reader should note that many of the steps in this proof process are highly creative: there are no straightforward algorithms for choosing representations or mapping functions. In general, sets, sequences, and multisets are the most common underlying abstractions, and arrays and vectors are the most common representations for the simple abstract data types that have appeared in the literature.

8.6 COMPARISONS AND EQUIVALENCES OF THE APPROACHES

The basic similarities among the three approaches (they are all nonprocedural and use sets of function definitions to specify the effect of operations in terms of known mathematical objects) raise the possibility that relatively straightforward transformations may exist between them. Such transformations do exist, and they are indicated in Figure 8.4. As the figure shows, two techniques that rely on explicit state descriptions (state-machine and abstract model) can be trans-

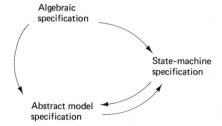

Algebraic
specification

State-machine
specification

Abstract model
specification

Figure 8.4 Approach transformations

formed into each other, and the technique that defines functions in terms of each other (algebraic) can be transformed into either of the other two. Inverses of the latter transformation are not straightforward, since the algebraic technique does not permit side effects; a set of functions defined algebraically (and therefore side-effect-free) can always be transformed one-for-one into functions in either of the notations that permit side effects, but a function with side effects (such as "push" in the examples) may have to be split into several visible and hidden functions when an algebraic approach is taken.

The transformation from algebraic to abstract model specification is described in [57]. Consider three functions f, g, and h whose "ok-ops" (see previous examples of algebraic specification) are

$$f: \quad \text{resulttype} \longrightarrow \text{resulttype}$$
$$g: \quad \text{argtype} \longrightarrow \text{resulttype}$$
$$h: \quad \text{argtype} \longrightarrow \text{resulttype}$$

Then an "ok-eqn," or rewrite rule, of the form

$$f(g(x)) = h(x)$$

can be "rewritten" to abstract model form by introducing an explicit state element y of type "resulttype." Then we can transform the rewrite rule into an abstract model function definition:

$$f(y: \quad \text{resulttype})$$
$$\underline{\text{pre }} y = g(x)$$
$$\underline{\text{post }} 'y = h(x).$$

This transformation takes advantage of the side-effect-free nature of algebraic specifications to specify the given data abstraction *in terms of itself*; that is, the semantics of a particular pre- or postcondition are determined, not by reference to an underlying abstraction, but by reference to some other function definition in the same specification. As an example, we give next the transformation of specification of the stack into this "recursive form of abstract model" specification.

ALGEBRAIC SPECIFICATION TRANSFORMED INTO ABSTRACT
MODEL SPECIFICATION

1. <u>type</u> stack;
2. stack <u>is modeled</u> as stack;
3. <u>invariant</u> depth ≤ 2;
4. <u>initially</u> $s = $ newstack
5. <u>functions</u>
6.   push (s: stack; item: integer)
7.   <u>pre</u> depth (s) ≤ 2;
8.   <u>post</u> $'s = $ push (s, <u>item</u>);

9.   pop (s, old_s: stack; item: integer)
10.   <u>pre</u> $s =$ push (old_s, item);
11.   <u>post</u> $'s =$ old_s;
12.   top (s, old_s: stack, old_item: <u>integer</u>) <u>returns</u> (item: <u>integer</u>)
13.   <u>pre</u> $s =$ push (old_s, old_item);
14.   <u>post</u> item $=$ old_item;
15.   empty (s: stack) <u>returns</u> (flag: <u>boolean</u>)
16.   <u>post</u> flag $= (s =$ newstack);
17. <u>aux</u> depth (s, old_s: stack; item: <u>integer</u>) <u>returns</u> (d: <u>integer</u>)
18.   <u>pre</u> $s =$ push (old_s, item) <u>or</u> $s =$ newstack;
19.   <u>post</u> $d =$ <u>if</u> $s =$ newstack
20.   <u>then</u> 1
21.   <u>else</u> 1 $+$ depth (old_s);

Note that push is defined in terms of itself; that is, the postcondition of a push is that a push has occurred. This condition arises because push is a "constructor function," the one function that can be used to generate all instances of the type being specified. As such there exists no rewrite rule in the algebraic specification with push at the outer level [for example, push $(\ldots) =$ $\ldots$]. By the transformation we are using,

$$f(g(x)) = h(x)$$

becomes

<u>function</u> $f(y$:   resulttype)

<u>pre</u> $y = g(x)$

<u>post</u> $'y = h(x)$.

There can be no postcondition for push other than the stated identity condition. Also, the two rewrite rules for the hidden function depth in the algebraic specification have been combined by disjunction of the preconditions and selection of the proper postcondition through a conditional expression. This change is necessary to meet the syntactic constraint that a function in the abstract model technique be defined only once. Also, the transformation has in this case altered the semantics of errors and exceptions. Following the OBJ model, our algebraic specification returned error values for invalid function references; the abstract model specification takes the other approach and constrains inputs to "acceptable" ones by means of the preconditions. Thus the precondition

<u>pre</u> $s =$ push (old-s, item)

in the definition of pop is the equivalent (with the above-mentioned change in approach) to the <u>error-eqn</u>

pop (newstack) $=$ underflow.

That is, the precondition states that at least one push must have been applied to the stack before a pop can be valid.

An elaboration of an abstract program for this specification will strongly resemble that of the algebraic specification, owing to the identical recursive nature of the function definitions.

Transformations between abstract model and state-machine specifications are essentially trivial, in that the preconditions are identical to the conjunction of the negation of the exceptions, and the postconditions to the conjunction of the effects. In fact, as has been observed [60], the state-machine technique can be viewed as a variant of the abstract model technique—a variant using the "built-in" underlying abstraction of unbounded arrays with symbolic indices. This observation must be tempered with the further note that the exception semantics of the state-machine technique are value-returning and not proscriptive. Transformation between the two techniques may yield identical semantics for "normal" function behavior but will involve a shift in meaning of exceptions.

9

STATE OF THE ART
AND SUMMARY

9.1 INTRODUCTION

In this chapter we describe the current state of development of formal methods, and to do so we alter our perspective somewhat from that of the previous chapters. In earlier chapters we deliberately chose very small examples and manual methods of analysis and proof, so that the principles would stand out from the detail. In this chapter we will consider formal methods in the context of practical systems, which are orders of magnitude larger and more complex. Our expanded context requires the consideration of automated tools, as well as an awareness that assessments such as those presented below are necessarily subjective. There currently exists considerable disagreement among observers and practitioners of formal methods as to progress, technical merit, and applicability to software engineering.

Enough is now known about formal development of software to permit the sketching of a hypothetical formal development method. We shall outline such a method and describe the theory, languages, and tools it would require. We then discuss the current state of development in each area in terms of the defined requirements. Note that the result is an assessment of formal methods against the requirements of formal methods and *not* against the more traditional, test-oriented methods of software engineering. This latter comparison must await the accumulation of much more experience with the use of formal methods.

9.2 FORMAL DEVELOPMENT OF SOFTWARE

Our hypothetical method follows Figure 1.2. The steps can be summarized as follows:

1. The system is initially described by a formal specification.
2. The formal specification is shown to be well formed, by being passed through automated checks for syntactic correctness and semantic consistency.
3. Once confidence is gained that the specification is well formed, it is validated, or shown to describe a system that satisfies the goals of the developers. Validation is performed primarily by inspection. It may be aided by "symbolic execution" (interpretation of specifications) or by automated interpreters for specification. These tools permit input values to be submitted to functions in a specification and then return the output values that the specification defines for these inputs. Validation may also include formal proofs of properties such as security and fault tolerance.
4. After confidence is gained that the formal specification is well formed and describes the intended system, it is used to guide the implementation (programming) of the system.
5. The programs are verified by proofs of correctness which show that they correspond to the validated specification. Proofs are carried out using the methods of Chapters 3 through 6, heavily supported by automated tools.
6. Testing is used selectively to double-check the proofs. Test strategies are automatically developed from the specifications, using tools that embody the principles sketched in Sections 2.5.1, 3.5, and 3.6.1.

Such a development process will require an integrated set of theories, languages, and tools; each of these elements is discussed in the subsequent sections. Each discussion includes (1) an overview of the role the particular element plays in formal development; (2) the requirements; (3) the state of the art as given by current efforts in the context of the requirements; and (4) known directions of evolution and research.

The choice of which theories, languages, and tools to use as examples is naturally subjective. Our selection criteria were formality, existence of tools, and use, even if only for evaluation, in practical applications. The criterion of formality requires that an example element be based on a mathematical foundation, and that concerns for rigor override more traditional concerns such as familiarity, or readability by the traditionally trained software engineers.

In addition, we have naturally limited our discussion to systems and approaches that are discussed in the open literature. This precluded inclusion of INA JO [144, 145], which is maintained as a proprietary system by the System Development Corporation.

9.3 THE ROLE OF THEORY IN FORMAL SOFTWARE DEVELOPMENT

Theory is the intellectual bedrock upon which a formal method is built. There are two distinct theories in this foundation. One, the *logical theory*, provides the means whereby reasoning about specifications, properties, and programs is carried out. The other, the *structuring theory*, provides an "expanded model of computation" that describes the essential aspects of the systems being developed. The model of computation is as important as the ability to reason correctly, for it defines the elements being reasoned about: the formal equivalents of modules, machines, and processes.

Once logical and structuring theories are defined (or assumed), their influence on the program development process is pervasive. The theories literally define the universe of discourse of the method—that is, the set of objects and relations that can be handled by the method.

9.3.1 Logical Theory

A logical theory used in a formal system must satisfy the following three requirements (a similar list of requirements is presented by Cohn [146]):

1. The theory must be formal. This means that the truth or falsity of a statement in the theory must be determinable solely from the form of the statement—that is, syntactically. This requirement reflects both the modern definition of mathematical rigor and the need to construct complex proofs by mechanical means.
2. The theory must be sound. All statements in the theory that are derived from theorems (true statements) by the rules of inference of the theory must be true.
3. The theory must be relevant. It must permit reasoning about the semantics of objects and constructs encountered in nontrivial computer systems.

The requirement of formality carries with it the problem of decidability. Formal theories of any complexity are typically undecidable; that is, it is possible to make well-formed statements in the theory whose truth or falsehood cannot be established by the decision rules of the theory (see [148]). As a practical matter, the limits of automated tools (for example, mechanical theorem provers, see Section 9.5) are reached long before the limitations of formal undecidability are encountered. A worker attempting to prove the truth of a statement (such as a verification condition) will often have to simplify the statement (typically, by rewriting the program or being satisfied with a looser assertion) to accommodate the mechanical theorem prover being used; such simplifications usually keep the workers well within the decidable fragment of possibly undecidable theories.

The requirement of soundness is readily met by theories based on known logical systems such as the first-order predicate calculus [147]. Soundness is a problem for theories that contain special-purpose or ad hoc logic.

The pressure to incorporate new logic forms arises from attempts to meet the third and most difficult requirement of relevance. None of the classical formal logical systems, for example, permit satisfactory reasoning about concurrency, side effects, or exceptions.

9.3.2 The State of the Art in Logical Theory

Most existing systems use theories based on some variation of the first-order predicate calculus, often without qualification (that is, "for all" and "there exists"). The AFFIRM verification system [144, 149] accepts quantifiers and the logical connectives not, or, and, implies, and equivalent, and it reasons about programs written in a Pascal-like language. The Stanford Pascal verifier [150] reasons in quantifier-free first-order predicate calculus. The Boyer-Moore theorem prover [151] uses a form of recursive function theory especially tailored to the needs of automated proofs; this theory is described in [152]. Boyer-Moore theory has been used in proofs about programs written in a major subset of FORTRAN [151]. Another system used to reason about programs, called LCF [153], uses the predicate typed lambda calculus.

Existing theories are adequate to deal with almost all relevant aspects of sequential programs; they do not handle concurrent programs except with great difficulty. Recently, Pneuli [154] has put forth a temporal logic with temporal quantifiers (for example, "always" and "at some time"), which permit statements about temporal conditions to be made that are similar to statements in the first-order predicate calculus, with "always" acting similarly to "for all," and "at some time" acting similarly to "there exists." A variation of temporal logic has been developed by Owicki and Lamport [155] and used to draw conclusions about network protocols [156]. The use of temporal logic, while showing promise, is in its very early stages, and no conclusions about its general merit can be reached at this time.

9.3.3 Structuring Theory

Since the adequacy of a structuring theory depends heavily on the application being structured, we do not attempt to state any general requirements but instead are content with a survey of existing approaches.

9.3.3.1 Programs as Structuring Elements

Some methods, such as the Stanford Pascal verifier [150], operate on the basis of programs as the unit of structure. These methods typically verify programs based on assertions written in the underlying logic theory. These assertions are the specification for the program; in the specification structure described in Section 8.1 they are concrete specifications with no abstract specifications above them.

Similarly, the Gypsy language [143, 144] integrates the specification and the program into a single text. The programmer places specification statements as formal statements of intent at appropriate points in the program. Statements called "dynamic external specifications" act as assertions. "Entry" and "exit" specifications act as input and output assertions, and "block" specifications act as assertions that describe the conditions when the routine is blocked. The concrete specification statements "centry," "cexit," and "cblock" perform the same functions for concrete representations of abstract data types. In addition to these "public" specifications, a routine may have "private" or "internal" specification statements that are not visible outside it: "assert," which must be true at a specific point, and "keep," which must be true throughout (an invariant). In addition, there is a "hold" specification statement, which expresses a constraint on the values that may be assumed by an abstract data type. Specification statements are quantified boolean expressions that use actual program objects as operands and are therefore concrete specifications. The specifier can state whether a given specification statement is to be used in verification, checked at run time, or both.

Approaches such as Gypsy and the Stanford verifier, and in general all approaches based on concrete specifications mixed with program text, seek to strike a middle position between extreme formality and "usability" with practical programming problems. They generally facilitate program construction and verification at the expense of specification and validation. The expense is incurred because no free-standing specification exists as an object that can be checked for well-formedness or have properties proven for it. This has led to some difficulty in demonstrating that a system exhibits a given property, such as security [144].

9.3.3.2 Abstract Data Types as Structuring Elements

Abstract data types can also, obviously, be used as structuring elements, as for example is done in the AFFIRM system [48]. Abstract data types, which are objects described in terms of the operations performed on them, are specified using the algebraic approach. The concrete objects of the programming language are also defined as types. Mapping functions can be defined to relate concrete and abstract objects. The overall use of abstract data types in specifications and verification closely follows the examples given in Chapter 8.

9.3.3.3 Abstract Machines as Structuring Elements

Another structuring theory is that of the *hierarchical development methodology* (HDM) [157, 144]. The HDM model of computation is a generalization of the concept of abstract and concrete specifications described in Section 8.1. A set of functions is specified in the state-machine language SPECIAL and becomes an *abstract machine* or interface. In contrast to the abstract data type theory of program structure, there is no necessary relation between an abstract machine and an abstract object.

The functions of a given abstract machine can, therefore, be referenced by an *abstract program*, precisely as the "using" program in Figure 8.1. Abstract programs can be written in any language, although a specific language called ILPL (interlevel programming language) [157] has been defined with features that facilitate references to functions defined in SPECIAL, notably the recognition of exception values.

The behavior of the abstract program can, of course, be formally specified in SPECIAL. If this is done, a two-level *hierarchy* of *abstract machines* results. The formal specification of the abstract program is called the upper-level abstract machine. The formal specification whose functions are referenced by the abstract program is called the lower-level abstract machine. The abstract program is said to implement the functions of the upper-level machine in terms of the functions of the lower-level one. The theory also includes *mapping functions*, which relate state transitions of the two abstract machines.

The hierarchy of abstract machines can naturally be extended to more than two levels. The purpose of such an extension is to reduce a complex system to a set of abstract machines, each simple enough to be manageable. The complete HDM theory of structure is presented in [157], and an example of the decomposition of an operating system into a hierarchy of abstract machines appears in [158].

The HDM theory of structure is applied to the development of a system in two steps. First, the lowest-level abstract machine is carefully specified so that its functions define behavior that is duplicated by the "operational" semantics of the real machine on which the system is to run. Second, the abstract programs are written in the language chosen for implementation. The abstract programs therefore become the real programs. Verification that each abstract machine is correctly implemented in terms of the machine below it proceeds as described in Section 8.4.3.2.

Application of HDM requires that the lowest-level abstract machine be able to characterize the semantics of a "real" machine, whether that be hardware or a virtual machine defined by a compiler. Verification also requires that the programming language be able to reference* functions defined in SPECIAL. Both these steps have proven difficult in practice, largely because of the rigid approach taken in SPECIAL toward errors, or "exceptions" as they are called in that language.

SPECIAL requires that exceptions be checked before the operations of a function are performed. If an exception is taken, the operations are not

---

*The reference to functions, or defined behavior, is for purposes of verification. The programs would naturally reference the implementing programs for the functions when executing. (See Section 8.1.)

performed and the function instead returns a value of predefined type "exception," which designates the exception. This exception mechanism is built into the language and cannot be altered by the specifier. It presents difficulties in terms of both the specification of low-level abstract machines and the use of operational programming languages to implement abstract machines.

Abstract machines, such as hardware, which are low in typical hierarchies, often delay the check for exceptions until immediately before the specific, detailed operation that would be in error if performed with the exception condition in effect. As a consequence, a function that consists of several operations may be partially completed before the exception is taken, and the effect of the partial completion may not be reversible (as, for example, when a register content is overwritten). A function that partially changes state before taking an exception cannot be precisely characterized in SPECIAL, and a machine whose operational semantics behave in this fashion cannot be precisely duplicated by an abstract machine in HDM. The specifier is faced with the unpleasant choice between specifying each operation that takes an exception as a separate function, or having the abstract system used for verification deviate from the operational one. The first choice complicates the low-level specifications and adds unnecessary layers to the hierarchy of abstract machines. The second choice introduces uncertainty about the worth of the verification precisely in an area, exceptions, that is historically the source numerous, obscure errors.

Programming languages typically have their own semantics for the detection of and response to exceptions. These semantics seldom, if ever, correspond to those in the structuring theory of HDM. The programmer is then faces unpleasant choices: either duplicate the HDM/SPECIAL semantics, with possible performance penalty, or have the implementing programs for functions operate differently from their specifications, with a lowering of confidence in the worth of verification.

The structuring theory associated with the AFFIRM system confines exceptions or error values to the domain of implementing programs only and does not include them in specifications or verifications. This approach permits a simpler theory at the expense of omitting a potentially significant source of errors from the rigors of verification.

In addition to the above-mentioned problems with exceptions, current theories of structure omit or deal only superficially with concurrent operations. HDM has a concept of an abstract process, and the SPECIAL language has a primitive that permits functions referenced by abstract programs associated with different abstract processes to achieve synchronization. This primitive requires that the functions share an element of state space, which practically requires that the implementing programs for them share memory. Distributed systems are thereby effectively excluded. The structuring theory of AFFIRM contains no concept of concurrency at all.

9.4 THE ROLE OF LANGUAGES IN FORMAL SOFTWARE DEVELOPMENT

Languages are used in formal development to communicate and to capture results. Communication may be human to human, as when a specification is submitted to inspection as part of validation, or human to machine, as when a program is submitted to a verification condition generator (see Section 4.4). Results are captured when a validated formal specification is later used to verify implementing programs, or a verified property of a program is used in the verification of a second program that calls or uses it in some way.

Three classes of languages are used in formal development: specification languages, programming languages, and logic languages. Specification languages, discussed in Chapter 8, are used to describe the behavior of functions in nonprocedural form. Programming languages describe the implementing programs for the functions in procedural form; they have both a formal semantics used in verification and an actual semantics exhibited during execution as defined by the runtime environment. Logic languages are used to make statements in the logic theory of the formal method, such as verification conditions or assertions, which, if true, indicate that a specification exhibits a given property.

Existing logic languages have seldom, if ever, been explicitly treated as "problems" in language design, and very little can be said about them, except to lament this oversight. Logic languages are primarily used for "machine-to-machine communication"—that is, for communication between verification condition generators and theorem provers, or "formula generators" (used in proofs of properties) and theorem provers (see Section 9.5 for a discussion of these tools). In its primary role any language, no matter how cryptic, is adequate so long as it is unambiguous. Shortcomings of hastily designed and arbitrary logic languages become visible to users as soon as the first verification condition or assertion that cannot be proven is encountered. The user must then examine statements in the logic language, which may be pages long [159], and attempt to determine the cause of the failure.

Specification and programming languages have, of course, been treated as exercises in language design, and accordingly we are able to discuss their requirements and current status in detail.

9.4.1 Specification Language Requirements

An adequate specification language should satisfy four basic requirements:

1. It should be intuitively understandable to specifiers (writers) and validators (readers).
2. It should have a rigorous mathematical semantics, defined in the logical theory of the formal method of which it is a part.

3. It should be compatible with the structuring theory and the programming language of the formal method.

4. It should have expressive power and be generally applicable.

These are difficult requirements to satisfy, and they are now only partly satisfied by programming languages that are in their fourth or fifth generation of evolution; the reader should not be surprised to note that existing, first-generation specification languages fall short of achieving these requirements.

9.4.2 The State of the Art in Specification Languages

Specification languages were discussed at length in Chapter 8; here we only summarize the various aspects of existing languages.

Extensive experience has been gained using only the algebraic and state-machine language approaches. No major systems have been specified or verified using the abstract model approach.

In general, the algebraic techniques have sacrificed expressive power and ease of intuitive understanding for rigorous semantics; the state-machine languages have accepted less rigor in exchange for a more "natural" mode of expression.

The general problem of formalizing a state-machine language is described by Principato [60]. A small subset of SPECIAL was given a formal semantics by Boyer and Moore [59]. The algebraic language CLEAR was given a complete formal semantics by Burstall and Goguen [160]; Goguen [161] asserts that this seems to be the only complete semantics ever given for a specification language. The absence of a formal semantics is only an annoyance when specifications are used for human-to-human communication, where ambiguities can be resolved by mutual agreement. It is a major problem when tools are to be built to mechanize proofs of properties and formal verification. The situation with regard to tools will be discussed in Section 9.5.

The relative expressive powers of the specifications languages have been covered in Chapter 8. It is interesting to note that Goguen, developer of the algebraic languages CLEAR and OBJ, has admitted that algebraic languages appear difficult to users who are not mathematically sophisticated and has selected the state-machine approach for the proposed successor to SPECIAL, called ORDINARY [161]. An important goal of ORDINARY is an ability to vary its expressive power with the application area being specified. The mechanism for doing so is called *institutions*. In very superficial terms, an institution is a mechanism for defining a special-purpose logical theory that is then used to express the formal semantics of the specification using the institution. The approach generalizes and makes rigorous the way we presented examples in Chapter 8 for abstract model specifications, where we used the algebraic method to provide underlying semantics. In ORDINARY this would be called the use of the *equational institution*. A fuller discussion of the use of institution appears in [161].

The principal shortcoming of existing specification languages is in the ability to express concurrency in a useful manner. To a large extent this reflects the corresponding shortcomings in logical theory. Tentative efforts have been made to incorporate generalized concurrency primitives in a state-machine approach [166], and the Gypsy language has a message-passing model as part of its operational semantics.

9.4.3 Programming Language Requirements

To be useable in formal development, a programming language must be consistent with both the logical and structural theories of the formal development method. This means that the semantics of the language must be expressible in the selected logical theory, and the features of the language must interface clearly with the structuring theory.

The first requirement is sometimes expressed as a requirement that the language be "axiomatizable." This means that the consequences of executing any statement in the language must be expressible formally in terms of verification conditions (assertions). The second requirement means that the programming language must recognize the basic structuring entities (modules, abstract data types) as well as effectively handle any objects, such as exceptions, that may be integral to the theory.

9.4.4 State of the Art in Programming Languages

Efforts in formal development have centered around the Algol family of languages, notably Pascal and its derivatives, although some work has been done with FORTRAN [145, 151]. The principal difficulty in axiomatizing such languages is called "aliasing" and is a consequence of name-scoping rules that permit variables to be known by different names in different parts of the program.

Two responses were made to the aliasing problem. One response modifies existing languages; an example of this approach is given by a version of Pascal accepted by the Stanford Pascal verifier [150]. The other approach calls for language designs that avoid the problem; examples of such languages include Alphard [46], Euclid [65], and Ada [162].

Both Alphard and Euclid were designed specifically to be part of a formal development method. The Alphard effort resulted in a language definition but no compiler. Euclid compilers have been constructed and used in evaluation efforts [163]. All preceding languages have been overshadowed by Ada, which has behind it the impetus of a standardization effort by the United States Department of Defense. The Stanford verifier group is constructing an Ada verifier, and it reports difficulties in axiomatizing the Ada concepts of packages (the mechanism that supports separately compiled modules), exceptions, and concurrency [164]. The last feature of Ada is the only one for which the language does not possess a formal semantics. It is unlikely that the force behind Ada will be diminished by these difficulties, and it is fairly certain that the structure and features of Ada will have a major influence on the next generation of specification languages and structuring theories.

9.5 THE ROLE OF TOOLS IN FORMAL SOFTWARE DEVELOPMENT

Tools are the physical embodiment of language structuring theory and logical theory. They mechanize complex operations, reduce the occurrences of error, and enable formal development to be applied to problems that exceed the scope of manual methods.

Language tools support the use of specification and programming languages. They perform checks for syntactic correctness and semantic consistency. A tool was developed for the specification language OBJ [49] that permitted "symbolic execution" of specifications; that is, the tool accepted a formal specification and a set of inputs and produced as output the results the specification defined for that set of inputs. The difficulties that have been encountered in reading formal specifications in practice indicate that such a tool would be a useful adjunct to any formal development method.

Tools to support structuring theory, if they exist at all, are usually associated with language tools. An example is given by the mapping functions in HDM [157], which are written in a subset of the specification language SPECIAL.

The tools that are unique to formal methods are the formula generators that generate statements in the logical language of the method and the theorem provers that decide the truth or falsity of the generated statements.

Formula generators can be constructed to support proofs of properties or proofs of correctness. The tools that support proofs of correctness are typically called "verification condition generators" and perform a straightforward mechanism of the procedures described in Section 4.4. Formula generators that support proofs of properties are considerably rarer than verification condition generators. Perphaps the most prominent example is the formula generator developed by Feiertag to automate the proof of the security property for specifications written in SPECIAL [64, 144, 165]. This formula generator automates the method outlined in Section 8.4.3.1.

An important consideration for formula generators and theorem provers is their correctness; a faulty tool can propagate misleading results in subtle and disastrous ways. An example of the application of formal methods to demonstrate the correctness of a simple verification condition generator can be found in [94].

Formula generators are specific to the languages being used and the property being proven and therefore resist generalization. Such is not the case with theorem provers, and the remaining discussion will be limited to their requirements and their current state of development.

Theorem provers mechanize the process of producing a formal proof. Such proofs differ considerably from the informal proofs encountered in mathematics, which suppress detail in the interests of clarity and are basic tools for gaining insight and refining intuitive conclusions [70]. A critique of mechanical proofs and formal methods in general is given in [14].

Cohn [146] makes the useful distinction between "proof systems" and "verification systems." A proof system aims to prove arbitrary theorems in its logical theory. Verification systems are designed to prove the consistency of programs with a set of assertions. Verification systems generally accept a great deal of manual guidance (for example, in the induction strategy used) and act primarily as expression simplifiers.

We have not given a set of requirements for theorem provers because many different (distinct) approaches have proved effective in practice. Instead, we shall simply survey the field without any predefined criteria of adequacy.

The simplest form of theorem prover is the so-called "proof checker." Numerous examples of proof checkers have been constructed, both as part of program verification systems and as exercises in computational logic [66]. At their simplest, proof checkers accept a series of inferences in some logical theory, such as the first-order predicate calculus, along with the rule of inference (for example, modus ponens) to be used, and as output they ensure that the logical formula obtained does indeed result from the designated rule of inference. Such proof checkers are on a level of complexity with a parser for a well-formed higher-order language.

An example of a verification system is the theorem prover associated with AFFIRM. This tool, in the words of its developers, is "not exactly a proof checker, not is it a proof finder" [149]. Instead, it mechanizes the simplifying transformations applied to logical formulas and captures the results as the user explores various avenues of proof (by splitting an initial conjecture into subgoals, attempting various induction schema, and backing up frequently).

A well-known proof system is the Boyer-Moore theorem prover [151, 152]. This tool mechanizes proofs in a logical theory especially developed by Boyer and Moore to facilitate mechanical proofs [152]. Primarily an induction machine, it incorporates many ad hoc proof strategies and expression simplifiers. It has been used for many proofs, including the correctness of a "toy" expression compiler, a recursive descent parser, a decision procedure for the propositional calculus, the arithmetic simplifier used in the theorem prover, and several working FORTRAN programs, including an implementation of the fastest-known string-searching algorithm. The tool operates without user intervention, although it accepts "coaching" in the form of lemmas, which it proves and then incorporates into its "theorem" library.

Another proof system is the Edinburgh LCF system [153], which operates in the predicate typed lambda calculus. LCF differs from the Boyer-Moore tool by being interactive and taking its overall proof strategy from the user. Other technical differences are discussed in [146].

An important aspect of any theorem prover is the manner in which proofs can or cannot be "assisted" by the introduction of lemmas by the user. As mentioned above, the Boyer-Moore theorem prover will accept only lemmas that are accompanied by proofs or that can be proven. Other theorem provers accept arbitrary formulas as true and use them in the construction of "proofs," which may then be subtly but definitely in error if the formulas are in error.

To take an obvious example, any well-formed formula can be "proven" by a tool that unblinkingly accepts the lemma

$$\text{false} = \text{true}.$$

More subtle errors are possible. A lemma of the form

$$(\forall x)(x + 1 \leq x)$$

may facilitate a given "proof," but a proposition thus "proven" may not be consistent with the rules of integer arithmetic. Likewise, a lemma such as

$$(\forall \text{ stack } s)(\text{depth } (s) \leq 3)$$

is a great aid to the "proof" of the "correctness" of a set of implementing programs for the bounded integer pushdown stack example given in Chapter 8; the amount of confidence gained as a result of such a "proof" would, however, be negligible. Verification systems typically rely on unproven lemmas, much more than proof systems, and for this they have been criticized [14].

9.6 CONCLUDING REMARKS

The development of formal methods has been typified by a large number of relatively small and disjointed efforts to develop theory, languages, and tools. A small number of projects have attempted to assemble elements into a more-or-less integrated whole and then to apply them to practical problems, with mixed results. Such a situation is characteristic of first-generation technology.

The most likely forces for improvement will come from the language elements. Research sponsorship for formal methods oriented toward other than Ada will likely be difficult to obtain; as a consequence, cross-fertilization of technology and wider use of tools will be possible. Also, the next generation of specification languages should eliminate many of the present practical difficulties encountered in specification, validation, and verification. Application

of the next generation of formal methods, and especially tools, will produce
"results" that will permit full assessment of the contribution of formal methods
to software engineering. Until then, formal methods remain worthy of study
as an intellectual challenge and as a way of deepening our insight into the craft
of programming.

REFERENCES

1. "Special Issue: Program Testing" (guest editor: E. F. Miller, Jr.), *Computer*, Vol. 11, No. 4, 1978.
2. Elspas, B., Levitt, K. N., Waldinger, R. J., Waksman, A., "An Assessment of Techniques for Proving Program Correctness," *Computing Surveys*, Vol. 4, No. 2, 1972.
3. Popek, G. J., Farber, D. A., "A Model for Verification of Data Security in Operating Systems," *Comm. of the ACM*, Vol. 21, No. 9, 1978.
4. Boyd, D. L., Pizzarello, A., "Introduction to the WELLMADE Design Methodology," *IEEE Trans. on Software Engineering*, Vol. 4, No. 4, 1978.
5. Spitzen, J. M., Levitt, K. N., Robinson, L., "An Example of Hierarchical Design and Proof," *Comm. of the ACM*, Vol. 21, No. 12, 1978.
6. Stoy, J. E., "*Denotational Semantics: The Scott-Strachey Approach to Programming Language Theory*," The MIT Press, Cambridge, Mass., 1977.
7. Wegener, P. "The Vienna Definition Language," *Computing Surveys*, Vol. 4, No. 1, 1972.
8. Van Wijngaarden, A., and others, "Revised Report on the Algorithmic Language ALGOL 68," *Acta Informatica*, Vol. 5, 1975.
9. Church, A., "The Calculi of Lambda-Conversion," *Annals of Mathematical Studies*, Vol. 6, Princeton University Press, Princeton, N.J., 1951.
10. Floyd, R. W., "Assigning Meanings to Programs," *Proc. Symposium on Applied Mathematics*, American Mathematical Society, Vol. 19, 1967.
11. Euclid, *Elements*.
12. Gödel, K., "Über formal unentscheidbare Sätze der Principia Mathematica and verwandter Systeme I," *Monatsheft für Mathematik and Physik*, Vol. 38, 1931.
13. Kolata, G. B., "The Four-Color Conjecture: A Computer-Aided Proof," *Research News, Science*, Vol. 193, No. 13, 1976.

14. DeMillo, R. A., Lipton, R. J., Perlis, A. J., "Social Processes and Proofs of Theorems and Programs," *Conf. Record Fourth ACM Symposium on Principles of Programming Languages*, Los Angeles, 1977 (also *Comm. of the ACM*, Vol. 22, No. 5, 1979).
15. Elspas, B., Levitt, K. N., Shostak, R. E., Spitzen, J. M., "In Support of Program Verificiation," unpublished manuscript.
16. Clarke, E. M., Jr., "Programming Language Constructs for Which It Is Impossible to Obtain Good Hoare-like Axiom Systems," *Proc. 4th Symposium on Principles of Programming Languages*, 1977.
17. Liskov, B. H., Zilles, S., "Programming with Abstract Data Types," *SIGPLAN Notices*, Vol. 9, No. 4, 1974.
18. Hoare, C. A. R., "An Axiomatic Approach to Computer Programming," *Comm. of the ACM*, Vol. 12, No. 10, 1969.
19. Knuth, D. E., "Structured Programming with Goto Statements, "*Computing Surveys*, Vol. 6, No. 4, 1974.
20. Darringer, J. A., King, J. C., "Application of Symbolic Execution to Program Testing," *Computer*, Vol. 11, No. 4, 1978.
21. Milner, R., "An Algebraic Definition of Simulation Between Programs," *Proc. 2nd Int. Joint Conf. on Artificial Intelligence*, London, 1971.
22. Manna, Z., "The Correctness of Programs," *Journal of Computer and System Sciences*, Vol. 3, No. 2, 1969.
23. Dijkstra, E. W., *A Discipline of Programming*, Prentice-Hall, Inc., Englewood Cliffs, N.J., 1976.
24. Gries, D., "An Introduction to Current Ideas on the Derivation of Correctness Proofs and Correct Programs," *IEEE Trans. on Software Engineering*, Vol. 2, No. 4, 1976.
25. Manna, Z., Pnueli, A., "Axiomatic Approach to Total Correctness of Programs," *ACTA Informatica*, No. 3, 1974.
26. Wegbreit, B., "Constructive Methods in Program Verification," *IEEE Trans. on Software Engineering*, Vol. 3, No. 2, 1977.
27. Flon, L., "On the Design and Verification of Operating Systems," Ph.D. Thesis, Department of Computer Science, Carnegie-Mellon University, 1977.
28. Hanson, P. B., *The Architecture of Concurrent Programs*, Prentice-Hall, Inc., Englewood Cliffs, N.J., 1977.
29. Flon, L., Habermann, A. N., "Towards the Construction of Verifiable Software Systems," *SIGPLAN Notices*, Vol. 8, No. 2, 1976.
30. Owicki, S., "Axiomatic Proof Techniques for Parallel Programs," Ph.D. Thesis, Department of Computer Science, Cornell University, 1975.
31. Howard, J. H., "Monitors," *Comm. of the ACM*, Vol. 19, No. 5, 1976.
32. Saxena, A. R., "A Verified Specification of a Hierarchical Operating System," Ph.D. Thesis, Department of Computer Science, Stanford University, 1976.
33. Owicki, S., Gries, D., "Verifying Properties of Parallel Programs: An Axiomatic Approach," *Comm. of the ACM*, Vol. 19, No. 5, 1976.
34. Franta, W. R., *The Process View of Simulation*, Elsevier North-Holland, New York, 1977.
35. Owicki, S., Gries, D., "An Axiomatic Proof Technique for Parallel Programs," *ACTA Informatica*, Vol. 6, 1976.

36. Clint, M., Hoare, C. A. R., "Program Proving: Jumps and Functions," *ACTA Informatica*, Vol. 1, 1972.
37. Laver, H. C., "Correctness in Operating Systems," Ph.D. Thesis, Department of Computer Science, Carnegie-Mellon University, 1973.
38. Boehm, B. W., McClean, R. K., Urfreg, D. B., "Some Experience with Automated Aids to the Design of Large Scale Reliable Software," *IEEE Trans. on Software Engineering*, Vol. 1, No. 1, 1975.
39. Rubey, R. J., Dana, J. A., Biche, P. W., "Quantitative Aspects of Software Validation," *IEEE Trans. on Software Engineering*, Vol. 1, No. 2, 1975.
40. Howden, W. E., "Methodology for Generation of Program Test Data," *IEEE Trans. on Software Engineering*, Vol. 2, No. 3, 1976.
41. Flon, L., Suzuki, N., "Consistent and Complete Proof Rules for the Total Correctness of Parallel Programs," Xerox PARC Report, CSL-78-6, 1978.
42. Francez, N., Pnueli, A., "A Proof Method for Cyclic Programs," *ACTA Informatica*, Vol. 9, 1978.
43. *John von Neumann, Collected Works*, Vol. 5, A. H. Taub, ed., Pergamon Press, Oxford, 1963, pp. 91–99.
44. Wegbreit, B., Spitzen, J. M., "Proving Properties of Complex Data Structures," *J. ACM*, Vol. 23, No. 2, 1976.
45. Dahl, O. J., Nygaard, K., Myhrhuag, B., "The SIMULA 67 Common Base Language," Norwegian Computing Centre, Forskningsveien 1B, Oslo, 1968.
46. Wulf, W. A., London, R. L., Shaw, M., "An Introduction to the Construction and Verification of Alphard Programs," *IEEE Trans. on Software Engineering*, Vol. 2, No. 4, 1976.
47. Guttag, J. V., "The Specification and Application to Programming of Abstract Data Types," Ph.D. Thesis, University of Toronto, Department of Computer Science, 1975.
48. Musser, D. R., "Abstract Data Type Specifications in the AFFIRM System," *Proc. Specification of Reliable Software Conf.*, Cambridge, Mass., 1979.
49. Goguen, J. A., Tardo, J. J., "An Introduction to OBJ: A Language for Writing and Testing Formal Algebraic Program Specifications," *Proc. Specification of Reliable Software Conf.*, Cambridge, Mass., 1979.
50. Guttag, J. V., "Notes on Type Abstraction," *Proc. Specification of Reliable Software Conf.*, Cambridge, Mass., 1979.
51. Birkoff, G., Lipson, J. D., "Heterogeneous Algebras," *Journal of Combinatorial Theory*, Vol. 8, 1970.
52. Knuth, D. E., Bendix, P. E., "Simple Word Problems in Universal Algebras," *Computational Problems in Abstract Algebra*, J. Leech, ed., Pergamon Press, Elmsford, N.Y., 1969.
53. Majster, M. E., "Treatment of Partial Operations in the Algebraic Specification Technique," *Proc. Specification of Reliable Software Conf.*, Cambridge, Mass., 1979.
54. Guttag, J. V., "The Specification and Application to Programming of Abstract Data Types," CSRG-59, Department of Computer Science, University of Toronto, 1975.
55. Majster, M. E., "Limits of the Algebraic Specification of Data Types," *SIGPLAN Notices*, Vol. 12, 1977.

56. Guttag, J. V., Horowitz, E., Musser, D. R., "Abstract Data Types and Software Validation," *Comm. of the ACM*, Vol. 21, No. 12, 1978 (also USC Information Sciences Institute Technical Report, 1976).

57. Flon, L., Misra, J., "A Unified Approach to the Specification and Verification of Abstract Data Types," *Proc. Specification of Reliable Software, Conf.*, Cambridge, Mass., 1979.

58. Parnas, D. L., "A Technique for Software Module Specification with Examples," *Comm. of the ACM*, Vol. 15, No. 5, 1972.

59. Boyer, R. S., Moore, J. S., "A Formal Semantics for the Hierarchical Program Design Methodology," unpublished manuscript, 1978.

60. Principato, R. N., "A Formalization of the State Machine Specification Technique," MIT Laboratory for Computer Science Report, MIT/hcs/TR-2-2, 1978.

61. Roubine, O., Robinson, L., "SPECIAL (SPECIfication and Assertion Language): Reference Manual," TR-CSG-45, SRI International, Menlo Park, Calif., 1977.

62. Scheid, J., Presentation on INA JO, at Air Force Summer Study on System Security, Cambridge, Mass., 1979.

63. Yourdon, E., *Structured Walkthroughs*, Prentice-Hall, Inc., Englewood Cliffs, N.J., 1979.

64. Feiertag, R. J., Levitt, K. N., Robinson, L., "Proving Multilevel Security of a System Design," *Proc. ACM Sixth Symposium on Operating Systems Principles*, 1977.

65. Popek, G. J., Horning, J. J., Lampson, B. W., Mitchell, J. G., London, R. L., "Notes on the Design of Euclid," *Proc. ACM Conference on Language Design for Reliable Software*, in *SIGPLAN Notices*, Vol. 12, No. 3, 1977.

66. Weyhrauch, R. W., "A User's Manual for FOIL," Stanford Artificial Intelligence Laboratory, Memo AIM-235, 1975.

67. Hoare, C. A. R., "Proofs of Correctness of Data Representations," *Acta Informatica*, Vol. 1, No. 4, 1972.

68. Blikle, A., Mazurkiewicz, A., "An Algebraic Approach to the Theory of Programs, Algorithms, Languages and Recursiveness," *Mathematical Foundations of Computer Science*, Warsaw, Poland, 1972.

69. Wood, W. T., "States and Relations: A Model for the Program Calculus of E. W. Dijkstra," Honeywell Corporate Computer Sciences Center Report, 1978.

70. Lakutus, I., *Proofs and Relations: The Logic of Mathematical Discovery*, Cambridge University Press, New York, 1976.

71. Joyner, W. H., Carter, W. C., Leeman, G. B., "Automated Proofs of Microprogram Correctness," *Micro 9 Proceedings*, IEEE Catalog No. 76 CH 1148-6C-1976.

72. Arbib, M., Alagic, S., "Proof Rules for Gotos," *Acta Informatica*, Vol. 11, No. 2, 1979.

73. Ashcroft, E. A., "Proving Assertions about Parallel Programs," *Journal of Computer and System Sciences*, Vol. 10, No. 1, 1975.

74. Burstall, R. M., "Proving Properties of Programs by Structural Induction," *Computer*, Vol. 12, No. 1, 1969.

75. Clint, M., "Program Proving: Coroutines," *Acta Informatica*, Vol. 2, No. 1, 1973.

76. Dershowitz, N., "The Schorr-Waite Marking Algorithm Revisited," *Information Processing Newsletter*, Vol. 11, No. 3, 1980.

77. Deutsch, L. P., "An Interactive Program Verifier," Ph.D. Thesis, University of California at Berkeley, 1973.
78. Dijkstra, E. W., "The Structure of the 'THE'—Multiprogramming System," *Comm. of the ACM*, Vol. 11, No. 5, 1968.
79. Dijkstra, E. W., "Notes on Structured Programming," in O. J. Dahl, E. W. Dijkstra, C. A. R. Hoare, *Structured Programming*, Academic Press, New York, 1972.
80. Duijvestijn, A. J. W., "Correctness Proof of an In-Place Permutation," *BIT*, Vol. 12, No. 3, 1972.
81. Ernst, G. W., "Rules of Inference for Procedure Calls," *Acta Informatica*, Vol. 8, No. 2, 1977.
82. Ershov, A. P., "Axiomatics for Memory Allocation," *Acta Informatica*, Vol. 6, No. 1, 1976.
83. Floyd, R. W., "Algorithm 245, TREESORT 3," *Comm. of the ACM*, Vol. 7, No. 12, 1964.
84. Foley, M., Hoare, C. A. R., "Proof of a Recursive Program—Quicksort," *Computer*, Vol. 14, No. 4, 1971.
85. Galler, B. A., Fisher, M. J., "An Improved Equivalence Algorithm," *Comm. of the ACM*, Vol. 7, No. 5, 1964.
86. Gerhart, S. L., Yelowitz, L., "Observations of Fallibility in Applications of Modern Programming Methodologies," *IEEE Trans. on Software Engineering*, Vol. 2, No. 3, 1976.
87. Goldstine, H. Y., von Neumann, J., "Planning and Coding Problems for an Electronic Computing Instrument, Part II, Volume 1," in *John von Neumann, Collected Works*, Vol. 5, A. H. Taub, ed., Pergamon Press, New York, pp. 19–104, 1963.
88. Good, D. I., London, R. L., "Computer Interval Arithmetic: Definition and Proof of Correct Implementation," *Journal of the ACM*, Vol. 17, No. 4, 1970.
89. Goodenough, J. B., Gerhart, S., "Toward a Theory of Test Data Selection," *IEEE Trans. on Software Engineering*, Vol. 1, No. 2, 1975.
90. Gries, D., Levin, G., "Assignment and Procedure Call Proof Rules," *ACM Transactions on Programming Languages and Systems*, Vol. 2, No. 4, 1980.
91. Gries, D., "The Schorr-Waite Graph Marking Algorithm," *Acta Informatica*, Vol. 11, No. 3, 1979.
92. Habermann, A. N., "The Correctness Proof of a Quadratic-Hash Algorithm," Department of Computer Science, Carnegie-Mellon University, 1975.
93. Hantler, S. L., King, J. C., "An Introduction to Proving the Correctness of Programs," *Computing Surveys*, Vol. 8, No. 3, 1976.
94. Elspas, B., "Specification and Proof of Consistency for Verification Condition Generators," *Proc. Specification of Reliable Software Conf.*, Cambridge, Mass., 1979.
95. Hoare, C. A. R., "Proof of a Program: FIND," *Comm. of the ACM*, Vol. 14, No. 1, 1971.
96. Hoare, C. A. R., "Procedures and Parameters: An Axiomatic Approach," in *Lecture Notes in Mathematics*, E. Engler, ed., Springer-Verlag, New York, 1971.
97. Hoare, C. A. R., "Proof of a Structured Program: The Sieve of Eratosthenes," *Computer*, Vol. 14, No. 4, 1972.

98. Hoare, C. A. R., Wirth, N., "An Axiomatic Definition of the Programming Language PASCAL," *Acta Informatica*, Vol. 2, No. 4, 1973.

99. Hoffman, C. M., "Design and Correctness of a Compiler for a Non-Procedural Language," *Acta Informatica*, Vol. 9, No. 3, 1978.

100. Jones, C. B., "Formal Development of Correct Algorithms: An Example Based on Earley's Recognizer," *Proceedings of the ACM Conference on Proving Assertions About Programs, SIGPLAN Notices*, Vol. 7, No. 1, 1972.

101. Jones, C. B., "Constructing a Theory of Data Structure as an Aid to Program Development," *Acta Informatica*, Vol. 11, No. 2, 1979.

102. Keller, R., "Formal Verification of Parallel Programs," *Comm. of the ACM*, Vol. 19, No. 7, 1976.

103. King, J. C., "A Program Verifier," Ph.D. Thesis, Carnegie-Mellon University, 1969.

104. Kowaltowski, T., "Axiomatic Approach to Side Effects and General Jumps," *Acta Informatica*, Vol. 7, No. 4, 1977.

105. Lamport, L., "A New Approach to Proving the Correctness of Multiprocess Programs," *ACM TOPLAS*, Vol. 1, No. 1, 1979.

106. Lanzarone, G. A., Ornaghi, M., "Program Construction by Refinements Preserving Correctness," *Computer*, Vol. 5, No. 1, 1975.

107. Lee, J. A., "The Definition and Validation of the Radix Sorting Technique," *Proceedings of the ACM Conference on Proving Assertions About Programs*, in *SIGPLAN Notices*, Vol. 7, No. 1, 1972.

108. Levitt, K. L., "The Application of Program-Proving Techniques to the Verification of Synchronization Processes," *AFIPS Conference Proceedings*, Vol. 41, 1972.

109. London, R. L., "Proof of Algorithms: A New Kind of Certification (Certification of Algorithm 245, TREESORT 3)," *Comm. of the ACM*, Vol. 13, No. 7, 1970.

110. London, R. L., "A Correctness Proof of the Fisher-Galler Algorithm Using Inductive Assertions," in *Formal Semantics of Programming Languages*, R. Rustin, ed., Prentice-Hall, Englewood Cliffs, N.J., 1972.

111. London, R. L., "Correctness of a Compiler for a LISP Subset," *Proceedings of the ACM Conference on Proving Assertions About Programs*, in *SIGPLAN Notices*, Vol. 7, No. 1, 1972.

112. London, R. L., Guttag, J. V., Horning, J. J., Lampson, B. W., Mitchell, J. W., Popek, G. J., "Proof Rules for the Programming Language Euclid," *Acta Informatica*, Vol. 10, No. 1, 1978.

113. Luckham, D., Suzuki, N., "Verification of Array, Record, and Pointer Operations in PASCAL," *ACM TOPLAS*, Vol. 1, No. 2, 1979.

114. Luckham, D., Polak, W., "Ada Exception Handling: An Axiomatic Approach," *ACM TOPLAS*, Vol. 1, No. 2, 1980.

115. Manna, Z., Waldinger, R., "A Deductive Approach to Information Flow in Programs," *ACM Transactions on Programming Languages and Systems*, Vol. 2, No. 1, 1980.

116. Moore, J. S., "Automatic Proof of Correctness of a Binary Addition Algorithm," *SIGART Newsletter*, 52, 1975.

117. Morris, J. H., "A Correctness Proof Using Recursively Defined Function," in *Formal Semantics of Programming Languages*, R. Rustin, ed., Prentice-Hall, Englewood Cliffs, N.J., 1972.

118. McCarthy, J., Painter, J. A., "Correctness of a Compiler for Arithmetic Expressions," in *Mathematical Aspects of Computer Science*, J. T. Schwartz, ed., American Mathematical Society, Providence, 1967.

119. McGowan, C. L., Kelly, J. R., *Top-Down Structured Programming Techniques*, Petrocelli Charter, New York, 1975.

120. Naur, P., "Proof of Algorithms by General Snapshots," *BIT*, Vol. 6, No. 4, 1977.

121. Naur, P., "Programming by Action Clusters," *BIT*, Vol. 9, No. 3, 1969.

122. Newton, G., "Proving Properties of Interacting Processes," *Acta Informatica*, Vol. 4, No. 2, 1975.

123. Ragland, L. C., "A Verified Program Verifier," Ph.D. Thesis, University of Texas at Austin, 1973.

124. Redish, K. A., "Comment on London's Certification of Algorithm 245," *Comm. of the ACM*, Vol. 14, No. 1, 1971.

125. Schorr, H., Waite, W. M., "An Efficient Machine-Independent Procedure for Garbage Collection in Various List Structures," *Comm. of the ACM*, Vol. 10, No. 8, 1967.

126. Sokolowski, S., "Axioms for Total Correctness," *Acta Informatica*, Vol. 9, No. 1, 1977.

127. Spitzen, J., Wegbreit, B., "The Verification and Synthesis of Data Structures," *Acta Informatica*, Vol. 4, No. 2, 1975.

128. Topor, R. W., "The Correctness of the Schorr-Waite List Marking Algorithm," *Acta Informatica*, Vol. 11, No. 3, 1979.

129. Waldinger, R., Levitt, K. N., "Reasoning About Programs," *Artificial Intelligence*, Vol. 5, 1974.

130. Walker, B., Kemmerer, R., Popek, G., "Specification and Verification of the UCLA Unix Security Kernel," *Comm. of the ACM*, Vol. 23, No. 2, 1980.

131. Wirth, N., "The Programming Language PASCAL," *Acta Informatica*, Vol. 1, No. 1, 1971.

132. Zelkowitz, M. V., Shaw, A. C., Gannon, J. D., *Principles of Software Engineering and Design*, Prentice-Hall, Englewood Cliffs, N.J. 1979.

133. Buxton, J. N., Randell, B., *Software Engineering Techniques*, NATO, Scientific Affairs Div., Brussels, 1970 (see p. 21).

134. Blikle, A., "On the Development of Correct Programs with the Documentation," Polish Academy of Sciences, Institute of Computer Science, 1970.

135. Hoare, C. A. R., "Communicating Sequential Processes," *Comm. of the ACM*, Vol. 21, No. 8, 1978.

136. Levin, G. M., "A Proof Technique for Communicating Sequential Processes," Cornell University, TR 79-401, 1979.

137. Apt, K., Francez, N., deRoever, W., "A Proof System for Communicating Sequential Processes," University of Utrecht, The Netherlands, TR RUU-CS 79-8, 1979.

138. van Lamsweerde, A., Sintzoff, M., "Formal Derivation of Strongly Correct Concurrent Programs," *Acta Informatica*, Vol. 12, 1979.

139. Lamport, L., "The 'Hoare Logic' of Concurrent Programs," SRI International, Tr-CSL-79, 1980.

140. Lamport, L., "A New Approach to Proving the Correctness of Multi Process Programs," *Trans. on Prog. Langs. and Systems*, Vol. 1, No. 1, 1979.

141. Wensley, J. H., "Sift: Software Implemented Fault Tolerance," *AFIPS Conference Proceedings*, Vol. 41, 1972.

142. Weinstock, C., "Sift: System Design and Implementation," *Proc. of FTCS 10*, 1980.

143. Ambler, A. L. and others, "Gypsy: A Language for Specification and Implementation of Verifiable Programs," *ACM Conference on Language Design for Reliable Software*, 1976.

144. Cheheyl, M. H., Gasser, M., Huff, G. A., Millen, J. K., *Secure System Specification and Verification: A Survey of Methodologies*. MITRE Corp., MTR-3904, 1980.

145. Scheid, J., "Ina Jo: SDC's Formal Development Methodology," *ACM SIGSOFT Software Engineering Notes*, 1980.

146. Cohn, L., "Remarks on Machine Proof," *ACM SIGSOFT Software Engineering Notes*, 1980.

147. Suppes, P., *Introduction to Logic*, Van Nostrand-Reinhold Company, New York, 1957.

148. Hofstader, D. R., *Godel, Escher, Bach: An Eternal Golden Braid*, Basic Books, New York, 1979.

149. Gerhart, S. L., Musser, D. R., Thompson, D. H., Baker, D. A., Bates, R. L., Erickson, R. W., London, R. L., Taylor, D. G., Wile, D. S., "An Overview of AFFIRM: A Specification and Verification System," USC Information Sciences Institute, PR–79–81, 1980.

150. Luckham, D. C., "Program Verification and Verification Oriented Programming," *Proc. IFIP 77*, Elsevier North-Holland, New York, 1977.

151. Boyer, R. S., Moore, J. S., "A Theorem Proven for Recursive Functions," *ACM SIGSOFT Software Engineering Notes*, 1980.

152. Boyer, R. S., Moore, J. S., *A Computational Logic*, Academic Press, New York, 1979.

153. Gordon, M., Milner, R., Wadsworth, C., "Edinburgh LSF: A Mechanized Logic of Computation," *Lecture Notes in Computer Science*, Vol. 78, Springer-Verlag, New York, 1979.

154. Pnueli, A., "Temporal Logic of Programs," *Proc. 18th Ann. Symp. on the Foundations of Computer Science*, 1977.

155. Owicki, S., Lamport, L., "Concurrent Program Verification," *ACM SIGSOFT Software Engineering Notes*, 1980.

156. Hailpern, B., Owicki, S., "Verifying Network Protocols Using Temporal Logic," *Proc. Symp. Trends and Applications, Computer Network Protocols*, 1980.

157. Robinson, L., Levitt, K. N., Silverberg, B. A., *The HDM Handbook*, SRI International Project 4628, 1979.

158. Neumann, P. G., Boyer, R. S., Feiertag, R. J., Levitt, K. N., Robinson, L., "A Provably Secure Operating System: The System, its Applications, and Proofs," SRI International, Final Report, Project 4332, 1977.

159. Silverman, J., "Proving an Operating System Kernel Secure," Honeywell Systems and Research Center, Report 81SRC31, 1981.

160. Burstull, R. M., Goguen, J. A., "The Semantics of CLEAR, A Specification Language," *Lecture Notes in Computer Science*, Vol. 86, Springer-Verlag, New York, 1980.

161. Goguen, J. A., Burstall, R. M., "An Ordinary Design," *ACM SIGSOFT Software Engineering Notes*, 1980.
162. Honeywell Inc. and CII-Honeywell Bull., *Reference Manual for the Ada Programming Language*, 1980.
163. Craigon, D., Boyun, D., "Two Projects in Program Verification," *ACM SIGSOFT Software Engineering Notes*, 1980.
164. German, S., von Heuke, F., Luckham, D., Oppen, D., Polak, W., "Program Verification at Stanford," *ACM SIGSOFT Software Engineering Notes*, 1980.
165. Feiertag, R. J., "Automated Proof of Multilevel Security," *ACM SIGSOFT Software Engineering Notes*, 1980.
166. Franta, W. R., Boebert, W. E., Berg, H. K., "An Approach to the Specification of Distributed Software," *The Use of Formal Specification of Software*, Informatik Fachberichte, Vol. 36, Springer-Verlag, New York, 1980.

INDEX